THE
TeamNet
FACTOR

Other Books by Jessica Lipnack & Jeffrey Stamps

The Networking Book: People Connecting with People
Networking: The First Report and Directory
Holonomy: A Human Systems Theory (*by Jeffrey Stamps*)

THE
TeamNet
FACTOR

Bringing the Power of Boundary Crossing Into the Heart of Your Business

Jessica Lipnack & Jeffrey Stamps

THE OLIVER WIGHT COMPANIES

Oliver Wight

Oliver Wight Publications, Inc.
5 Oliver Wight Drive
Essex Junction, VT 05452

To our parents, Ethel (1911–1989) and Marvin (1907–1964),
and Ann and Jim, and for our children, Miranda and Eliza

Acknowledgments

In the beginning, there was our literary agent, Mike Snell. When we first contacted Mike, we had more of a desire for a book than a fully formed idea for one. With his help, the idea became this book. Mike shepherded us through the proposal process, discussing ideas, and reading drafts. Then he found us our incomparable editor, Jim Childs at Oliver Wight Publications.

What a handoff. Jim belongs in the Editors' Hall of Fame. He taught us how to write (not insignificant, given that we already thought we were writers); encouraged us to tell stories; convinced us to speak our own ideas; and maintained his sense of humor through numerous long phone calls. Thank you, Jim. You are one-of-a-kind.

Before the writing began, Jean-Pierre Pellegrin materialized in our office and pointed us toward the extraordinary business developments among small companies in Europe. His afternoon visit turned into two chapters of this book, and led us to meet many people who've assisted us in writing the "flexible business network" story: Gregg Lichtenstein, Stuart Rosenfeld, Anne Heald, and Bob Friedman. They led us to the folks who are making it happen in Arkansas: Sandra Miller, Jim Benham, Chuck Myers, Clayton Franklin, Brian Kelley, and Bob Graham.

As we finished drafts, two people really pitched in, both spending hours with us on our porch, going through the manuscript on a line-by-line basis. Pam Johnson occupies a special place in our hearts: as a top engineering manager at Digital Equipment Corporation, she sponsored two years of our research on how groups can become smarter using technology. Roy Rezac, now at the Protocol Division of Zycad Corporation, was a longtime colleague at Digital who implemented many of our teamnet ideas in his software group.

Charles Savage, another Digital colleague and author of *Fifth Generation Management*, receives the most-prompt reader prize.

Acknowledgments

He was the first to return a fully marked-up manuscript, loaded with good ideas. Another Digital manager, John Manzo, read the how-to chapters in detail, and told us how-to. Bob Glorioso gave the first half of the book a thorough reading through the eyes of the executive who built Digital's first mainframe. George Metes has been a longtime conspirator on many of these ideas (his *Enterprise Networking* book, written with Ray Grenier, led Jean-Pierre Pellegrin to us). Ulf Fagerquist is a tireless visionary who included us in many fascinating projects where we tried out ideas.

The last shall come first at Digital: Bill Johnson, who originally introduced us to the company, sponsored project after project, year after year. He was the first executive we met who understood the value and power of networking in all its dimensions. All words but these fail: Keep the faith, B.J.

Elizabeth Lorentz, the grand doyenne of resource exchange networks (so grand that she did two books about them with Seymour Sarason at Yale), has been a godmother of sorts. She encouraged us month after month, line-edited the manuscript, sent us new material, and called every few days to bolster our spirits as we approached the end.

Two men with similar names probably are our mentors of longest standing. Robert Kirk Mueller of Arthur D. Little reviewed the whole manuscript and made helpful suggestions in regard to areas that would trouble CEOs. Thanks, Bob, for many years of serving as informal chair of our nonexistent Advisory Committee. Robert Muller, Chancellor of the UN University for Peace in Costa Rica, and former Assistant Secretary General of the United Nations, guided us to "decide to network."

Ron Cordes, architect of TeamFlow, read the practice and tools sections in detail, providing several valuable ideas that make those chapters flow. Steve Bennett, Rick Berenson, Josh Hyatt, Andrew Young, and Phil Halstead also positioned certain key ideas in unique ways for our consideration. Nick Gall found a critical piece of information just in time. Bob Randolph, an old friend from our Oxford days, helped with the Afterword.

David Ryder of CSC Index engaged us in a challenging project that put our ideas to the test while we were writing them, then helped us improve the manuscript.

Lisa Carlson of MetaSystems Design Group, a truly talented networker, highlighted the importance of "messiness" in teamnets, and encouraged us to write more boldly about it.

Dana Ducharme taught us that the ability to navigate electronic highways has nothing to do with physical sight. With a sophisticated voice recognition system, Dana tracked down hundreds of articles in no time at all.

Debra Church-Smith of The Networking Institute helped launch this book before giving birth to her second child, then came back to help us bring it to a close. Thanks, Deb, for sharing the vision. Judy Woods, our newest employee at TNI, is a prodigious information finder, who can locate the fastest answers to the oddest questions. Kim Hogan, a psychologist in the making, showed up at precisely the right moment full of energy for keeping our family functioning.

Family members—extended and immediate—have encouraged us for more than the length of this book: Judy and Irving Bazer, Emilie Farnsworth, Priscilla Harmel and Alan Shapiro, Erwin and Marianne Jaffe, Lucrecy Johnson, Tom and Emily LaMont, Eric Lipnack, Jack and Mary Merselis, Jimmy and Holly Morris, Carole and Guy Page, Judy Smith, Ann Stamps, Jim and Joan Stamps, Susan Stamps, Andrea Rogers and Avery Hall, and Kate and Ben Taylor. Who bring us to our two favorite people, our magnificent daughters, Mirmy and Liza, eternal sources of excellent advice, knowledge, love, amusement, and the endless parade of teenagers through our house. Your first response to the idea for this book was to sit down together that very morning and start to write a teenage version. You two are just what the world needs.

Do any authors ever thank themselves? Maybe we can because there are two of us, a little teamnet. Thank you, Jeff, for the snow plowing. And thank you, Jessica, for wallpapering the dome with confetti.

Jessica Lipnack and Jeffrey Stamps
West Newton, Massachusetts
January 1993

Contents

Chapter 9

**Launching Teamnets: Taking Off by Thinking
It Through**

Chapter 10

Those That Do, Plan: Bringing Discipline to Teamnets

Illustrations

Introduction

In many ways, we started this book 25 years ago at 46 Leckford Road in Oxford, England, where we met as American students in 1968. We shared a vision that seemed like a dream in the 1960s: a world that works. For all the nightmarish interludes that continue to plague the world, we still hold to our original inspiration.

"A World That Works"

We believe the teamnet factor can help solve the world's problems.

To paraphrase Archimedes, "Give me a lever and a place to stand on, and I will move the earth." Our teamnet lever increases people's ability to do things together. By improving how new horizontal organizations operate, we complement the traditional prescriptions of vertical hierarchy. By offering new tools to manage change, we help people tackle all kinds of problems and opportunities with greater effectiveness.

Piecemeal solutions to urgent crises are monstrously time consuming. In the end, they are ineffective because real problems don't come one-by-one. Problems are messy creatures. They appear in untidy clumps, hooked to other quagmires near and far.

Problems cross boundaries. While distributed across places and situations, they also interconnect. With a big enough view, you ultimately can tie together most problems in business as well as in every other important part of life.

Together, we stand in many places. Together, we can move the world with the teamnet lever. The fulcrums we use are the multiple interconnected opportunities for constructive change. You know about some of these points of possibility in your own world. You have your own special contribution to make with teamnets.

Teamnets meet the need to work faster, smarter, and more flexibly to solve problems and gain competitive advantage. The need for boundary crossing organizations dovetails with expanding technological capabilities. With new ways to connect continuing to explode throughout the 1990s, people who work apart are becoming increasingly productive.

Teamnets offer an *organizational advantage*. It's available to be reaped by all sizes of companies:

- Today, no company can go it alone all the time. It's too complicated and too expensive. Right now, it means missed opportunities. Tomorrow, it means going out of business.
- The right organization gives you the right edge—the power of partners, speed of multiple decision-makers, and flexibility of voluntary links.
- Teamnets are networks of teams. They're the new organizations that companies use to do business across boundaries—inside and out. Teamnets are about *crossing* boundaries.
- Co-opetition is key to future vitality—when companies cooperate and compete at the same time.
- Successful teamnets have fewer bosses and more leaders. Hierarchies limit the number of power seats. Teamnets increase them.
- Use teamnets to shrink hierarchies and replace bureaucracies.
- Teamnets between companies—sharing costs and pooling talents—create business. More business means more jobs. Teamnets can drive economic development.

The TeamNet Factor is 20 years in the making. We have lived teamnets as well as studied them. We have endured and delighted in them, created and buried them. And we have learned, practiced, revised, and revisited teamnet ideas as a full-time job for the last decade.

The Road to Teamnets

When we returned from Oxford, we took a path we hadn't anticipated. Instead of taking jobs in big companies or universities (or moving to a farm to grow organic vegetables), we started our own business, simply by developing and selling our expertise. Our first foray was in the field of cable television. It appealed to us because of its promise for distributed, two-way communication. In 1971, we bought a computer—and so many since that we could start a museum—that radically changed our ability to process information. With this programmable calculator, we developed an econometric model that assessed the viability of cable television franchises. We found ourselves competing for contracts against RAND Corporation and Mitre, and when we sometimes won, we realized that we were in the consulting business.

It's been more than 20 years, and we're still in the consulting business. We've always been self-employed, and we've always had to face the same problems other small business people have. Fortunately, our parents and grandparents on both sides of our families also owned their own small businesses, which gave us certain advantages. We knew from family experience what it was like to have employees, worry about cash flow, satisfy customers, and do the books. This life education was very different from what we learned from our Oxford tutors.

Through an unpredictable series of extraordinarily lucky, often last-minute, breaks (one dear friend describes our lives as "The Perils of Pauline"), we've had the chance to work on some very large-scale projects. In the mid-1970s, we worked for three years as consultants to the U.S. Department of Commerce Fire Administration's new effort to develop a fire prevention education program throughout the United States. This gave us the chance to think about solving national problems while working in such diverse localities as Dade County, Florida; Tulsa, Oklahoma; Salem, Oregon; and downtown Chicago.

Introduction

In the meantime, our consulting business flourished, but grew simultaneously boring and frantic. Then, one day, we saw the results of our research on another project used for purposes that clashed with our ethics. Burned out, within a few months (the same time as the birth of our first child) we stopped all consulting, and retreated to our house to rethink our purpose. We studied systems theory, finished a doctorate (and had it published), wrote some articles (and a book that was never published), and generally anguished over what would come next.

About a year later, we began to write a book about networks—informal, peer-based, horizontally structured organizations. We started our research in 1979 by writing to one person whom we knew to be interested in the idea. Robert A. Smith, III, who died in 1990, was our first network correspondent. Having recently retired from NASA, Bob then was living quietly in Abbeville, Alabama, but his network reached around the world. Using letters as his primary medium of communication, Bob had a network unlike anyone else's: at one time or another, he sent us Ted Koppel's and Alvin Toffler's home addresses, put us in direct communication with Warren Bennis and Norman Cousins, and led us, literally, to a list of people that numbers in the hundreds of thousands.

Bob responded to our initial inquiry by sending us the names of nine other people. We wrote to them, and six wrote back, suggesting more people to contact. We followed up on those names, and within 18 months, we received the names of 50,000 people around the world interested in networking. We wrote to 4,000 of those people, and 1,600 wrote back, a remarkable 40 percent response rate. (In the midst of all this, our second daughter appeared.) Those were the people whose organizations we chronicled in our first book, *Networking: The First Report and Directory* (New York: Doubleday, 1982). Since that time, people in more than 70 countries have contacted us about their networks.

The reaction to our first book astonished us. Although we did our initial research largely in the grass roots and counterculture, our response came from the mainstream, particularly corporate America. With hindsight, this does not now seem surprising. Published the same year as *Networking*, John Naisbitt's best-seller *Mega-trends* had identified "Hierarchy to Networking" as the 8th global megatrend and cited some of our early research in the area.[1] A decade later, this trend is no longer the stuff of future prognostication. It is the shape of fundamental change happening now.

While leading-edge thinking pointed to the emerging organizational form of networks, little was known about what makes them work. Even less was known about how to manage them. After *Networking* came out, our core mission became to learn what makes networks tick and how to improve them. Late in 1982, we started a business again, The Networking Institute, Inc. Soon we were back into full-time consulting, this time with Fortune 500–type clients. We became small business people who lived in the big business world.

One opportunity came in 1984 when we served as faculty at the Western Behavioral Sciences Institute's executive management program in La Jolla, California. Among the students were executives from a number of high-tech firms, including Bill Johnson of Digital Equipment Corporation, the vice president who led Digital's computer networking effort for many years. He saw a fit between his company's products and our work. For the next eight years, we worked closely with Digital, both on internal projects and with Digital's customers, among the world's largest users of computer networks.

Another 1984 surprise came when Japan's Economic Planning Agency translated our book; Toppan Printing Company, the third-largest publisher in the world, printed it; and President-sha, one of Japan's largest houses, published it. The book caused a small group in Japan to form the Networking Research Society. Supported by the Toyota Foundation, the country's largest philanthropy, they started study groups throughout the country using *Networking* (also its title in Japanese) as the study guide. Their mission was to understand a first in the country's history: the sudden spontaneous appearance of thousands of small independent voluntary associations all over Japan. Over the next five years, the group surveyed thousands of groups and hundreds of municipal governments. *Asahi*

Journal, the Japanese weekly magazine comparable to *The Atlantic Monthly*, published 200 consecutive stories about the country's networking movement.

In 1989, Toyota Foundation invited us to keynote the First Japan Networkers' Conference along with numerous other gatherings. During that tour, we met people from all walks of Japanese life— disability rights activists, farmers, artists, students, teachers, journalists, business executives, doctors, lawyers, and government officials. In Kanagawa Prefecture, Japan's second largest "state," we met Governor Kazuji Nagasu, described to us as "Japan's Mario Cuomo," who said, "We use networking to run the Kanagawa government."

Businesses and institutions in many other parts of the world also are taking great strides with the idea. For the past 10 years, we have worked on one project after another developing networks in large companies in North America, Europe, and Australia. At the same time, we've accumulated voluminous files of information about small companies' achieving success, particularly in Europe, by working together in "flexible business networks."

In the fall of 1991, we began work in earnest on this book. In December of that year, Jean-Pierre Pellegrin, a French official at the Organization for Economic Cooperation and Development (OECD) in Paris, visited our offices at The Networking Institute in Boston. On leave from OECD at the time, he was doing research at the Kennedy School at Harvard. Jean-Pierre had a very strong message to deliver: pay attention to flexible business networks. More accurately, he pounded the table and demanded that we start writing immediately about this little-reported breaking business story. As a result of Jean-Pierre's urging, we have connected with scores of business people and policy makers actively engaged in networks in both Europe and the United States.

At a time when business looks bleak, jobs are dwindling, and even the world's powerhouse economies are in recession, successful business ideas are very good and very welcome news. Flexible business networks of companies of all sizes are doing very well. Successful businesses create jobs. Jobs provide income to meet people's needs. Full stomachs enable full minds. Creativity flourishes. Cutthroat competition gives way to compassionate cooperation.

On Thanksgiving Day, 1989, an editorial entitled "Networking Concept" ran in *The Daily Yomiuri*, Japan's largest newspaper with a circulation of 10 million. Its message is pertinent to business.

> Today, we have almost endless problems. . . . It is sometimes difficult if not impossible to properly tackle problems within the framework of existing isolated organizations. . . . Networking emphasizes horizontal human relations among those who share common values, beyond ideological differences and geographical locations. . . . This new concept was introduced seven years ago in a book titled *Networking*, coauthored by an American couple, Jessica Lipnack and Jeffrey Stamps. . . . Networking aims at rejuvenating the spirit of mutual help among people unknown to each other and linking diverse groups together.

A quarter of a century after our Oxford vision, we see a world that works rising above the horizon.

Understanding Teamnets and What They Can Do

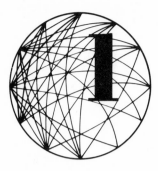

Teamnets: The Great Competitive Advantage of Boundary Crossing

According to conventional measures, a country of small traditional businesses like Denmark should be at the bottom of Europe's heap, a $28 billion global giant such as Asea Brown Boveri in a commodity industry should be in a slump like many other multinationals, and a small, old-fashioned manufacturing firm such as western Pennsylvania's Erie Bolt Company should be out of business.

Instead, Denmark, Asea Brown Boveri, and Erie Bolt all are doing quite well. What is it that a little country (population 5 million), a megaglomerate with 220,000 employees around the world, and a tiny bolt maker have in common? They all are using a new, powerful, and flexible form of organization.

- Beginning in 1989, 3,500 Danish firms organized into networks, small groups of businesses that work together. In just a year and a half, they contributed significantly to completely reversing a three-decade-long deficit in the country's trade exports.

- Instead of conducting worldwide operations from a top-heavy "headquarters," Asea Brown Boveri, a distributed global network of more than 1,300 mostly traditionally organized companies, houses only 100 professional staff people in Zurich.
- Rather than go bankrupt, the likely alternative in 1985, today Erie Bolt thrives as a network hub for cooperative vendor/supplier partnerships, choosing to "ally not buy."

Businesses that form *teamnets*—networks of teams that cross conventional boundaries—will be winners in the 21st-century global economy.

Denmark, Asea Brown Boveri, and Erie Bolt are not isolated examples. From the smallest to the largest companies, businesses are climbing over their own walls. Customers, competitors, and even people in different industries traverse their traditional limits to work together. When business teams cross boundaries, benefits accrue. Whether three-person shops or multinationals, these companies can achieve something that by themselves would be impossible. By definition, teamnets are on a mission for mutual benefit.

The effect of an economy teeming with teamnets is dramatic: Emilia-Romagna's teamnets among small companies have made that previously impoverished region of Italy the country's second wealthiest. Acting together, groups of businesses become small giants.

Although the need is different, large firms in many industries are doing the same thing, using *internal* teamnets to bridge barriers inside their companies, and *external* teamnets to bridge boundaries with suppliers, customers, and competitors.

Dateline: Denmark

Nowhere have teamnets had greater effect than in Europe, a tremendous story that remains largely unreported.

Small business in Europe is doing business differently. Instead of starting small and growing big, small businesses employ a different strategy. They form networks and together produce results far beyond the abilities of any single company. These networks have saved jobs and spurred economic growth, precisely what all local economies need in the world of the 1990s.

For all practical purposes, companies in these "flexible business networks" are in business together. But instead of merging, they remain independent with their own financials, employees, and areas of expertise. At the same time, they act as one to pool resources and exchange complementary skills. Together, these networks generate higher profits for all by:

- Gaining access to larger markets;
- Benefiting from economies of scale; and,
- Competing with the best of the big companies.

When the flexible business network movement began in Italy's Emilia-Romagna region during the mid-1970s, that region ranked 18th in income among 21 administrative regions. A decade later, powered by networking and an explosive growth in small businesses, the region was the country's second wealthiest. Its unemployment rate went from 20 percent to effectively 0 in the same period.

In 1989, the Danish government announced a $25 million program to develop "flexible manufacturing networks." The word "manufacturing" translates loosely—lawyers, accountants, and even landscape architects all participate in Danish networks.

- Within 18 months, a number equivalent to nearly half of the country's manufacturing companies joined networks.
- In 1991, Denmark, alone of the Common Market countries, reported a positive trade balance with Germany, the mammoth economy to Denmark's south, a first in Denmark's recent history.

Subsequent independent studies show that *flexible networks* provided one key competitive advantage for this little nation. Denmark starts the 1990s with the highest per capita balance of trade in the world, surpassing even Japan's.

As northern Italy's success spread to Denmark's troubled industries, so have the Danes inspired Iceland, Portugal, Spain, Canada, the United Kingdom, and the United States. By the early 1990s, networking efforts are under way in most states, notably North Carolina, New Hampshire, Oregon, Arkansas, Michigan, Washington, Florida, and Ohio.

European governments play an important role in promoting networks: they target broad industries for development among the existing manufacturing and service base—such as textiles, metalworking, and tourism. By investing relatively small amounts of money,[1] the Europeans have leveraged significant results.

Around the globe, plant closings take great visible bites out of the job market, dramatizing the reality that for years big business has been steadily shrinking its workforce. In 1990, Oregon reported what so many other regions around the world have experienced. In the previous eight years, big business had shed jobs in the state, while small firms had created new jobs in all economic sectors, including manufacturing and services. In a 1991 measure, Oregon became the first U.S. state to pass "networking laws," encouraging companies to form networks. Modeling its program after Denmark's, Oregon trains network "brokers" and provides incentive grants for businesses to explore the potential of networking.

Flexible networks represent a new but proven approach to economic recovery with true *trickle-up* power. By relocating work back to small companies, the manufacturing base can be revitalized, and as a result, the service sector grows. The employment math is simple. As more small firms work together to create more business, flexible networks will put more people back to work. New jobs drive down unemployment and provide relief to empty government coffers.

As contributions to local revenues increase, more money is available for education. This meets the increasing need for trained workers and professionals. A better-educated workforce means access to better jobs and higher personal income, which decreases the demand for publicly funded social services.

Flexible business networks offer a new vision of economic opportunity.

Crossing the New Frontiers

Teamnets bring together two powerful organizational ideas:

- *Teams*, where small groups of people work with focus, motivation, and skill to achieve shared goals; and
- *Networks*, where disparate groups of people and groups "link" to work together based on common purpose.

While teamnet means "network of teams," the two ideas are complementary; each brings a unique element to the other. "Teams" imply small, in the same place, and tightly coordinated; "networks" have a sense of large, spread out, and loosely linked. "Teamnet" brings the best of both together:

- Teamnet applied to small groups means more networked teams.
- Teamnet applied to large groups means more teamlike networks.

In an ideal teamnet, people work in high-performing teams at every level, and the network as a whole functions as though it were a highly skilled and motivated team.

> *The teamnet factor is about organizational advantage.*

Denmark, Asea Brown Boveri, Erie Bolt, and Japan clearly represent the power of people to organize for competitive advantage. Japan has few natural resources or other traditional industrial advantages. Its advantage is organizational.

> *The right organization gives you the right edge.*

Teamnets are an *intraenterprise* way to leverage small empowered business units and an *interenterprise* way to leverage partnerships with other businesses.

By using the power of boundary crossing for mutual competitive advantage, companies can organize to tap people's potential, enter new markets, expand their product base, and invest in the future. Teamnets are organizations for the new economy of the 21st century.

BENEFITS OF BOUNDARY CROSSING

How does a boundary crossing teamnet differ from a conventional team?

> *A boundary crossing teamnet crosses traditionally guarded organizational borders. Borders remain, benefits are gained.*

Boundary crossing teamnets offer a critical edge for dealing with the speed of change and the new decentralized, globalized economy. Teamnets boast three basic competitive advantages: power, speed, and flexibility.

Power

With more than one organization working toward the same purpose, boundary crossing teamnets benefit from the power of the part *and* the power of the whole. In concert together, they share knowledge, learning, skills, and resources. In Louisville, Kentucky, the Ford Explorer and Mazda Navajo come off the same assembly line; Ford does most of the styling while Mazda provides the engineering. At the other end of the scale, small businesses acting together have the buying power of big companies.

Speed

Boundary crossing teamnets streamline decision making. Multiple decision-making leaders work in parallel on different aspects of the same problem. A few phone calls replace 15 levels of signatures. Rapid realignment of resources to respond to opportunities is the order of the day. Information disseminates rapidly through person-to-person contact rather than official forms and unread memos.

Flexibility

Unlike their rigid bureaucratic relatives—organizational "stovepipes," "silos," and "chimneys"—that prevent creative response to opportunities, teamnets are highly "plastic." They bend, conform, and contort, configuring and reconfiguring to respond to the needs of the moment. Because such teams depend upon many connections among members at many levels, they are always "at the ready" to take on a new shape.

Rigid functions are so destructive at one Fortune 50 firm that some employees dread the intervention of other parts of the company with their customers. Recalling too many lost opportunities because of battles among the functions, one engineering manager feared what he called "the Sales Prevention Effort."

Perhaps the biggest impediment to success for boundary crossing teamnets is fear of change. It takes courage to believe that working with competitors is mutually good for business, that working with other internal groups is the best thing for the enterprise when it means *your* group may have to give up a degree of control.

Every culture has its own view on why cooperation is "unnatural," why the idea "can't work here." Ironically, a fierce strain of independence is one of the necessary ingredients that make these arrangements viable. There's a healthy tension between autonomy and integration in boundary crossing teamnets. Both attributes weave through the invisible infrastructure that permeates teamnets of all sizes—from the global scale of McDonnell Douglas's proposed new jumbo jet to the local success of a woodworking network, The Philadelphia Guild.

If the ideas in the chapters ahead prove to be the trend of the future, many companies and people in many countries all will be winners.

"Seeing the Obvious," chapter 2, and "Linoleum, Furniture, and Electrical Systems," chapter 3, provide the five principles and key examples you need to understand "the teamnet factor." In "In It Together," chapter 4, and "Inside-Out Teamnets," chapter 5, we explore how large firms use these principles. "Small Giants," chapter 6, and "Instead of Layoffs," chapter 7, describe how small companies use teamnets to astonishing bottom line advantage.

In "Harnessing the Power of Teamnets," section II, we show you how to develop teamnets. We build from a "Quick Start," chapter 8, which addresses small teams, to a more detailed methodology in "Launching Teamnets," chapter 9. "Those That Do, Plan," chapter 10, and "Transforming Bureaucracies and Systems," the Reference Section at the end of the book, provide concepts and tools for addressing large and complex teamnets. Failure is the theme of "Rascals in Paradise," chapter 11, to emphasize the "use with caution" warning that comes with our teamnet prescriptions. In "Fighting

Fire with Organization," chapter 12, we wrap the major themes, examples, and conceptual tools together. "The Risk of Democracy," our Afterword, pushes the envelope of teamnets and steps up to look at business networks in a larger context.

Co-opetition: When Competitors Cooperate

Compete *and* cooperate. Many businesses will not survive into the 21st century unless they resolve this apparent contradiction. Will yours?

There is a great strategic change under way in the way the world does business.

Companies cooperate and compete at the same time.

The competitive advantages of cooperation come from doing things together that cannot be done alone. The cooperative advantages of competition arise from innovation and striving for excellence.

"Co-opetition" is the oxymoron that combines the words "cooperation" and "competition." You may have already heard the term, perhaps used in a context like this TV story about the auto industry:

> The Big 3 auto makers meet with their Japanese counterparts on May 18, 1992, in Chicago. They are setting up "a number of task forces to explore areas where Americans and Japanese can work together for mutual benefit," Peter Jennings explains on ABC News. "Cooperation between U.S. and Japanese companies has produced a new word—'co-opetition'—which industry analysts say may be the wave of the future," reporter Al Dale tells the viewers using this newly minted word. "[It] may be the only way for some car makers to survive in years to come."[2]

Coined word or not, co-opetition perfectly captures the difficult-to-describe dynamic of independence and interdependence. This dynamic is at the core of the new, emerging flexible organization style that so many companies are attempting to emulate. Fast replacing the old, hierarchical bureaucratic organizational machine, the flexible organization uses cooperation to cross boundaries, instead of competing to dissolve them.

CAUTION: PARADIGM SHIFT AHEAD

The word "co-opetition" is the sort of strange made-up concoction that drives linguists crazy. Cooperation and competition are not usually strung together in the same sentence or even the same thought. Usually, they are opposites: If you cooperate, you can't compete. If you compete, you can't cooperate. Even so, people use the word to describe something important about a new way of doing business.

- When Siemens Nixdorf announces its entry into the $16 billion U.S. systems integration market, Heinz Kagerer, vice president, says they "will follow a policy of co-opetition—the ad hoc cooperation even with competitors."[3]
- When Luc de Brandere, whom the Belgian press describes as "the iconoclast of the stock exchange" (he was once head of Belgian Friends of the Earth and "writes obscure scientific books"), takes control of the Brussels Bourse in 1990, he says he will restructure the Bourse around "co-opetition, a mixture of cooperation and competition."[4]
- Novell's chairman Ray Noorda calls co-opetition his "business philosophy. . . . We decided we would partner with anybody and everybody that made sense." Instead of a sales force, the company uses 13,000 independent distributors. The strategy works: sales and earnings have soared.[5]
- Ted Engkvist, president of NYNEX's Information Solutions Group, says the word "co-opetition" means "We're a competitor

today, a loyal customer tomorrow, a buyer the day after and a joint partner the day after that."[6]

While "competition" is an easy word to swallow, "cooperation" can make some business people choke.[7] Boundary crossing teamnets are an easy, palatable way of bringing the two ideas together.

WHAT IS A BOUNDARY CROSSING TEAMNET?

Boundary crossing teamnets are the business wave of the future. They include independent members who voluntarily coordinate their activities. Most people already participate in cross boundary groups, perhaps without realizing it. Any task that involves plans, meetings, and joint actions with people outside your own organization—suppliers, customers, or competitors—requires a boundary crossing teamnet. Formal arrangements, that require two or more groups to work together on an ongoing basis, operate through a boundary crossing teamnet.

The trick is to: work together without giving away key trade secrets; share openly in well-defined areas while not being naive about unique differentiating advantages; and to cooperate without caving in to least-common-denominator thinking.

Members of boundary crossing teamnets work across conventional boundaries, cooperating for mutual benefit while retaining competitive independence.

Teamnet features appear in many new management innovations that have popped up at all levels of organization in the past quarter century:

- Small groups in companies use quality circles, self-managed work groups, and cross-functional teams as participatory, flexible organizations.
- Big companies institute total quality management programs, high-performance work systems, and internal markets to introduce large-scale changes inside.
- Joint ventures, alliances, consortia, and flexible manufacturing networks remake the maps of external corporate relations.

All these innovations are variations on common teamnet themes, people crossing boundaries that are normally "off-limits." It's easier than you might think.

Teaming Inside and Out

Traditionally, most people have worked for one company with other fellow employees. Within their company, people have worked in a particular area, almost exclusively with co-workers from their department. At least, this is the official version of how work gets done, as given by the formal organizational chart. Well, good-bye order, and hello messiness.

The demand for greater speed and flexibility turns the organized world of work inside out. "Inside" and "outside" depend on multiple points of reference. Gail Snowden, a financial services executive, in effect holds four "badges" simultaneously: at Bank of Boston, where she is president of First Community Bank, the bank's inner city urban network of branches and lenders in three New England states; at the City of Boston, where she represents the bank as a board member of the Boston Local Development Corporation, an urban economic development project; at Fleet Bank, where she works with her competitor both on that board and on the Massachusetts Minority Enterprise Investment Corporation, a multi-bank-owned vehicle for providing small business loans to minority- and women-owned businesses throughout the state; and at Simmons

Graduate School of Management, where Simmons is following Snowden in its first case study on a woman of color in a significant position of power. Multienterprise relationships such as Snowden's cross all kinds of "state lines."

Today, people regularly work across divisions in their own firms, forging new links with people from other groups, departments, or subsidiaries of the company. Toyota, in the interest of quality, has developed all kinds of cross-functional teams. Toyota's success inspired similar efforts at Ford, and, later, scores of other companies outside the auto industry. These multiunit teams cross internal organizational "city limits."

Whether inside companies or between companies, these teams and alliances require a new kind of thinking to be successful. For instance, beware competitor bashing: today's competitors may be tomorrow's colleagues. Remember Super Bowl 1984? You may have forgotten the game, but you remember the commercial. Apple Computer launched its "1984" ad campaign George Orwell style: a perfectly fit young woman runner hurls a fatal weapon against the only thinly disguised old men running Big Blue. Seven years later, Taligent is under way, IBM and Apple's joint venture. In the '90s, the youthful Cupertino upstart in jeans works side by side with the aging Armonk blue suit.

It's too complicated and too expensive for any size company to go it alone all the time. Today, going it alone means missing opportunities. Tomorrow, it means going out of business.

The "little people" are doing exactly as the big companies. While the restaurants in our Boston-area neighborhood compete for the lunch-time crowd—Brigham's, Cherry Tree, and even Captain Marden's, the local fish store—they all cooperate to promote "Square Dollars," a local economy good only in West Newton Square. To enhance your business opportunities, think differently about all your relationships:

• Customers, once the passive distant receivers of products, now are part of their vendors' product and service development programs.

Kodak's Black and White Film organization (nicknamed "Team Zebra"), which has produced a continuous stream of breakthrough products in record time, has regularly included customers on its teams. Steve Frangos, former manager of Black and White Film manufacturing, eschewed what he calls the "hand grenade" principle on Team Zebra—"throwing the design over the wall." Instead, customers "were in on the design from the beginning, including people from other parts of Kodak, like the marketing organization, and outside customers who bought the products."

• With cash flow slowed and credit extremely hard to come by, suppliers become partners.

Instead of buying the major parts for its new plane, the MD-12, Douglas Aircraft came up with a different plan of partnering with its suppliers. Partners would *invest* their components—the wing, the tail, the engines—and get paid when the airlines bought the planes.

• Supplier-customer relations also exist inside the company, between interdependent departments and in the groups that provide products and services to one another.

Cross-functional teams coordinate across the sometimes great walls of internal politics in Conrail's Strategic Managers Group and across borders in Armstrong's five global management networks. Even the smallest of firms specialize functions—one person does the books, another does the purchasing, a third does the deals—but they all have to work together to make the business successful.

Boundary crossing teamnets are businesses' potential secret weapon.

They offer greater diversity of expertise, experience, and skills as problems become more complex and increasingly difficult for one person, one small group, or one company to solve. Quality circles at Komatsu, autonomous work groups at GM's Saturn plant, and project teams at Arthur D. Little, Inc., the international consulting firm,[8] all interact cooperatively, drawing people from across their companies. At the same time, they give people more freedom to contribute and to balance home and work life.

Colleagues, vendors, customers, and competitors are all members of boundary crossing teamnets. These new alliances allow groups and companies to quickly configure and reconfigure their relationships to take advantage of changing business realities.

Why is this happening? How have we gone from the steady state of a single boss and strict allegiance to one chain of command to the dynamic challenge of working in many places across traditional boundaries?

Why? Because things are getting faster, more complex, and more global. No matter how big we are, we can't do it all, all by ourselves.

Whether they are well known—as in Armstrong, once synonymous with the word "linoleum"—or not known at all—as in ACEnet, a network of small firms that design and build kitchen appliances for the disability equipment market, companies today depend upon *boundary crossing teamnets*. Whereas not so long ago working with the competition was an unthinkable sin, today not figuring out how to work with the competition may be a deadly one.

"SMALL IS BOUNTIFUL": TEAMNETS AMONG THE LITTLE PEOPLE[9]

In the United States, small business, when taken as a whole, is really big business. The country's 20 million small business entrepreneurs employ half the nation's workforce, account for 40 percent of GDP, and create the majority of new products and technologies. Small businesses are also now the major contributors to new employment: in some areas, small business creates two out of every three new jobs or more.

This time a revolution in management practices is not passing by small business. In the new world that emphasizes speed and flexibility, smart combinations of small firms have real global competitive advantages, and create benefits that dramatically appear on the bottom lines of nations.

Flexible business networks among even the smallest of companies can yield dramatic results. From Denmark to Denver, small companies create boundary crossing teamnets to compete in markets that traditionally lock out individual firms as the cost of business goes up. In the United States, networks among small firms exist in all parts of the country:

- On Florida's north coast, 16 member companies of TEC-NET (Technopolis Network/Silicon Coast Corridor), which previously competed fiercely for defense contracts, set aside their differences. Instead, they collaborate to design, manufacture, and market a high-quality laser printer.
- In Pennsylvania, five small woodworking firms, seriously threatened by the recession, join forces in The Philadelphia Guild, which markets a new line of home office furniture.
- In southern New Hampshire, Team Nashua, 10 electronic component manufacturers, band together to offer "electronic packaging" for their customers. Joseph Roberts, CEO of Advanced Circuit Technologies, Inc., the convener of Team Nashua, anticipates that its first big contract for $1.2 million with Compaq is

the harbinger of things to come. "We expect to do $4 to $10 million in additional business in 1993," he says.[10]

In textiles, metalworking, landscape architecture, woodworking, plastics, secondary wood products, disability devices, apparel, waste management, software, golf courses, and even cemeteries, companies are finding it is better to grow together than to go it alone.

TEAMNETS SOLVE SOME BIG PROBLEMS FOR LITTLE COMPANIES

Teamnets can solve many different problems for small businesses. For businesses locked out of markets that favor economies of scale, teamnets of allied companies are the answer. By sharing costs and knowledge in areas that only the big companies can traditionally afford, small companies can do the work of giants. Their competitive parity is achieved without giving up the independence and benefits of a small enterprise. Companies don't form boundary crossing teamnets in the abstract. Teamnets are most often created for specific purposes. Some typical reasons are to:

Purchase Cooperatively

The Southeastern Massachusetts Sewn Products Network buys thread together at a 15 percent discount, which means $100,000 per year in savings to one member.

Market Jointly

The nine black American artists who own stores in 1800 Belmont Arts in Washington, D.C., where they sell products reflecting African-American culture and heritage, found their combined mailing list numbers 100,000. "We've already done radio interviews together and plan to do joint promotion," says Diane White, the owner of Blackberry, a small chain of stores in the Washington, D.C., area offering Afrocentric gifts and clothing.

Combine Research and Development

Five Massachusetts metalworking firms pool resources to research solvents for parts cleaning.

Co-sponsor Training

Twenty Arkansas high-end furniture-finishing companies share training on new finishes and their environmental regulation implications.

Set Up Quality Programs

Some 35 high-tech companies—ranging from Bolt, Beranek and Newman to Polaroid to Carrier Corporation—cooperate to form the Center for Quality Management, which teaches quality concepts at all levels of the corporate hierarchy.

By combining forces with other companies, businesses benefit from economies of scale. Working with others provides access to complementary products and services, which, when combined, provide a much larger offering to customers.

Can We Partner?

Among large companies, teamnets make for some complicated arrangements. For example, Deutsche Aerospace, a partner in Europe's Airbus consortium, announces at the 1992 Berlin Air Show that it now exchanges engineers with Boeing. The obvious complication here is that Boeing and Airbus, as the only players besides Douglas Aircraft left in the world's commercial aircraft business, are arch competitors. Deutsche Aerospace and Boeing face a major challenge in managing their boundary crossing teamnets—both on the corporate level and on the ground as small groups of engineers get together to implement the agreement.

Aerospace is particularly predisposed to "teaming" since costs are so great and customers are so few. With the high cost of new product development, no single company can afford to be the sole investor. As the military buildup topped out, defense firms found themselves forced to partner with arch rivals: Rockwell and Boeing, Northrop and General Dynamics, Lockheed and McDonnell Douglas, found themselves in partnerships. On NASP, NASA's space plane, five major competitors jointly developed the first designs.

"There are many more engagements than there are marriages among big companies," says Pamela Johnson, a Digital Equipment Corporation engineer turned management consultant. "There are more marriages than there are good marriages. And because of the enormous capital investments, companies cross-supply each other in all kinds of specialties." Her company specializes in certain technologies that the public is not even aware of, such as thin film heads, for example, which the other big computer companies buy from Digital. Digital in turn buys small computer memory tape systems from Hewlett-Packard and large ones from IBM, while also supplying information storage assembly components to other storage manufacturers.

In Silicon Valley, networks among start-ups in the semiconductor field are as common as new generations of chips: some 350 strategic alliances have been formed since 1979.

To get an idea of how complex these relationships can be, consider the emerging field of multimedia, the electronic combination of words, images, sight, sound, and motion. Apple has at least six major relationships that are so complex they nearly defy being put into words. Apple partners with:

- AT&T/NCR to invest in Echo Logic;
- AT&T/NCR and Sony to invest in General Magic;
- IBM to invest in Kaleida;
- IBM and Motorola to invest in Taligent;
- Sony directly in a strategic alliance; and,
- Toshiba directly in a strategic alliance.

Meanwhile, Sony has a separate strategic alliance with Microsoft, Matsushita has a separate alliance with AT&T/NCR, and Toshiba has an alliance with IBM, which in turn has separate alliances with both Hewlett-Packard and Intel. Although not every high-tech arrangement has been successful—and some among the megafirms are downright suspect as efforts to squelch the competition—technology companies are important testing grounds for many of these new business ideas.

Some companies now appear to *specialize* in multiple partnering arrangements, like Corning, Inc., a self-described "global network," formerly known as Corning Glass Works (where perhaps, like us, you bought miniature glass animals when you were a child), the company that makes Corning Ware, the dishes you can drop on the floor without breaking. Corning now participates in nearly 40 joint ventures. Likewise, Perstorp, the Swedish specialty chemical firm, has a similar number of entrepreneurial partnerships. According to a *Biotechnology 91* survey, the larger biotechnology firms, numbering 300 or more employees, participate in nine strategic alliances on average.

For big companies, working in teamnets is also the solution to many common problems inside the enterprise:

Running Into Walls, Stovepipes, and Silos

Internal groups wage war on a fragmented project that crosses functional borders; and departments become so protective of their turf that they refuse to appropriately work with other parts of the company.

Moving a Centralized Bureaucracy

Key projects and strategic programs that require multigroup collaboration are stymied by the central group's slowness, rigidity, and unwillingness to change.

Getting a Life

As the need for creativity sharpens, the tradition-bound organization with no spirit of initiative or innovation wants to "do this one just like we've done all the others," as the company goes out of business.

Big company or small, teamnets provide the infrastructure to get things done.

PROBLEMS IN PARADISE

Teamnets may sound like the answer to all business problems—they increase competitiveness, profits, and jobs. But don't the same problems that exist within companies and groups plague them when they move to this new style of doing business?

Of course they do. Not every boundary crossing teamnet succeeds. Some networks have gone belly-up the minute their government funding ran out. Their purpose was never completely clear, and so without the influx of cash, there was nothing to keep the teams working together to survive. Six of Corning's strategic alliances have failed, some for market reasons, some for lack of organization. One particularly high-profile alliance highlights unanticipated problems with independent partners: Dow Corning took some heavy hits in 1992 when the silicon gel breast implant controversy moved to the front page.

A boundary crossing alliance in-the-making shows the not necessarily successful application of the teamnet principles on a very large corporate scale. The early story shows both the necessity of looking for new partners by even the biggest companies, and the enormous difficulty an old-line company has in re-creating itself. Although it remains to be seen whether the company will be able to pull off its challenging teamnet idea, its proposal is a harbinger of many projects to come.

BUILDING A NEW PLANE IN MANY PLACES

The situation that Douglas Aircraft faces as it sets out to build its new plane in 1990 is that it has no capital. The MD-12 is designed to be the successor to an illustrious line of airplanes stretching back through the DC-10, DC-9, and Donald Douglas's first great hit, the DC-3.

If history were to repeat itself, sometime in 1997, the first in the next generation of jumbo jets designed to compete with Boeing's aging 747s will roll out onto the tarmac in Long Beach, California. Lakewood Avenue, where Douglas Aircraft's headquarters is situated, is a strange sight at night, with the stadium lights flooding the huge iron birds. The company paints its behemoths next to the football-field-sized hangars where they build the planes. The noise level is so intense that most people in the hangars wear ear protectors.

Outside on the tarmac, crews on three-story-high ladders transform the nearly completed vehicles from their mottled Army-fatigue hue to the sleek, attractive color-coordinated airborne *objets d'art* that we associate with jet airliners. However, not a single MD-12 will roll out of the Long Beach hangars, change colors, then glide across the street (in the middle of the night so as not to disturb traffic) to the takeoff runways. Douglas will not build its new plane in Long Beach at all. Rather, it will be built in pieces all over the world and assembled in a "greenfield," a brand-new industrial park of 30 tenants gathered just to manufacture MD-12s.

Building a jumbo jet is a daunting process. To be state-of-the-art, this plane will consist of at least 700,000 designed parts, ranging from the very large like the fuselage, wing, and engines, to the very small, like knobs in the cockpit and fixtures for light bulbs at service points.

It costs a lot to build a new plane, probably far more than you would guess unless you're in the aerospace industry. Douglas Aircraft projects the cost to build the first copy of its next-generation, wide-body, long-haul vehicle at *$5 billion*. Very few companies anywhere in the world are able to foot the product development bill for such a gigantic project—even if the plane's sticker price is $130 million, and the total market size (of which Douglas hopes to capture 30 percent) is estimated at $300 billion over the next 20 years.[11]

In the early 1990s, Douglas certainly is not in that position, even though until the MD-12 (and since the early 1920s, when Douglas first set up shop in Long Beach), it has built every one of its planes by itself—from the DC-1 to the MD-11. (They switched acronyms from DC to MD after the DC-10, which was the last plane that Douglas itself designed before St. Louis–based McDonnell Aircraft bought it in 1967.)

Each manufacturer of the plane's major parts—the wing, the tail, the avionics, the computer systems—will not be a supplier, vendor, or contractor, traditionally adversarial relationships in aerospace. Instead, the manufacturers become risk-sharing partners: they invest the up-front capital needed to build their part. Then, when the planes sell to the airlines, the partners reap their share of the rewards.

Imagine a plane built with a Taiwanese tail, a Canadian fuselage, Spanish wings, English engines, and American computer systems. Some of the estimated 30 global risk-sharing partners are Douglas's fiercest competitors. The MD-12 "campus," as large companies affectionately refer to their corporate settings, will be globally distributed, a virtual place where the sun never sets.

Does inevitable failure doom such an undertaking? Douglas can succeed only if it concentrates as much on its organizational problems and opportunities as it does on its technical ones. Like its competitors, Boeing and Airbus, Douglas knows how to build very good planes. Neither Douglas nor Boeing is a world leader, however, in the new management required to coordinate work across corporations, time zones, cultures, and continents.

Airbus, the upstart newcomer that has surpassed Douglas as the world's second largest commercial aircraft producer, may have a leg up on its competitors in this regard. Airbus is an entrepreneurial consortium funded by a group of European nations, a very large-scale boundary crossing teamnet.

Douglas's new plane is one development program to watch, not for the MD-12's metrics on its thrust and loft, but rather on its innovation in designing and coordinating its partnerships.

So, if Douglas Aircraft is able to pull off its ambitious plan and you someday find yourself on board an MD-12, take a look around. You'll fly on a bird built by what is likely to be a record number of boundary crossing teamnets. If Douglas attempts to build the MD-12 alone, it will not succeed. You'll never take that flight unless Douglas successfully learns the skills of co-opetition.

> The supreme challenge of the 21st century will be the ability to manage projects that transcend all the conventional boundaries, whether to produce global products or prevent global warming. The bureaucracies of the Industrial Age with their rigid focus on in-house protocols will appear to the new inter-corporate transcontinental networks as old Royal typewriters do to PC users.[12]

Barbecued Sushi and Competition Among Nations

Perhaps it is not surprising that teamnets are developing at a rapid rate in countries as historically different as Japan and the United States. Each of the different national characters—Japanese collectivism and U.S. individualism—carries strong seeds of the other.

East and West are moving to network organizations from complementary directions. In the East, the whole group has historically been considered more important than individuals. In the West, we put more emphasis on the individual than the whole group. So, in the United States, we find ourselves explaining networks as a way of developing more cooperative and group-oriented organization without diminishing the importance of individuals. We emphasize the importance of group factors like cooperation and planning in seeking a balance with individualistic cultural tendencies.

In Japan, the need is just the opposite. Networking becomes a way to foster personal development, enhancing individual creativity, initiative, and responsibility without diminishing the traditional importance of the group. In Japan, networkers emphasize the role of individuals in seeking a balance with group-oriented cultural tendencies.[13]

At the September 1990 meeting of the University of Michigan's annual automotive seminar, Alfred H. Peterson III, chairman of a relatively small auto spring manufacturer (sales under $100 million), finds a clever way to highlight the difference between America and Japan. "Sushi is beautifully presented and wrapped," he says, "with everything in place and perfect. Barbecue is made up of pieces of pork or beef swimming around in a big pot. The dissimilarity of these two dishes is symbolic of the great difference in the way our economies are organized and our auto industries function."

> *"The Japanese system relies on interdependence, while the North American is based upon independence."*[14]

Are the Japanese ahead in the race to uncover the secrets of successful co-opetition? If they are, should the United States emulate them?

Rather than calling for Americans to copy the Japanese system, at the automotive seminar Peterson suggests "much closer but better-balanced supplier relationships, rigorous pursuit of continuous improvement and a genuine re-evaluation of the true importance of people who get dirty while getting things done the right way."

Both Japan and America have something to learn from one another about independence and interdependence. Each has opposite strengths and weaknesses. Each starts with a cultural advantage: Japan's is cooperation, while America's is competition. Japan is learning the game of individual initiative against the cultural prohibition against being different. Americans are learning new ways to cooperate against the great historical resistance of die-hard independence.

Europe seems to occupy a middle ground. Europe is home to Western civilization's emphasis on the individual, but does not extend it to America's extreme. Europe's coordination often comes from the top down, from many small nations, principalities, city-states, and ethnic groups. The European Community is one of the planet's grand experiments at a supranation network designed to benefit all its members, national and individual. For small companies, Europe provides lessons for flexible business networks; for large companies, examples such as ABB's internal markets are cutting-edge management innovations.

Cooperation *and* competition. America, with its caldron of diversity, has the harder row to hoe than Japan or Europe to bridge differences with beneficial relationships. But if the highly heterogeneous United States succeeds, it may show the world how even the greatest extremes can work together productively and profitably.

Networking is a global business philosophy. It is being driven by the pace of change and the worldwide need to find flexible new ways of managing in the 21st century.

Seeing the Obvious:
Five Teamnet Principles

Stephanie Whitley is a strategic planner at TransOceania, a $6 billion international transportation company based in Asia. We had the chance to work with her team, the Transportation Scheduling Project. Their purpose was to develop a cross-functional network to plan the company's shipping schedules. A few weeks after our last visit to TransOceania, we received a letter from Stephanie with "some brief news on our progress":

> Although our status is unclear at the moment, our Friday afternoon meetings with Johann and Robert [two key vice presidents] are continuing. We're installing an electronic mail system that will link us to 15 other people who will be involved in delivering the new schedule. Richard, David, John, and I have become quite a determined foursome, each focusing on our own specialty. Our mission is "to increase profits by redesigning the way the company plans its schedules."

Stephanie gives a precise description of what makes teamnets work. A successful teamnet has:

- A clear *purpose*, which Stephanie calls a "mission";
- Independent *members* who want to be involved, "quite a determined foursome," in Stephanie's words;
- Ongoing *interaction* ("Friday afternoon meetings") and good communications *links*, in this case, an electronic mail system;
- Two or more *leaders*, in this case, four; and
- Connections to different *levels* of the existing hierarchy, in her case, the vice presidents.

The "Five Teamnet Principles" are fundamental to every successful effort that involves people crossing boundaries:

- *Unifying* **purpose;**
- *Independent* **members;**
- *Voluntary* **links;**
- *Multiple* **leaders;** and
- *Interactive* **levels.**

Each principle is found in every successful teamnet. A teamnet must have a reason to exist (purpose), a critical number of committed participants (members), a rich web of relationships (links), people who assume specific responsibilities (leaders), and connections at many levels in the environment.

Companies that understand how their teamnets operate have a distinct organizational advantage. In 1989, former Digital Equipment Corporation vice president Ulf Fagerquist, a nuclear physicist (who started the company's Swedish operation) with a special interest in strategic alliances, asked us to look at the teamnet features of five Digital projects. Digital was an especially interesting place for teamnets because in 1989, it was a $12 billion enterprise doing business in 97 countries. With its expertise and development activity scattered around the globe, for many years the company had the world's largest private telecommunications network at its disposal. For us, Digital has been a particularly fascinating, challenging environment in which to observe the Five Teamnet Principles in a wide variety of circumstances.

We began our studies of Digital's successful teamnets with its

1977 project (run by Fagerquist) that enabled Associated Press to network its stock quotations to newspapers all around the world every day. We ended with the most successful internal teamnet we had seen to date. "Calypso" took place in the mid-1980s at the company's peak and shows what 40 to 50 people can achieve when everything "clicks."

The One-Page Project: When Everything Clicks

It is late 1986 and Digital is riding high on its preeminence in the computer industry, second only to then-faltering IBM. Marketing strategists spot a "window of opportunity" opening in both the United States and Europe for a high-volume, high-ticket product. Time, however, is of the essence. Competitors crowd a shrinking market for mini-computers.

Can Digital plan, design, test, market, manufacture, deliver, and service a highly complex computer in a window with at most a two-year introduction horizon? Fifteen months later, Digital's 6200 computer pours out simultaneously from plants in New England, the Caribbean, and Europe. Code-named "Calypso," the computer generates the steepest revenue ramp in the company's history, eventually developing into a family of products. The window is wide open, the market loves the product, and the company reaps enormous profits.

How does this happen? Intuitively, the project's managers put into practice the five principles required for successful boundary crossing teamnets.

"In the beginning, there are just a handful of people from different large functional organizations," explains Pauline Nist, Calypso's overall project manager. "There are people from engineering, manufacturing, marketing, and service right from the start."

Like many boundary crossing teams, Calypso's members repre sent different levels within the organization. And the managers have a wide spectrum of staff sizes. Some people have large groups reporting to them. Others have none; they're on the project for their unique expertise.

Getting off the ground quickly, the small group begins with a brilliant vision. "It's compelling because it contains both the market insight and the creative technical approach," Nist says. "With our vision in hand, we take our show on the road to recruit people, looking for talent, enthusiasm, and commitment." Before long, several dozen people sign up.

Because Digital is such a large company, the "right" people for the project often are in the "wrong" place. "We don't have the time to move people and it's too expensive anyway. So, we decide to do this project in a distributed way," she says.

Eventually, the 50 core people who become directly identified with the Calypso team sit in 14 separate locations, including several in New England, California, the Caribbean, and Ireland.

Many methods of communication—rich links—connect Calypso's teamnet members. They phone one another often. The members use telephone conference calls and video conferences and hold scheduled and unscheduled meetings. They use electronic mail and computer conferencing.[1] A common database is created that contains all information necessary for the machine's design.

"We compensate for everyone not being in the same place all the time by setting up lots of ways to communicate," Nist says. "If I could have changed one thing about the project, I would have put in the Puerto Rico satellite dish sooner."

Even so, the teamnet members travel frequently. "There are a lot of project miles on these people," says George Hoff, then Nist's boss, underscoring the point that face-to-face contact is essential, contrary to what many think.

"You don't build trust over the wire," Nist allows, reaffirming that it's critical for people to meet periodically. "Building trust takes flesh and blood, but it doesn't take a long time to make that happen." Virtually every teamnet member stresses this point: trust is the first and most major stumbling block; once it's achieved, things can begin to click. With the core internal teamnet in place, Calypso is ready to talk with other companies, and form the external part of its team.

"Then we hit pay dirt," she says. "When we visit potential vendors of a key component, we notice that one of them shares our vision and enthusiasm. We propose joint development, which significantly reduces time and costs for both companies."

While anticipating a possible *supplier* partnership, the Calypso team is surprised when it suddenly finds itself in a *customer* partnership. "The next big break is that Raytheon, one of our largest customers, proposes an alliance," says Hoff. "We make an agreement: they'll do parallel development of a product for their military market. The goal is to release both products at the same time." The partnership succeeds. Both companies' presidents speak at the 6200's announcement, vastly increasing the first-day market for Digital's product while also ensuring ongoing customer review of the design. Here, Digital demonstrates an extremely important point that causes many companies problems when they try to do this. Being clear on who is doing what is critical for avoiding unhealthy friction. Companies often have different, conflicting views of what they both own.

This is not the success of skunkworks—where a group locks itself in a room and doesn't come out until they complete their project—but of teamnets. No driven boss with traditional levers of power manages this global boundary crossing teamnet. Although Nist, the engineering manager, has the designation of overall project manager, only a portion of Calypso's engineers report to her. Nist reports to the engineering chain of command (Hoff reports to the vice president of engineering and she reports to Hoff); the project's production manager reports to a manufacturing vice president; still other team members report into their own functional organizations or what Digital calls "stovepipes." Naturally, Nist has no direct control over the team members from the outside companies.

At first glance, it sounds like a prescription for disaster. None of the traditional management school principles seems to apply to this situation. Far from a disaster, Calypso is a smashing success.

Why does it work? "Why," indeed, is the key.

Calypso understands its purpose early on: to develop a multiprocessor mid-range computer in 18 months using existing technology.

And it continually tests it on prospective partners. Shared vision, common purpose, clear goals, and well-articulated tasks provide an overall picture and detailed direction. Jointly, all the stakeholders accomplish the shared work on schedule and within budget.

A shared view of a project's purpose drives a boundary crossing teamnet to excellence, not an authoritarian leader. In Calypso's case, they are able to reduce the purpose to a single graphic that fits onto an 8½-by-11-inch sheet of paper. This "one-pager" summarizes the project so well that people carry it around, along with their calendars.

When everyone works toward a shared, common purpose, boundary crossing teamnets work. Calypso achieves this. Without it, this team would have failed miserably.

> *"When you manage to get the goals lined up," Nist says, "the opportunity is there for great success. In this project, a number of goals came together simultaneously. They meshed in a unified way as opposed to an antagonistic one. Once a project like this gets momentum, there's no stopping it."*

A Handful of Principles

Calypso is an example of the new type of organization already at work within and between companies. It illustrates the basic principles of teamnets: members of the Calypso team include people and organizations that cross conventional lines of authority, both within Digital and outside the company, and cooperate on the basis of common goals without giving up their independence.

Teamnets combine the concepts of distributed teams and organizational networks. They apply across a range of different-sized companies, from micro-enterprises to macro-economies. And teamnets take a variety of forms, ranging from the very familiar to 21st-century technology-wave organizations, just emerging.

The Five Teamnet Principles mix learning from examples with the guidance of theory, a conceptual range from concrete to abstract. "Teams" make the here-and-now promise of practical ideas of value, while "networks" evoke vision, the ability to grasp wholes and weave pieces together.

People learn in different ways. Some prefer concepts, others examples. Our effort to mix these two styles may leave some readers a little impatient in places. Try to tolerate the discomfort. Use this book as a "scratch-and-sniff" experience, a taste of what it feels like to create a teamnet, integrating divergent views and cultures into a coherent whole.

Although the boundary crossing organization chart is hard to fit into a typical bureaucratic box design, it does have a structure. Unfortunately, if you use a conventional hierarchical perspective, it is generally all but impossible to see. Try looking for "The Boss" when there is more than one. When members must cross conventional boundaries to solve problems and accomplish goals, they are most likely to develop networks. Teamnets are not about "breaking" or "smashing" boundaries:

Teamnets are about crossing *boundaries.*

Boundary Crossing Teamnets

A teamnet is a group of people and groups that cross conventional boundaries for mutual benefit while retaining individual independence.

Inside organizations, these cross-boundary teams show up as specific forms like self-directed work groups; outside, they refer to concrete arrangements like corporate alliances. Teamnets are the *visible* people and groups who work together to get something done.

Networks represent the core logic that ties together the variety of boundary crossing organizations. The concept stands for the *invisible* infrastructure and processes that give life to teamnets of all sizes and styles. A general network concept is a powerful tool for increasing your boundary crossing capabilities and improving the effectiveness of your teamnets.

Networks are all about integrating global and local. It is imperative that the local parts of networks (teams) be able to adapt to local circumstances while providing global value. This can be achieved only by understanding general principles and how they can be applied to your unique situation. Our model, within which the Five Teamnet Principles play a major role, acts as an instrument for coping with the cacophony of confusion in the real world.

Organizational Network

An organizational network has independent members with multiple leaders, a unifying purpose with lots of voluntary links, and interacting levels.

When all five principles work together adapting to local circumstances, boundary crossing teamnets can be very successful. Without these principles, organizational success is left to luck in the face of coping with rapid change. Sometimes, millions of dollars and years of unrecoverable time evaporate with unnecessary failures.

In organizational networks, people and groups are the members, the independent nodes. Voluntary links across boundaries develop interdependence among members. Mutual benefits make unifying purposes tangible. Multiple leaders arise to serve different needs. And members interact across levels.

You cannot put these five principles together and come up with a "perfect" network. At least we've never seen one; have you? In reality, pure organizational forms do not exist. Mostly, the new organizations have fuzzy boundaries, with networks springing up in and between hierarchies. Sometimes they clash and occasionally they reinvigorate these central control systems.

There will be no wholesale replacement of hierarchy with horizontal structures. But there is coexistence; often hierarchies and networks can even thrive together. Alarming as it may sound to some, hierarchy has a critical role to play in organizations of the future. Hierarchy, bureaucracy, and networks mix to manage large organizations and small for different needs and purposes.

Our groups and organizational structures are in a transitional time. As people always do, we have one foot in the past and one in the future. The unique aspect of this transition is that the gap between our feet is widening faster than ever before. The Teamnet Principles bridge the gap between the old and new, and offer platforms on which to build flexible organizations that work.

THE DYNAMIC BALANCE OF COMPETITION AND COOPERATION

Purpose, members, links, leaders, levels—these are the features to look for in boundary crossing teamnets. Use them as a powerful tool for seeing these vital but fuzzy phenomena. The five principles are not a list. They are an interacting system, connecting members and leaders through links and purpose, creating new levels of organization.

Co-opetition Dynamic

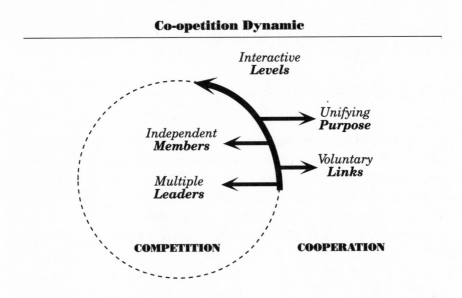

Networks exist in the creative tension between competitive and cooperative tendencies, ever-shifting between the self-assertion of individuals and the integration required for a group whole.

Two of the principles support competition, the self-assertive tendency:

- *Independent* **members**.
- *Multiple* **leaders**.

Two of the principles reflect cooperation, the integrative tendency:

- *Unifying* **purpose**.
- *Voluntary* **links**.

The fifth principle balances the opposing forces through:

• *Interactive **levels.***

The combination of "cooperation" and "competition" is not an awkward contradiction. The root of the two words, the conjunction "co-opetition," literally means "to work and seek together." It is the feisty combination of cooperative power and competitive zeal that offers people and companies organizational advantages.

As one word, "co-opetition" fuses complementary forces, single-handedly gripping a complex system of concepts. The five principles allow you to take the first steps in fusing opposites. Treat each principle as a valuable tool in its own right. Look at each independently and calibrate it for optimal effectiveness in specific teamnet circumstances.

Despite the power of the Teamnet Principles, each one has certain myths associated with it.

1. CLARIFY THE UNIFYING PURPOSE

Calypso is a project that is a huge success, bringing the company its fastest revenue ramp of any product to date. A major success factor is the team's initial clear view of *"why* it is doing what it is doing." The group understands the context within which it is working. Then the team nurtures, grows, and develops its idea into a powerful motivating force that guides the project. Were they simply lucky? Many people believe that success with decentralized, distributed organizations happens randomly, unpredictably, without cause.

Myth 1: It is just plain dumb luck when networks work.

Quite the contrary. When boundary crossing is successful, there is *always* a reason. In successful business networks, the reason is clear and benefits are tangible. People form teamnets around needs. A boundary crossing group strikes a spark and develops an internal motivation when it meets real needs. Common goals become so explicit that you can test them against feasible solutions and real products or services.

Teamnet purposes run the gamut from high-flying unifying visions to carefully crafted mission statements to lists of specific goals and concrete objectives to the details of tasks and work. People even wear their mission statements on lapel buttons, broadcast them from billboards along the highway, hang them on banners in cafeterias, and publish them in annual reports.

Our definition of this key teamnet ingredient admits to its intangible nature:

Purpose

Purpose is the vital spirit of a network expressed as a unifying aim and set of values shared by participants.

Be explicit. This hard-learned idea renders hard-to-see purposes more visible, more able to be used as guides—and debated when necessary:

Boundary crossing teamnets must express their purposes explicitly.

Purpose needs elaboration in a teamnet because it performs the coordination role traditionally played by centralized command and control.

While many networks spontaneously emerge to respond to a clear need, such as in crisis situations, most groups require some conscious motivation for formation. Without something that spurs the group to enthusiastically agree, many boundary crossing teamnets never get beyond the talking stage. They cannot articulate a clear-enough purpose that benefits a critical mass of participants. Even after successful formation, many networks later collapse when their unifying purpose splits into factions. Unless a shared purpose is renegotiated, the group begins a slide into disintegration.

> *The importance of clarifying purpose in boundary crossing teamnets is critical.*

Purpose—shared goals—is the vital core of teamnets. The term "vital" emphasizes the organic nature of teamnets. It contrasts with the mechanical metaphors that hierarchy and bureaucracy use.

Strength of purpose holds boundary crossing teamnets together. With links, purpose pulls together disparate elements acting as a centripetal force. Purpose replaces traditional glues—such as coercion in hierarchy and written instructions in bureaucracy—that are weak in fast-moving teamnets. In the face of rapid change, traditional control mechanisms falter. Purpose provides a context for action.

2. IDENTIFY INDEPENDENT MEMBERS

It's a misty May 1992 evening, just before dinner at the semiannual meeting of the Calvert Social Investment Fund Advisory Council.[2] We are out walking with a member of the Board of Trustees on the grounds of a Maryland conference center, the site of the dinner meeting.

"But don't you think Americans are too independent for networks?" Terry Mollner asks, when we tell him about this book. He is voicing the sentiment that people do all around the world when they first hear about the idea. Wherever you go, people say, "It won't work here." In Italy, people said the medieval guild mentality would prevent people from working across business boundaries. In Denmark, people said that Viking fierceness would get in the way. In the United States, depending on which part of the country you're from, people point to Yankee independence, Lone Ranger cowboys, or southern pride to explain why Americans can't, or won't, cooperate.

Myth 2: If you join a network, you give up your independence.

The opposite is true. No independence, no network! "When you join, you discover your independence," writes Charles Savage, author of *Fifth Generation Management.*[3] Healthy boundary crossing teamnets depend upon the healthy independence of their members. When direct command-and-control hierarchical structures are inappropriate or simply won't work, networks emerge to coordinate the activities of independent business units or people inside and outside companies. In the case of Calypso, the collaborative project forms in a corporate culture that has long prided itself on its strong Yankee individualistic traditions.

Teamnets thrive in the dynamic balance between self-assertion and integration. They seesaw between the decentralizing forces of independence and the integrating forces of cooperative interdependence. So long as teamnet participants continue to have some measure of real independence, you have a boundary crossing teamnet. When independence ceases, you have a hierarchy or a merger.

Members

Members are the people and groups that contribute specific capabilities to achieving the shared purpose.

Each member has something unique and different to bring to the group. With multiple leaders, independent members are the "pulling apart" centrifugal forces within teamnets. Members are also the most tangible aspect, the parts that are easier to grasp. It is easier to see members than it is to see purpose. Boundary crossing teamnets are known by their purposes and members, but without linking the parts together, a teamnet cannot exist.

3. CREATE VOLUNTARY LINKS

As Calypso demonstrates, boundary crossing teamnets tend to be spread out. Without the local water cooler or cafeteria as a daily meeting ground, these groups require very different work processes from those traditionally used by people located in the same place and same organization. "Working together apart" is how George Metes and Ray Grenier describe this.[4]

"Oh, I know what you're talking about," a telecommunications engineer says to us. "You people are writing about LANs [local area computer networks] and WANs [wide area computer networks]." In a sense, he is correct, but boundary crossing teamnets need a lot more than copper wire or fiber optics to be truly connected. Digital has a saying about this: "Just because the bits traveled around the world doesn't mean they were understood."

Myth 3a: Networks are just the channels of communication.

Some people, particularly those with a high-tech perspective, can only see the links of a network. They see the wires and completely miss the members. Other people are blind in another dimension: they cannot see the links that reveal trust and other invisible ties.

Myth 3b: Relationships are impossible to grasp. They are intangible, unreal, fleeting, short-lived, and can end on the turn of a sentence.

In a way, they're right, because it is very difficult to "see" the ineffable "stuff" of the relationships that bind teamnets together. *But relationships are real, and they do last. They are essential to the stuff of teamnets.*

Teamnets need interdependent links, both physical connections and voluntary relationships that people build over time. In order for a teamnet to achieve its goals, there must be sufficient connections among the people. "You do business with the people you know," says Jerry Nagel of the Red River Trade Corridor based in northern Minnesota.[5] First, people have to know and trust each other. Until there is trust, nothing happens. And they have to be able to communicate easily and effectively.

One way to see relationships is to follow these steps:

Step 1.

First, picture the physical communication links, the concrete connections between people like telephones, faxes, electronic mail, and the face-to-face exchanges.

Step 2.

Now, see people actively communicating through these channels, the interactions between senders and receivers. They are so "quantifiable" that communication researchers actually study them as discrete observable phenomena. Researchers break them down into such fine points as "acts," which someone initiates, "interacts," which involve sender and receiver, and "double interacts," which is what happens when responses start to multiply.

Step 3.

Finally, put all these interactions into motion over time and leap ahead to see relationships. They emerge in the repeated patterns of the exchanges. Relationships are like the patterned coherence that is natural in chaotic phenomena like human heartbeats and the weather.[6]

Relationships that develop over time seem to take on lives of their own. You can undoubtedly remember how some of your relationships with colleagues began, developed, and matured over time— say, from a first meeting, to follow-up contacts, to perhaps working on the same project and eventually saying good-bye in a job change.

Links

Links connect teamnet members through voluntary relationships, repetitive interactions, and physical ties.

Both bureaucracies and networks bind their members through interdependent links. In a bureaucracy, the decision-making relationships are nonvoluntary, while in networks they tend to be voluntary and more freely motivated.[7] It is this voluntary quality of relationships within networks that enables so many administrative mechanisms to be replaced with market processes.

Links complete our smallest set of core network concepts. The most rudimentary teamnet requires at minimum three elements:

- Purpose,
- Members, and
- Links.

Minimum Network Structure

If human networks could be cleanly and simply designed like a communications network, these three elements would suffice for a basic tool set.

You can see the members (nodes)[8] and physical links. You have to imagine purpose and relationships, which the shape of the numbers and links together suggests.

But the reality is that teamnets always have an irreducible "messy zone," which represents the freedom factor. The messy zone is where things get worked out in real time between real people who demand independence while calling for inclusion, cooperation, and a new vision. The messy zone springs from the inevitable struggles where the essence of networks meets the nub of hierarchy. Here, leadership is seized, granted, conferred, and otherwise established, and here the organizational levels inside and outside the teamnet meet and interact.[9]

4. RECOGNIZE THE POWER OF MULTIPLE LEADERS

As the Calypso project manager, Pauline Nist has influence without traditional authority, the ability to spend money but no control over paychecks, responsibility for overall project success but little power to fire people who do not perform. Many members of the team are independent decision makers, not dependent on the anointed leader for their survival. Each is an acknowledged leader in his or her own right.

No subject is more complex for the world's leading-edge organizations than leadership. No part of a teamnet experience is more fraught with uncertainty and clashes, minor and major, between the "old way" and "new way," than is establishing a successful leadership structure. While many successful networks have what appears to be a single identified leader, this conventional shape is just one way leadership structures form, even in rigid hierarchies.[10]

Myth 4a: All leadership comes to a single point.

Interestingly, the notion that hierarchy and other decision-making structures come to a single point has provoked a common misconception about networks, particularly prevalent among our friends who remember the myriad networks of the counterculture of the 1960s and 1970s.

Myth 4b: Networks have no leaders.

Multiple leadership that works is perhaps the most surprising feature of successful boundary crossing teamnets. Over time, most vital networks have many leaders. In example after example, you can soon read between the lines and figure out that most networks have more than one leader. The great network anthropologist Virginia Hine emphasized this point through use of the term "polycephalous," meaning "many-headed."[11]

> *Diversity and fluidity of leadership are hallmarks of boundary crossing teamnets. These groups sport a variety of leaders—like owners, brokers, experts, strategists, managers, networkers, and facilitators. Within any particular teamnet, multiple leadership arises from the multiple roles, skills, and knowledge required to address the complex problems taken on by the group.*

Be careful: There's a big difference between the network style of leadership and the hierarchical style. Unfortunately, many people believe that the old crack-the-whip, omnipotent command-and-control hierarch is the only effective way to lead.

In networks, leaders appear at the nexus of purpose and commitment, where responsibility is taken and shared work gets done. It is critical that leaders making decisions in one role not feel that they need to make all the group's decisions. Good network leaders are also good followers. This avoids both the hierarchy trap and its antithesis: Democratic paralysis from the dis-organization of everyone involved in everything.

We describe teamnet leaders this way:

Leaders

Leaders are members who make and keep commitments, know how to follow, and who may participate in the decision making of a network.

Note the subtlety that leaders *may* participate in decision making. Studies show that it is much more important for people to feel they have an *opportunity* to participate in decision making than it is to actually participate.

"Leaders are expert followers, mapping the needs, resources and agendas of network members, so as to create good matches among people and organizations," writes Elizabeth Lorentz[12] who with Seymour Sarason at Yale has studied resource exchange networks in depth.

With independent members, multiple leaders keep the pressure on for decentralization. They provide a good balance to the centralizing tendencies of unifying purpose and interdependent links.

How do teamnet leaders interact with traditional management? Intensively. One of the worst mistakes a teamnet can make is to ignore existing management. Teamnets also may have formal leaders, authority figures who occupy traditional roles.[13] In complex teamnets, leaders play pivotal roles in managing relationships among the different levels of the hierarchy. This entangling messiness needs interpretation; it isn't neat like the hierarchical tree structure on which it is easy to hang people.

In teamnets there are:

Fewer bosses, more leaders.

5. STAY CONNECTED AT ALL LEVELS

Calypso has a core group, some of whose members report to managers who are one, two, or three layers up in the hierarchy. Calypso is also a team of teams, a number of layers deep in places. As part of a larger company, Calypso has partnerships with other companies, so the core internal group also includes external members.

Myth 5: Networks are flat.

Like the flat-earth memory of the world before Copernicus, many people mentally picture a network as a flat, featureless, two-dimensional plane of horizontally connected members.

Perhaps the most common of all misconceptions is the idea that networks are only horizontal. This myth is so prevalent that people describe decentralized companies that deliberately have cut out layers of management as "a mile long and an inch high."

Appealing as this image of "flatness" is, especially in our bureaucracy-burdened society, it unfortunately is just plain wrong. Boundary crossing teamnets are lumpy, clustered, and multileveled forms of organization. People wear many hats, and act at many levels. One teamnet we worked with included a vice president, two senior managers, and a sales unit manager, along with a dozen other people reporting to people at similar levels.

This cross-level multiple-role feature of networks is one source of its power. It is also a major source of people's difficulty in being able to clearly see networks among the general tangle of relationships.

Luckily, there is a powerful conceptual tool available for understanding levels, which Herbert Simon called the "architecture of complexity."[14] Like everything complex in nature, networks are organized in levels of successive inclusion. In the context of systems, which networks are, levels mean sets within sets, like cells in tissues in organs in organisms, or pennies in dimes in dollars.

A network has at least two levels: the level of the member parts and the level of the network whole. A teamnet has at least three levels: a network of teams composed of members.

To use the levels principle to see networks of boundary crossing teams, you need a point of reference. One excellent point of reference is the corporate boundary, which is how we generally distinguish between "internal" and "external" networks. Departments, divisions, projects, and other typical internal boundaries also reflect levels. Anchor yourself to one of these points of reference, and you can roam the levels, going down into the depths of intrarelationships and out into the larger world of interrelationships.

Levels is the fundamental systems principle of "successive inclusion."[15] People live in levels. For example, people are parts of families, which in turn are members of communities that comprise regions that assemble into nations. People are also organisms made up of organs made up of tissues, cells, molecules, atoms, and so on. Everything in life is both part of larger things and can be broken down into smaller things.

> ## Levels
>
> Levels are the succession of parts and wholes that make up complex networks.

We do not include the principle of levels in the cooperative/competitive pairs. Rather, levels result from the dynamic itself: members retaining independence but integrating through the principles of purpose and links generate a multilevel organizational structure.

The Five Principles—purpose, members, links, leaders, and levels—are found in every successful teamnet. In the next chapter, we illustrate these principles with some stories. Throughout the rest of the first section, the principles provide the threads of consistency. They cover a variety of descriptions and situations. In the second section of the book, you put these ideas to work: we use the Teamnet Principles in a disciplined approach to starting and managing teamnets.

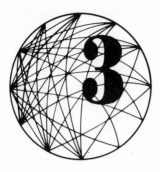

Linoleum, Furniture, and Electrical Systems: Three Different Boundary Crossing Teamnets

Companies of all sizes use teamnets in a variety of situations: a small group in a big company—like Armstrong World Industries' "global teams"; a group of small companies comprising a bigger group—such as The Philadelphia Guild, five independent woodworkers who produce one coordinated line of products; and a large group of companies comprising a larger company—like the 1,300 firms with nearly a quarter of a million employees at Asea Brown Boveri, the electrical systems and equipment giant. These three companies bring the Five Teamnet Principles to life: purpose, members, links, leaders, and levels.

Armstrong: How the Linoleum Company Became a Leader in People Networks

If you haven't walked all over its product, then you probably haven't set foot in the United States in the past half century. For many years, Armstrong was to flooring what Frigidaire once was to refrigerators. Armstrong was synonymous with linoleum. Unbeknown to the general public, in the 1980s, Armstrong became the classic example of a major firm in a somewhat traditional industry thrust into the fast lane of global markets. The twin dynamics of commoditization and "know no boundary" technology changes rapidly reshaped the once-stable floor covering industry.

The company's world headquarters, the seat of decision making as well as most research and development activities, is in Lancaster, Pennsylvania, the rolling hills of the Pennsylvania Dutch community. Even as the Amish routinely trot by the company's buildings in their horse-and-buggies, just as they have done for more than a century, Armstrong's world has been accelerating. To be successful in its global opportunities, Armstrong faces a challenge: to balance large economies of scale with local knowledge of customer needs in specific product and geographic markets.

For Armstrong, international growth has gone on somewhat haphazardly. At the close of the go-go decade, however, the company's management knows it must take a new approach to this burgeoning business. In 1989, senior management launches five "cross-border, cross-functional networks" to "globalize its businesses."[1]

GLOBALIZING THE BUSINESS

Members and Purpose

Rather than convert from one formal hierarchical structure to another, such as from a functional to a divisional arrangement, Armstrong sets up global boundary crossing teamnets to coordinate within worldwide product lines.

Networks form in building products, insulation, gaskets, textiles, and, of course, flooring. Their charge is to increase boundary crossing—they call it "cross-border collaboration"—and to make more effective global/local trade-offs. The networks also set up a self-evaluation system to assess the networks' benefits in an ongoing, open manner. The survey asks simple questions, such as "How often do you communicate with your team members?" The results lead directly to Armstrong's simplifying its global reporting structure.

Members of the building products network spend 18 months touring all the Armstrong factories in Europe. Out of the trip comes a common sourcing plan with the U.S. manufacturing operations as well as R&D. While looking to understand their customers' needs better, the network spots a window of opportunity in Asia, particularly in Korea. The team encourages Lancaster R&D to quickly develop new products to meet Pacific Rim needs. Within a year, Armstrong's share of the Korean building products market goes from essentially 0 to 15 percent.

Leaders and Links

By their nature, boundary crossing teamnets are spread out in different locations. So it is hard to get together face-to-face. While face-to-face communication is essential, especially at the beginning to help jump-start trust, every team must find ways to stay connected on an ongoing basis. Armstrong's building products team settles on one very simple way of maintaining group communication—regularly scheduled telephone conference calls. Every other Monday at 7:00 A.M. EST, 10 team members from the United States, Europe, and Asia get together for at least an hour on the phone.

Group vice president Henry Bradshaw, who is also one of the teams' leaders, describes the conference calls: "We talk about business conditions . . . competitors [and] service, which is especially important in the Pacific . . . particular orders [and] new products. Europe wants to know where the labs are with a new kind of ceiling board that they think will be a big hit in their market."[2]

Bradshaw then points out the broader value of these exchanges, beyond the obvious virtues of exchanging specific information.

"Simple as they sound, these conference calls have been very effective. Before we created the global network, I didn't know most of the guys on it. And we had complicated communication channels; important information got lost. Today we're on a first-name basis. The more we talk, the more we want to talk. The more information we share, the more natural it becomes to share it."

Levels

At Armstrong, higher-level boundary crossing teamnets naturally encourage more junior managers to network among themselves. Stimulated by the site visits in Europe, the plant managers call for a global conference of Armstrong plant managers to share technical information and operational insights. Success leads to a second face-to-face conference and further exchanges among the plants.

Influence of the multiple boundary crossing teamnets also trickles up. As concrete solutions to problems begin to show unmistakable benefits, it becomes apparent that the "hierarchy need[s] simplification." In 1991, Armstrong announces a corporate reorganization that, in particular, streamlines global reporting relationships.

The network simplifies the hierarchy.

The global networks have their effect. "The creation of the global teams and the measuring and sharing of members' perspectives on their work and the company help us make better decisions about people and organization," says Allen Deaver, executive vice president. "This change is designed to facilitate the work of the teams. It is natural, logical, and evolutionary—and perceived as such. So we expect it to generate energy rather than confusion."

Armstrong illustrates several critical lessons about teamnets:

- Geography is no barrier.
- Old-line companies can benefit just as much as fast technology start-ups and service firms.
- Practicing what you preach at the highest levels plows the path for others to follow.

Companies do not have to throw out their hierarchies to create teamnets. Good boundary crossing may lead to a better, leaner hierarchy. It does not inevitably lead to a winner-take-all shoot-out between the Old Machine Paradigm and the New Teamnet Paradigm.

The Philadelphia Guild: The Tale of the Five Woodworkers

Boundary crossing teamnets also cross company boundaries. Come with us now to the Cradle of Liberty, where the entrepreneurial spirit of Benjamin Franklin is alive and well in the furniture industry. On a bright spring Pennsylvania day in April 1992, The Philadelphia Guild features its new home office collection at a trade show. The Vassar Show House is an elegant and prestigious venue for furniture designers and manufacturers to display their work. Buyers receive the new line with great enthusiasm and a little curiosity.

More than a few people on the floor ask, "What is The Philadelphia Guild?" The show always features Delaware Valley companies, a relatively incestuous community in which most firms at least have heard of one another, but few people know of The Philadelphia Guild.

MIDWIFING THE BIRTH

Members

The Guild is a boundary crossing teamnet of five companies. Together, they have been developing a network of business relationships since January 1991. A sixth member of the team is the Delaware Valley Industrial Resource Center (DVIRC), a private nonprofit economic development organization funded by Pennsylvania's Department of Commerce. DVIRC serves as the facilitator for the network. The five companies include four production shops (some unionized and some not) and one design firm.

How did this disparate group grow from a glimmer in the eye to products on a show floor in less than a year and a half? Here, we have a rare meeting-by-meeting glimpse into the development of a boundary crossing teamnet of small businesses as seen through the eyes of Gregg Lichtenstein, one of the pioneer practitioners and researchers in this area.[3]

"The interaction among firms is not being mediated but facilitated by someone who brings them together for mutual interaction," he says, precisely the role he plays for The Philadelphia Guild. To describe his role, Lichtenstein uses the term "facilitator," also known as "network broker" or "mediator."

Links and Leaders

Like many stories of boundary crossing teamnets, this one begins with hard business times.

"In the fall of 1990, the recession finally hits the Philadelphia area real estate market, which slows business for all local woodworkers. Even six to eight months earlier, several members of The Guild have said, there would have been considerably less motivation to look for new opportunities," Lichtenstein explains.

By this time, business is so bad that people are open to all kinds of ideas that they previously wouldn't have considered. One such idea comes from the owner of a firm that ultimately does not become one of The Guild's members.

"He comes to DVIRC with the observation that many woodworking firms in Philadelphia face similar problems," Lichtenstein says. "He suggests that perhaps some firms could get together and address the issues collectively with DVIRC's help."

This seed idea then grows into a series of interviews. That leads to a succession of meetings, first hosted by the DVIRC and then rotated among the participating shops. As trust builds among the competitive firms who work to find ways to cooperate, the more neutral players from the DVIRC provide vital connective tissue. DVIRC takes responsibility for meeting preparation, information flow, and follow-up with individual firms.

"Do we have more than one leader? Yes, absolutely," Lichtenstein says. During the incubation period, several people lead the boundary crossing teamnet, some at the same time. "The man who initiates the idea for the network leads the first meeting but then he becomes ill and is not able to come to the next several meetings. So his partner comes instead. Another firm's owner, who is also an architect and active in woodworking industry associations, takes over as leader."

When the time comes for the owner from the largest company to host the group, he comes forward with a market study that he has conducted. "He volunteers the findings to the group," Lichtenstein says. By rotating meeting locations, each member leads the group in turn, and offers tours of the host's facilities after the meeting.

While the participation of industry leaders seems to be critical to the successful launching of boundary crossing teamnets among small businesses, so, too, is credible, energetic leadership from the outside, particularly at the beginning. In the case of The Philadelphia Guild, DVIRC plays a critical role: it initiates, develops, and maintains the business formation process until the group acquires its own self-organizing capabilities. Then, the DVIRC consultants develop expertise around the market that the firms need, thereby making a content contribution to the work of the network, becoming specialized task leaders.

Purpose and Levels

Although some groups arrive at a clear purpose relatively early, it isn't quite that easy for the group that would eventually form The Guild. For more than a dozen meetings, initially averaging about one a month, the group returns repeatedly to its purpose, working it from different angles and in greater and greater depth.

"The first idea was kind of vague," Lichtenstein says, "but we knew it had to do with collaboration. But collaboration for what purpose? So we start talking about common problems, which puts the focus on the need for expanding markets, which in turn leads to a desire for market research."

Wisely, they recognize that choosing a direction for the group will best result from understanding their new customers—who they are and what their needs entail. "But then we discover that we really don't have the information we want, which leads to an agreement to sponsor the specific regional research that the whole group needs."

In deepening their understanding of the market, the group also inventories their internal capabilities. This helps them better understand their own individual strengths and needs, which point to the areas in which collaboration might be particularly beneficial.

"This is an important step," Lichtenstein says, "because it helps us realize that we have complementarities in the group. We also realize that everyone can benefit from economies of scale if everyone pools their needs."

In June 1991, the group finally snaps into place and names itself, a highly important symbolic act for any new boundary crossing teamnet. "At the same time, we agree to prepare a letter of understanding, which is set to be signed at the next meeting in July," he explains. The group creates a new level of organization, a new whole born out of interacting parts. After an August review of the opportunities produced by merging the newly gathered customer research with a matrix of each firm's capabilities, the newly named Philadelphia Guild decides in early September to focus on a specialty line of home office furniture.

With even more definition of their joint purpose, the pace picks up, and the meetings begin to average two a month. The Guild initiates a product development process, prepares and revises plans, approves sketches, and forms working committees. When they decide to exhibit at the Vassar Show House in April, the external date propels the team to a new level of energy. Responsibility for meetings finally shifts fully from the DVIRC to the firms. The group is clearly launched, propelled by the dynamics of the process they have wrought together.

The Guild revisits its purpose time and again. From vague vision to clear goal to explicit detailed plans, purpose keeps The Philadelphia Guild alive and growing. Purpose is the spark of life in boundary crossing teamnets.

Asea Brown Boveri: Turning Contradictions to Advantage

At the other end of the scale from The Philadelphia Guild is Asea Brown Boveri (ABB), a global giant with almost a quarter of a million people working in 140 countries and 1992 revenues of more than $30 billion. ABB is a dramatic example of large-scale teamnets and the competitive advantages they bring.

Percy Barnevik is the visionary who forged ABB in 1988 by merging Sweden's Asea and Switzerland's Brown Boveri, two century-old pillars of European industry. "ABB is a company with no geographic center, no national ax to grind . . . a federation of national companies with a global coordination center," he says.[4]

ABB is not "multinational," he says, but *"multidomestic,"* evoking the local boundaries of "homes" and domestic markets rather than national borders. He says ABB is "not homeless . . . it is a company with many homes."

Asea Brown Boveri's story demonstrates both the good news and the bad news about what teamnets mean for hierarchy and bureaucracy. The good news: ABB's global network proves the incomparable value of a lean, focused hierarchy in internal coordination. The company cannot function without it. This is an example of how networks and hierarchy work as complements in a successful system. The bad news: ABB may well portend the probable fate of bureaucratic, centralized jobs: dramatic shrinkage is in store.

"Barnevik is the most insistent enemy of bureaucracy I've met," Tom Peters writes in *Liberation Management*.[5] He sees ABB's star as one likely direction of the future.

ABB uses the Teamnet Principles to structure a world-class megacompany. This is different from Digital's Calypso project or Armstrong's coordination group. There the companies use the teamnets in traditional organizations to address specific cross-boundary areas. In the early 1990s, ABB is a clear example of the large-scale effectiveness of internal networks in large companies. It exemplifies the idea in the way Denmark's economy shows the large-scale effects of external networks among small companies.

DESIGN FOR ORGANIZATIONAL ADVANTAGE

ABB has an explicit strategy for global success. It feeds on the creative tension between cooperation and competition that fuels teamnets. "ABB is an organization with three internal contradictions. We want to be *global* and *local*, *big* and *small*, radically *decentralized* with *centralized* reporting and control. If we resolve those contradictions, we create real organizational advantage," Barnevik says.

The teamnet factor is organizational advantage.

Without realizing it, ABB uses the Teamnet Principles, showing how to resolve contradictions such as these. Observing the principles gives ABB a real organizational advantage addressing the "contradictions" of:

- Global and local, big and small—through the principle of levels, and
- Centralizing and decentralizing processes—through the paired principles of purpose-links and members-leaders.

Levels

The place to start understanding ABB's level structure is in the middle. Anchor yourself at the company level, the 1,300-and-growing separately incorporated businesses of roughly 200 people with presidents, balance sheets, and career paths. Two levels above the company (the matrix and executive committee) provide ABB's global strategy and decision making, and two levels below the company contribute local strategy and decision making (profit centers and high-performance teams).

Here's how this teamnet's levels stack up:

1. ABB is governed by a 13-person *Executive Committee* headquartered in Zurich with a total professional staff of 100 people.
2. Directors of the 100 or so *Countries* through which the companies in 140 countries report, and the 65-plus *Business Areas* report to committee members, with the Areas grouping into eight *Business Segments*.
3. *Companies*, 1,300 and growing, with their own incorporated bottom line, have a dual report to Country and Business Area directors.
4. Within the companies are the 5,000 *Profit Centers* of 40 to 50 people, each with P&L responsibility.
5. Finally, there is an ongoing effort to segment Profit Centers into *High-Performance Teams* of 5 to 15 people, the basic small group structure that provides the foundation for larger forms and is to be found repeated at every more-inclusive level.

ABB's innovative transformation of the traditional bureaucratic matrix into an effective network matrix attracts much attention.

ABB Levels of Organization

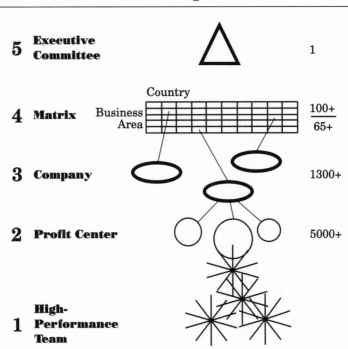

Barnevik believes ABB gains its organizational advantage at the Business Areas/Countries level. "This is where the matrix comes in. The matrix is the framework through which we organize our activities. It allows us to optimize our businesses globally and maximize performance in every country in which we operate," he says.

ABB's organizational advantage lies in its vast teamnet structure, its small local organizations with their own markets to manage, its very lean and mean hierarchy, and its ability to tap its true resource wealth, its people.

Purpose and Links

ABB is in the electrical systems and equipment business, which it divides into eight general Business Segments, such as "Power Plants" and "Power Distribution." Each segment holds five to seven

Business Areas focused around specific global markets that ABB believes it can lead. Every three weeks, the Executive Committee meets to set strategy and resolve any of the matrix issues that get to this level. *They revisit their purpose at the top in full-day meetings more than once a month.*

In January 1988, days after Barnevik formalized the merger of Asea and Brown Boveri, the new company's top 300 people met in Cannes, France, to plan its future. The "Policy Bible," the 21-page handbook that emerged from that meeting, is a model of clearly articulated purpose. "It communicates the essential principles by which we run the company. It's no glossy brochure. It's got tough, direct language on the role of Business Area managers, the role of Country managers, the approach to change we just discussed, our commitment to decentralization and strict accountability."

Barnevik gave the managers 60 days from the close of the Cannes meeting to communicate the policy document to ABB's then 30,000 employees. "Communicate" included personally sitting down with the people affected and hashing it out with them. The newly formed company paid attention to communication from the beginning. It also acknowledged that it is very hard to get the right amount of it in the right places. Barnevik's essential prescription is to "*over*inform. That means breaking taboos. There is a strong tendency among European managers to be selective about sharing information."

To foster open communications, ABB has its Abacus management information system, "the glue of transparent, centralized reporting . . . of performance data on . . . profit centers." This information infrastructure both gives the sparse hierarchy the information it needs to make fast globally sensitive decisions, and it keeps players "fully informed" on the basic operations of ABB's internal market mechanisms. The information system and market interactions supplant the vast administrative structures endemic to traditional organizations.

Members and Leaders

There are different "members" depending on which parts of ABB's teamnet you look at. Barnevik and a dozen others comprise the Executive Committee. ABB's big components are the (1) Business Areas, represented by their 65 or so directors who lead on average five-person management teams; and (2) the national businesses of the 100 Countries, traditionally structured, albeit with astonishingly slim central staffs.

Other than the top 250 executives with mandates to optimize globally, everyone else is part of Companies, Profit Centers, and operational work groups. They have mandates to optimize locally within their markets while negotiating a contribution to ABB's overall benefit. Depending on your perspective, each of these levels tells a different teamnet story, with its own players, purposes, communications processes, and leaders.

The matrix threatens to be the bulkiest form of bureaucracy. It's apt to get hideously bloated as it tries to keep up with complexity by spinning out countless rules and directives. ABB cuts this Gordian knot in one stroke by pushing autonomy and responsibility to the lowest layers of the global enterprise and opening internal transactions to external market forces. The need to balance global economies of scale with internal competition has caused massive reorganizations and sometimes wrenching restructuring of markets and layoffs.

Most ABB companies measure themselves against two or three other similar ABB companies as well as external competitors in their niche product or service areas. Sune Karlsson, director of the Power Transformer Business Area, believes that the intense pressure created by the internal comparisons is an even stronger motivator than the external competition.[6]

"We are fervent believers in decentralization," says Barnevik. Leadership flourishes at the Company, Profit Center, and team levels because much of the bureaucracy has been eliminated. "I believe you can go into any traditionally centralized corporation and cut its headquarters staff by 90 percent in one year." And he's done this often, starting with downsizing Asea's central staff from 2,000 to 200 when he arrived in 1980, and the decimation of Brown Boveri's Zurich headquarters staff from 4,000 to just 200. Barnevik calls his general approach to restructuring "30-30-30": 30 percent of the people are redeployed, 30 percent go to new spin-offs, and 30 percent are laid off (considerably higher than the standard 20 percent corporate layoff).

Different types of leaders have different types of roles. Business Area managers need vision, cultural sensitivity, and "the ability to lead without being dictators," wielding targets and influence instead of budgets and the power to fire. Country managers function like traditional CEOs in that country's culture. Presidents of local companies need the unusual ability to report successfully to two equally important bosses. They also need "the self-confidence not to become paralyzed if they receive conflicting signals and the integrity not to play one boss off against the other."

"Our most important strength is that we have 25 factories around the world, each with its own president, design manager, marketing manager, and production manager. These people are working on the same problems and opportunities day after day, year after year, and learning a tremendous amount. We want to create a process of continuous expertise transfer. If we do, that's a source of advantage none of our rivals can match," Karlsson says, referring to the interplay among the companies in his Business Area. ABB's bottom line focus on giving people responsibility and the opportunity to learn as only a global company can provide continuously increases the value of its human capital.[7]

Three Cases in Point

Armstrong, The Philadelphia Guild, and Asea Brown Boveri illustrate the five basic principles of boundary crossing teamnets. Each:

- Clarifies a different *unifying purpose*;
- Has *independent members*, including individuals, groups, and companies;

- Creates personal relationships through *voluntary links*, ranging from simple face-to-face meetings to sophisticated telecommunications technologies and fast-paced market mechanisms;
- Takes advantage of the power of *multiple leaders*, though key roles vary from one to another; and
- *Interacts among different levels* of organization from the internal micro-structure of each teamnet to the external macro-structure of the environment.

Purposes don't automatically come with a "good" tag on them. They may be grand or petty, sacred or profane, "good" or "bad," but all successful boundary crossing teamnets, whatever their sizes, have *some* purpose. All require independence in their members. Connections, both physical and relational links, are essential at both ends of the size scale and everywhere between. While one person or company often is the spark of teamnet life, the emergence of other supportive leaders leads to successful decision-making teamnets. And all successful teamnets operate at two or more levels—at minimum, the level of the members and the level of the network as a whole.

These five principles apply to groups of all sizes.

What *does change* is how complex boundary crossing teamnets become when they go from small to large.

The examples in this book run the complexity gamut. They are as simple as the five woodworkers who produce a joint line of furniture to as complex as ABB's 1,300 interacting companies or McDonnell Douglas's trying to produce a jumbo jet with a global partnership of 30 megafirms. To gain the advantage of scale, increased complexity results. The problem here is that as things become more complex, new boundaries appear, making the whole slower moving and less flexible. Principles remain the same as scale increases, but their application expands as internal market forces and other teamnet processes replace bureaucratic adjustments.

Teamnets need to put new systems into place to accommodate the complexities of scale. Weekly meetings and telephone messaging may suffice for some small groups to build interdependent relationships, whereas large global teamnets may need voice mail, a computer network, video conferencing, and a weekly newsletter as well to establish adequate links.

LEVELS WITHIN LEVELS WITHIN LEVELS

Larger groups are composed of smaller ones. Inclusive level structure is a fundamental characteristic of both networks and hierarchy.

Teamnets cannot be understood without levels. Every teamnet has several or more major levels of organization. The ability to see levels is an essential conceptual skill of practical systems thinking that grows increasingly valuable with use.

Whether your boundary crossing teamnet is big or small, global or local in extent, it has multiple levels of organization. We describe the overall teamnet world in five generic levels:

- Economic megagroups;
- Alliances;
- Enterprises;
- Large organizations; and
- Small groups.

Size is not the same as levels. Enterprises can be tiny or gargantuan. Some small groups may have complex level structures, while some large groups may seem comparatively flat. In a given context, however, a more inclusive level involves a "larger" organizational form.

Picture yourself standing on a boundary at each level, a perch from which to look both inward, or "down," and outward, or "up." Cooperation and competition, complementary "inner-outer" dynamics, operate at each level.[8]

Levels of Organization

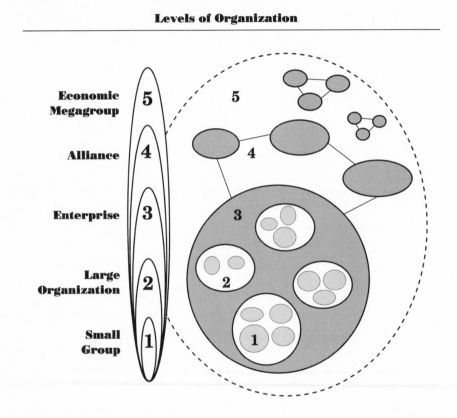

Level 1—Small Group

No matter where it occurs in an organization—from top to bottom—people usually do real collaborative work in *small groups*. Boards of Directors, Executive Committees, staffs, and work units are all small groups. Knowing how to increase small group performance is a critical competitive advantage with potential benefits for all processes involving people who need to cooperate.

In small groups, people know one another by their group roles, their responsibilities and behaviors. Pauline Nist, certainly a unique person, is a member of the Digital Calypso team. She is a team member on the merits of her overall managerial expertise, and her position as manager of the engineering group. Armstrong's Henry Bradshaw is a group vice president as well as a team member with a small group role.

Level 2—Large Organization

Most companies of almost any size have major components that make up the whole enterprise—functions, departments, divisions, programs, or projects. At this second level, internal organizations are a primary source of "walls" that require climbing over. This level also comprises the thick layers of middle management found in traditional management structures.

Looking inward, large groups decompose into smaller groups. Internal organizations live in a world filled with peer organizations. Calypso is one project among hundreds of projects at Digital. To gain attention and resources from the enterprise as a whole, they directly compete with a number of other projects.

Level 3—Enterprise

The third level is the enterprise, an incorporated legal body— private, public, or governmental. This level is a key point of reference: it anchors the middle of the teamnet scale.

CEOs traditionally have responsibility for the two-faced Janus-view sitting on the company's boundary. The person in charge looks inward and sees an enterprise composed of a handful of organizations, divisions, or departments, which may, in turn, break into a cascade of groups-within-groups. Looking out, the enterprise is enmeshed in a world of enterprises, with many external relationships to manage, including links with customers, suppliers, and market competitors.

In successful teamnets, everyone adopts the "CEO view" from

time to time. This helps people to understand their part in the whole, or to seek a new perspective for solving a problem at another level. "Do what's right for the company" is a good answer to a teamnet many layers below the enterprise boundary struggling to resolve an issue—*if* the company has well-understood strategies and values.

Level 4—Alliance

Relationships among a group of enterprises generate a fourth level of organization: alliances. Alliances are small sets of multinational corporations, teams of tiny companies, or "winning combinations"[9] of large and small enterprises.

The contributing enterprises are internal to the alliance. What's important to the alliance is the role played by each member enterprise. Like personal roles in small groups, company roles in alliances reflect only some parts of their strategic interests.

External to the alliance perspective are other alliances and large-scale economic collaborations. Markets, industries, and the world economy provide an environment just teaming with interenterprise teams. Ford and Mazda team up. Sony and Apple ally. The Guild is only one of a number of small business networks facilitated by DVIRC.

Level 5—Economic Megagroup

The broadest level of teamnet we consider is the "economic megagroup," encompassing such large-scale forms as keiretsu, regional networks, and an integrated national small business strategy. From a global perspective, a rich soup of alliances and relationships in all stages of formation and disintegration simmers within the fuzzy bounds of a megagroup. At this level, you can see macro-networking benefits that accrue to the bottom line on a grand scale, as northern Italy and Denmark demonstrate.

CALIBRATING CO-OPETITION

Everyone is a player in many teamnets. To play your part as only you can, keep the Five Teamnet Principles in mind—unifying purpose, independent members, voluntary links, multiple leaders, and interactive levels. But having the principles in mind is not enough. You need to balance cooperation and competition in boundary crossing teamnets. Otherwise, failure follows.

No teamnet forms when arrogant independence and unrelenting parochial pressure overwhelm a feeble mission and weak ties. Worse, a once-healthy teamnet can fall apart. When persistent peer pressure and a barrage of messages overwhelm individual good sense and silence natural leadership, teamnet structures give way to traditional control forms.

There is no magic meter to calibrate exact doses of independence and interdependence. Each of us makes judgments and acts in ways that bring out the co-opetition dynamic in groups. You can greatly enhance your contribution by learning the lessons of others who have been down similar paths.

In It Together: Crossing Boundaries in Groups

On the ground floor of the British Museum of Natural History in London, a small sign that incites critics of genderized language points upstairs to an exhibit called "Evolution of Man." Here, in a few moments, visitors can trace the history of our species, through physiology, anthropology, and even a few shards of archaeology. What the exhibit makes clear is that, regardless of how we prefer to view ourselves, people are herd animals.

From the dawn of time, life has lived in groups: colonies of invertebrates, societies of bees, and troops of bonobos. Increasingly complex social forms of life have evolved alongside increasingly complex individual forms. As humanity evolves, so do our groups.

"Working in groups" is one of our foundation skills. Whether we are good or bad at it, we all participate—no matter how towering the edifices of the globe-girdling organizations that we occupy. In business, real work always gets done in a small group of people.

The fundamental relationship in business is a transaction between buyer and seller. It generates a temporary team laced with the tension of cooperation and competition. Both buyer and seller compete for the "best price." Making a deal requires that each cooperates in a mutually beneficial exchange.

David and Goliath Have Common Interests

Big and small companies have a lot to learn from each other, which is why many already have teamnets among them. Big companies have expertise in technology and planning methods; small companies hold clues for entrepreneurialism and alliances.

Big companies are downsizing toward core competencies and outsourcing many peripheral parts and functions. This creates more opportunities for small companies, *and* it puts greater pressure for quality, state-of-the-art technology, and cost containment of the overall product or service in many small hands.

Small business networks located upstream and downstream in the value chain can recover some of the good jobs that big business eliminates when it slims down. Indeed, a more flexible disaggregated big-and-small business structure may net more jobs overall.

As business people, we want our companies to run lean and do more with fewer people. As citizens, we want a vibrant economy constantly creating many good jobs. To accomplish both goals, more, smaller companies must move quickly and flexibly to meet niche needs that fit into a larger competitive mosaic.

Lessons also transfer across the Teamnet Scale—small group, large organization, enterprise, alliance, and economic megagroup—from internal to external endeavors. High performance at more inclusive levels, like the enterprise and alliance, requires high performance at the small group and organization levels. Strategists cannot concoct brilliant enterprise-level teamnets without knowledge of how small teams work and what motivates people.

Historically, businesses began as small groups. Small businesses are still a major part of the economy. Naturally, new businesses start small; a few grow larger. As they grow, they make internal divisions so that work still gets done in small clumps of people. Work clumps on the shop floor and the mail room, and it clumps in small groups all the way up the chain of command. Supervisors meet with a manager, who is on the staff of a general manager, who is on the staff of a VP, who meets every Wednesday morning with the small group in the executive suite. Small groups permeate organizations of all sizes at all levels.

Small groups must adapt to accelerating change just like all other organizations. The training ground for boundary crossing on larger scales is how we manage our affairs in our own small groups. Boundary crossing teamnets begin at home.

When two multinationals negotiate an alliance, they usually begin with a meeting of a few top people from each side who know each other. They "agree to agree" if things can be worked out. Small cross-functional teams from each side work out details, then other small teams work on the projects. On paper, it is a relationship between enterprises; practically, it is a process of many small boundary crossing teamnets forming and reforming.

Small groups are good places to learn basic boundary crossing skills. They are also wonderful laboratories to experiment in new forms of competition/cooperation relationships.

In this and the next chapter, large companies are the focus, comprising many internal levels and many external relationships. In the two chapters following these, small companies are the focus, moving from the small group to the economic megagroup scale.

Teamnets do not have to be big to have great leverage. They need only be strategically situated. Conrail's story shows how.

This Is a Way to Run a Railroad

Railroads symbolize the Industrial Revolution, chugging along, moving raw materials from their source to refineries to manufacturers to distributors and eventually to customers. By the mid-1970s, trucks, highways, aircraft, and high-speed telecommunications

completely eroded the monopoly railroads once held over transportation. In 1976, Conrail emerges when it resurrects one of the
country's premier rail lines, the Penn Central, from bankruptcy
(along with a handful of assorted smaller lines). Unfortunately, the
newly organized freight transportation company is the epitome of
the rigid industrial age hierarchy, burdened with bloated bureaucracy. In the next 13 years, Conrail shrinks its work force by an
astonishing 70 percent—from 100,000 to 28,000. Eliminating people, however, does not solve Conrail's problems.[1]

In May 1989, James Hagen comes aboard a still-struggling Conrail. To turn the company to profitability, Hagen forms two networks from the 450 top managers.

"There are no more than 25 people in this company whose close
horizontal collaboration will have a dramatic impact on the bottom
line," he says. "There are the seven assistant vice presidents in the
marketing department responsible for our lines of business—steel,
autos, intermodal . . . six general managers responsible for railroad
operations . . . some key people at headquarters—the chief mechanical officer, the chief engineer, the head of customer service—as well
as the senior management group. . . . On their own, none of these
managers can move the business decisively. As a network, they
[can]."

The 13-member senior planning team comprises 11 people from
top management and two from middle management. Hagen selects
the "Strategy Management Group" (SMG) as "the smallest working
group whose interlinking can significantly affect both the operation
and selling of our basic services."

The SMG soon forms "subnetworks" to tackle key problem areas.
One subnetwork's story shows some of the real life drama generated
by co-opetition—the combination of cooperation and competition.
Its Customer Service Subnetwork (CSS) undertakes to solve Conrail's longtime customer service problems.

Customer service is spread out in three separate departments
and 10 locations. Previous attempts to improve service and cut costs
have gone down in "painful and demoralizing" turf battles. However, the six middle manager stakeholders—from customer service,

information systems, regional station management, labor relations, corporate finance, and general station management—face the disturbing reality that few want to admit. To do the right thing by the company means consolidation, which will cost two members their positions. They make the hard decisions.

As the CSS pulls together its recommendations for the whole SMG, some senior managers make it clear that they oppose any consolidation proposal. CSS declares it will dissolve rather than put forward an unworkable proposal. No way, says the SMG, recommending that CSS take its proposal to Hagen's other boundary crossing group, the Senior Planning Team. In short order, the six middle managers find themselves presenting their case to Conrail's top management—and winning!

In late 1990, a seemingly routine public announcement—that Conrail will consolidate customer service operations in Pittsburgh—goes unnoticed. Internally, however, the announcement signals a massive change in the way Conrail makes decisions. In particular, the SMG, virtually unknown to the public, is smiling, for this is their triumph. It is a common corporate vignette, but in the life of Conrail, it is a rite of passage. Its new boundary crossing teamnets have come of age, bringing into effect corporate strategy and making decisions that stick. In just 18 months, they are able to do what the bureaucracy could not accomplish in 15 years.

As the new year begins, Conrail's operating committee, a 19-member subset of the SMG, takes formal responsibility as the railroad's "core network for profitability." Members meet for two hours every Monday morning to make key tactical decisions around price, schedule, and service consistency. Senior management joins in discussions and receives reports, but does not chair or dominate the proceedings. The boundary crossing teamnet generates a five-year plan for the first time in the company's history, to provide a clear context for their daily decisions.

Conrail is an example of how small teamnets can be very effective in even the most traditional organizations. What happens when the teamnet idea shapes a whole company? One fascinating case is the company known for its water-repellent fabric that "breathes."

Meet the Lattice: The Free-Form Organization That Makes Gore-Tex

Gore-Tex™ is a miracle weave in the fabric of the world's outdoor life. It evaporates sweat while protecting its wearer from the drench of rain. Gore-Tex is a visible, distinctive partner with producers of ski gloves, tents, and clothing of all descriptions. Like Dolby™ sound, Gore-Tex is known for the special contribution it makes to a wide range of products.

If ever there were a company whose product mirrored its culture, it is W. L. Gore & Associates. This lattice textile is made by a *lattice organization*, a company designed for horizontal interactions where employees are known as "associates."

In 1982, *Inc.* magazine runs a cover story on the Newark, Delaware, company best known for its popular product Gore-Tex. Headlined "The Un-manager: Without Ranks and Titles," the story describes Bill Gore's "not your average" almost-billion-dollar company. By 1991, the company is among the "400 largest private U.S. Companies."[2]

The name "W. L. Gore & Associates" captures the essence of this remarkable enterprise. The design of the company is that of a network. Its core glue is the philosophy of its husband-and-wife founders, Wilbert ("Bill"), who died in 1986, and Genevieve, who remains involved in the company. *Business Week* features their son Robert in 1990 in an article titled "No Bosses. And Even Leaders Can't Give Orders."[3]

The 1982 *Inc.* story so excites us that we call its author, Lucien Rhodes, who in turn forwards us a poorly typed document with a few handwritten notes on it that Bill Gore has sent him. "The Lattice Organization—A Philosophy of Enterprise" describes the Gore "bureaucracy":

*People group around projects undertaken
on the basis of commitment.*

The firm's 5,600 *associates* (not employees)—now in 46 plants in six countries—have *sponsors* (not bosses), who serve as their mentors and advocates.

Gore's projects are boundary crossing teams. "The mathematician, engineer, accountant, machinist, chemist and so on provide a combination of capabilities of a much broader scope . . . than the mere sum of their number. This synergism . . . impels us to join together for mutual benefit."

STUMP SPEECH TO THE TRIBES

Bill Gore's paper, written in 1976, was the basis for many talks that he gave over the years to the company's associates.[4] (Which brings us back to the name: *everyone* who works at W. L. Gore & Associates is an associate.)

It's not your typical corporate speech. With his ponderous, sometimes mystical tone, Gore sounds more like a 19th-century transcendentalist than the late-20th-century entrepreneur that he is. He begins with the "Nature of Man," the starting point, usually unstated, of every corporate culture.[5] One part of our heritage, he says, comes from hunters and predators with the urge to attack, destroy, loot, vanquish, and overcome competitors. Fortunately, humans evolved new social capabilities that carried the species far beyond this endowment. "A further great evolutionary invention is the cooperation of groups made possible by friendship and love. . . . The tribal group . . . combines aggressive capability welded together by emotional interactions." To Gore, the essence of human nature is co-opetition.

Besides being capable of friendship and love, he says, people are also dreamers. He asks what would happen if people doubled their brain capacity. "If the norm in our society is the utilization of say 10% of our inherent human capabilities, what would be the result if we were able to restructure . . . this to double to 20%?"

People participate in groups because together they can accomplish more than alone, he says. Gore believes accomplishment peaks with about 150 people in the same group. After that, results decline, and it's time to form another group, a principle that the company puts into practice. Gore breaks plants apart when they exceed 150 to 200 people. This is, roughly, a tribal size, the upper-limit size of groups that people lived in after the invention of language but before the development of agriculture and cities.

When groups pass out of the realm in which everyone knows everyone else, Gore believes "we" quickly translates into "they." This tiny language signal announces the beginning of turf wars, the identification of enemies, and win-lose maneuvers that eventually bring down even great companies.

THE LATTICE BEHIND THE FAÇADE

There's another downside to groups of more than 150 to 200, Gore says. "Beyond some such level, it becomes necessary to impose rules, regulations, procedures and the like that dictate how the cooperation shall be done. Special teams evolve within the lattice structure usually led by someone particularly competent in the discipline or activity of the team. One individual may participate on several such teams and have a leadership role in them. These multi-participant people serve an important liaison function and are often involved in . . . a number of different teams," Gore says.

To avoid bureaucracy and to reach for that doubling of human capabilities, the company uses the lattice, which has these characteristics:

- No fixed or assigned authority;
- Sponsors, not bosses;
- Natural leadership defined by followership;

- Person-to-person communication;
- Objectives set by those who must make them happen; and
- Tasks and functions organized through commitments.

Leadership "evolves" at the company, according to Daniel D. Johnson, who eventually followed in his former co-worker's footsteps, leaving Du Pont to join Gore. "You look behind you, and you've got people following you."

In Gore's view, "Every [successful] organization has a lattice organization that underlies the façade of authoritarian hierarchy. It is through these lattice organizations that things get done. . . . Most of us delight in 'going around' the formal procedures and doing things the straightforward and easy way. The legendary subversion of official military procedures by the 'non-coms' is an example of this. All astute military leaders utilize this *sub rosa* lattice."

For all his unusual ideas, Gore is not a romantic. He doesn't propose replacing every aspect of hierarchy with lattices because of what he calls obvious difficulties:

- "Stability and long-term constancy require a firm hand at the helm;
- "Decisions must be made. Complete consensus is never achieved;
- "There seems to be some upper limit for which the lattice is effective; and,
- "It's unrealistic for people to set their own salaries."

VOW TO AVOID BUREAUCRACY

"The rest of Corporate America is only beginning to think about how to motivate employees now that there's a shrinking hierarchy to slot people into," Joseph Weber says in the 1990 *Business Week* article. "But Gore, a quirky, family-held plastics company, has never had much of one: It has been experimenting with an almost free-form management structure for 32 years. . . . Gore isn't some little countercultural outfit, mind you. By turning a flexible form of Du Pont's Teflon into Gore-Tex, used in fabrics and assorted medical, electronic, and industrial products, the company has grown into a nearly $700 million a year outfit, whose return on assets and equity puts it in the top 5%, whose sales quintupled in 8 years."

As irony would have it, of course, Gore started his own company because "as a Du Pont chemist, he couldn't get his innovation—Teflon coating for electrical wires—marketed by the big company. When he left, he vowed to avoid stifling bureaucracies, so he tossed out the traditional chain of command for a 'lattice' system. In it, any staffer may take an idea or complaint to any other: A machine operator can talk directly with plant leaders."

In his lattice organization paper, Gore gives Du Pont credit for inspiring his "ahead of the time" ideas. "The concept of the lattice originated from my consideration of the operation of 'Task Forces' created during the 1950s to carry out research and development within the Du Pont Company. The original ideas have been refined and extended over the past 18 years. . . . The record supports the belief that a lattice organization releases and promotes the creativity of human beings."

Task forces at Du Pont and lattices at Gore are just two expressions of the worldwide, simultaneous, uncoordinated "experiment" with boundary crossing teamnets in the past few decades.

A Teamnet for Every Occasion

THE TEAM AS HERO

In business, people form groups to do work and accomplish goals together. That is the genius of the firm. How people organize themselves to do work gives them their organizational advantage or disadvantage, as the case may be. To see the world of groups, you must be able to shift your focus from individuals to groups of people—*without losing the individual perspective*! It's much harder than it sounds.

"If we are to compete effectively in today's world, we must begin to celebrate collective endeavors in which the whole of the effort is greater than the sum of individual contributions. We need to honor our teams more, our aggressive leaders and maverick geniuses less," writes Clinton administration Secretary of Labor Robert Reich, in his 1987 *Harvard Business Review* article, "Entrepreneurship Reconsidered: The Team as Hero," famous in team circles.[6]

That Lee Iacocca is reputed to have saved Chrysler obscures the larger network of Chrysler, labor, government, and other major contributors to the rescue and recovery. If the hero gets single-handed credit for saving a horrendously complex and risky situation, the actual group and countless commitments that really made the success are ignored.

"[E]conomic success comes through the talent, energy, and commitment of a team—through *collective* entrepreneurship," Reich says in his article, pointing to the American blind spot created by the ideology of individualism. He uses Tracy Kidder's *Soul of a New Machine*[7] as an example of a team-as-hero, "a tale of how a team—a crew—of hardworking inventors built a computer by pooling their efforts."

Reich has a grave warning if we ignore teams. "To the extent that we continue to celebrate the traditional myth of the entrepreneurial hero, we will slow the progress of change and adaptation that is essential to our economic success."

A team is different from a group; a team adds value. A group associates people by anything, whether deeply like a family or superficially like a group of mostly random passengers on Flight 108. A team is more than individuals; it has synergy. It has an organizational advantage.

Reich calls for new team-as-hero myths, and they're already being written. Dean Tjosvold and Mary Tjosvold open their book, *Leading the Team Organization: How to Create an Enduring Competitive Advantage*[8] with such a vision:

You are part of a team committed to a common cause in which you help and are helped to be as effective and fulfilled as possible. You can get close to your colleagues and depend upon each other for support, encouragement, and information. You and employees form project teams to combine expertise and join task forces to explore problems and conflicts and to implement solutions that further mutual benefit. You feel united and loyal to your team and company.

Real life, of course, unfolds a bit more rockily than this, so the Tjosvolds contrast this idyllic picture with scenarios of "competitive outdoing" and "independent work."

Teamnets are networks of teams.

Teams may have widely varying internal styles, yet form into larger teamnet groups. Hierarchies often form coalitions, alliances, and even networks to emphasize their autonomous nature. Whether a command-and-control firefighting team or partners in a professional firm, teams allow people to do more together than they can accomplish alone.

Teams also carry the implication of smallness, as a particularly coherent form of small group. Teams are the level where it gets real personal.

BOUNDARIES: GET A GRIP ON A POINT OF REFERENCE

Without boundaries, there is nothing: no distinctions, differences, or diversity to make up complex things. Teamnets need boundaries to work, to be logical. Some boundaries are easy to see, such as a person who has a unique name, personality, and face; legal corporations, which require that you wear a badge while within their borders; and nations, to which you present papers before entering.

Borders provide "hard" boundaries. They are visible and typically exclusive—either you are in or out. Membership is clear.

Business teamnet boundaries are either sharp or *fuzzy*. As in traditional hierarchy-bureaucracy, teamnets can use sharp boundaries, borders that create a need for free trade agreements and membership fees. Teamnets also have fuzzy boundaries, which sometimes arise from particularly porous borders created by great "gray" areas of employees, part-timers, flex-timers, contract workers, consultants, colleagues, and, yes, suppliers and customers. Sometimes they are fuzzy because a central idea, person, or group with concentric circles of increasingly less involved peripheral relationships defines the teamnet.

TEAMNETS ACROSS THE LEVELS

Teamnets apply across the organizational range: from small groups of only a few, to larger organizations, to enterprises as a whole, to alliances, which are groups of enterprises, to economic megagroups, which cross industry, corporate, political, and geographic boundaries.

Small groups often have quite informal boundaries. Large internal organizations tend to have more formal boundaries, but less so than a corporation. External alliances—with the exception of joint ventures—tend to have less formal boundaries than enterprises. Economic megagroups mix many formal and informal relationships.

> *The personal challenge is to cross boundaries no matter what the level or size.*

Each of the five levels—from small group to economic megagroup—represents a general organizational type. Everyone in business belongs to one and usually more of these types. In the Teamnet

Organization Scale chart, examples of teamnet forms at each level appear on the right. These are not the only examples, but each contributes a different message about the emerging nature of teamnets.

Teamnet Organization Scale

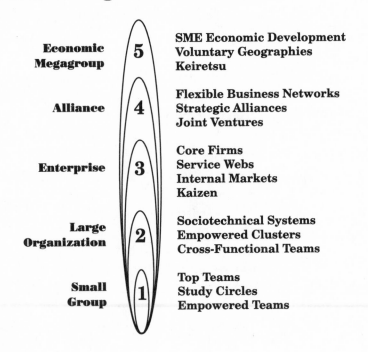

Economic Megagroup — 5 — SME Economic Development / Voluntary Geographies / Keiretsu

Alliance — 4 — Flexible Business Networks / Strategic Alliances / Joint Ventures

Enterprise — 3 — Core Firms / Service Webs / Internal Markets / Kaizen

Large Organization — 2 — Sociotechnical Systems / Empowered Clusters / Cross-Functional Teams

Small Group — 1 — Top Teams / Study Circles / Empowered Teams

Small Group

The size of a small group starts with two and can be as big as a few handfuls. With more than 20 or so people, you are pushing the limits. "The rule of seven," give or take a few, provides a good average size. In teamnet terms, this is the team level.

- *Empowered teams* emphasize the quality of independence.
- *Study circles* demonstrate the self-help power of peers.
- *Top teams* show that teamwork works at every level.

Large Organization

Beyond the small group size, there is another typical cluster around 40 to 50 people. This seems to be some natural size for an administratively self-sufficient business unit. A further clumping happens at around 150 to 200 people, the average size of ABB companies and Gore factories, which seems to be a typical size in many industries for a fully functional, cost-effective, autonomous business division. The teamnet concept, rooted in small groups, expands into larger organizational frameworks.

For teamnets, the large organization level represents middle management. It encompasses clusters of 50, business units of 200, and other major internal departmental and/or divisional boundaries.

- *Cross-functional teams* underscore cross-enterprise needs and processes.
- *Empowered clusters* have administrative self-reliance and other bottom line responsibilities.
- *Sociotechnical systems* make the critical point of fit between technology—particularly information and communications technology—and organizational structure.

Enterprise

To understand teamnets in their full scope, you must travel the levels in your imagination. But it is easy to get confused without a firm point of reference in a complex situation involving many levels. Our advice: Set yourself up at the enterprise level and use it as a base camp for exploring multilevel teamnets. Clarity is greatest in the middle of the scale; fuzziness is greatest at the extremes.

> *Level does not mean size. Adjust your teamnet scale to a typical enterprise size in your context.*

An enterprise, which we're defining as an "incorporated legal body," can be as small as one and theoretically as large as humanity as a whole. China alone incorporates a quarter of the world's people. The teamnet factor applies to huge macro-enterprises and tiny micro-enterprises, and everything in between.

- *Kaizen* shows the value of continuous improvement applied to the whole company.
- *Internal markets* replace many internal controls with the discipline of external markets.
- *Service webs* are distributed and entrepreneurial.
- *Core firms* illustrate how outsourcing can become networking.

Alliance

Alliances are notable for their incredible variety but generally small numbers of partners. This is the small group level of enterprises. Bilateral alliances are most common. Groups of "a few" companies make up most of the rest. Some alliances, of course, involve hundreds or thousands of enterprises. As numbers increase, either the meaning of partnership becomes severely diluted, or the alliance tends to become an organized megagroup.

- *Joint ventures* create a new business that quite literally represents the "something more" synergy of an alliance.
- *Strategic alliances* underscore interenterprise needs and processes, like external cross-functional teams.
- *Flexible business networks* leverage the advantages of scale while retaining the power of small.

Economic Megagroups

Economic megagroups are very big agglomerations of teamnets of every size and point on the scale. They represent the economic power available to those that learn the art of cooperating and competing on a very large scale, focused on a geographic region, an industry, or a funding source.

- *Keiretsu* illustrate the family approach to multitiered business alliances.
- *Voluntary geographies* capture the value of whole regions and industries of alliance ferment.
- *SME economic development* shows how public-private efforts can catalyze large numbers of flexible business networks with a great impact on the macro-economic bottom line of nations.

Next, we will look at the first two levels of the Teamnet Scale: small groups and large organizations. In the following chapter, we look at the next three levels: enterprise, alliance, and economic megagroup levels.

Teaming with Life

Economic
Megagroup **5**

Alliance **4**

Enterprise **3**

Large
Organization **2**

Small
Group **1**   Top Teams
Study Circles
Empowered Teams

Teams are stretching the limits of what small groups can do to-gether. People at every level need to work in teams, and can improve performance by using the teamnet organizational advantage.

Small group teamnets have many labels. *Empowered teams* tackle manageable chunks of work and take shared responsibility for results. *Study circles* are simple, voluntary peer-based associa-tions to solve problems and improve processes. *Top teams* remind us that all levels of organization are inclusive, with smaller forms continuing into larger forms.

P&G PIONEERS IN GROUPS, NOT JUST SOAP

What makes a teamnet different from a committee? It is empowered in some substantial way by its empowered members. Otherwise, neither the group nor the members would meet the teamnet criteria of independence. "Empowered" is the difference between a team that fixes a problem and a committee that recommends options.

"Empowered" can be very narrowly defined in terms of specific problems and opportunities. It can extend to mean an autonomous group or self-directed work team: groups of from 5 to 20 multiskilled and often highly trained employees responsible for turning out a well-defined product or service. The self-directed idea implies that members work together, planning, controlling, and improving their work.[9]

> *For Americans, today's team issue is empowerment. The dream of being your own boss in a big company comes close to being realized in autonomous teams.*

In the mid-1960s, Procter & Gamble (P&G) begins to explore what they will later call "high-commitment team systems." After three decades, P&G still promotes these teams, reporting productivity improvements of 30 percent to 40 percent in the 18 plants using them. Until recently, P&G considered these teams such a competitive advantage that they provided little public information about them.

"The reason I am enthusiastic about self-directed teams is simple: they really do work," says David Hanna, P&G's manager of organizational development. "In fact, if they are designed properly and nurtured well, they almost always outperform other organizational forms. I say this, having been a line manager myself who once wandered in the dark on this issue, not knowing what the outcome might bring."

In the mid-1970s, other American experimenters with self-directed work teams are Cummins Engine and General Motors. In the 1980s, a slew of companies including Ford, Digital Equipment, Tektronix, General Electric, LTV Steel, Boeing, and Caterpillar follow suit. In most cases, the idea shows up in isolated experiments, albeit ones that generally involve whole plants, such as Digital's Enfield facility in Connecticut. Unfortunately, none of these companies has yet been able to take the step from experiment to policy.

Self-directed work teams have not taken off from lack of success. Rather, the enormous blinders of skepticism hold them back.[10] It often comes down to issues of trust: will people work without supervision? It also comes down to issues of power, and middle management is generally more threatened than senior management.

HOW "MADE IN JAPAN" CAME TO MEAN QUALITY

While the Gores and Percy Barnevik have applied the teaming idea to whole companies, the Japanese have applied teamnets to a whole *country*. One widely known type of small group, the quality circle, is the child of the 1960s, Japanese-style.

The work of American W. Edwards Deming catalyzed Japan's overall quality movement. Deming's statistical control techniques, his people-based philosophy of business, and his visits to Japan beginning in 1950 crystallized a focus that grew into a management practice cooperatively developed throughout a whole country.

The Japanese did not invent small teamnets in business, nor are they the source of all the current array of organizational innovations. But Japanese success in the 1970s and 1980s drew new attention to the nitty-gritty small group details of business. Many of the buzzwords of the 1980s are standard operating procedure in the 1990s. Cross-functional teams, for example, are now in the repertoire of every modern manager. Few American companies, however, have a truly *cross-function* organization throughout the enterprise, such as Toyota has perfected.

Quality circles were born with the 1962 publication of *Quality Control for Foremen*, a magazine started by the Japan Union of Scientists and Engineers 12 years after Deming's first visit to the group. With so much new information about the then-nascent quality movement available in one place, groups of supervisors and workers spontaneously spring up all over Japan to study it. These study groups soon become known as *quality control circles*. Their common purpose is to change the 1950s perception that "Made in Japan" means cheap and shoddy.

Quality circles[11] are part of a larger enterprisewide quality management strategy that also puts emphasis on individual self-development. They are self-empowered, peer-based groups of limited scope with intense local focus on shared work.

Komatsu, the Japanese heavy equipment manufacturer, begins its odyssey with quality circles in 1963 in response to a crisis sparked by its major competitor. Caterpillar, the American giant then 10 times Komatsu's size, signs a joint production agreement with Mitsubishi Heavy Industries in 1961. In response, hundreds of quality circles form all across Komatsu. In 1992, Komatsu is a formidable competitor to the ailing Caterpillar with comparable revenues and net worth. Quality circles are still integral to the company's culture, with astonishingly high participation rates in these voluntary, informal organizations: 95 percent of all manufacturing groups and 89 percent of all sales and service groups participate.

For the Japanese, quality circles are simply the application of good sense to manufacturing processes. That is, the people most knowledgeable and responsible for a local process solve problems together as a small group. Over the years, quality circles have spread like a positive virus from the factory floor to other parts of the organization—to administration, sales, and service functions.

Quality circles merely are the most famous of Japan's many small group industry efforts: no-error movements, level-up movements, big-brother groups, big-sister groups, ZD movements, mini-think tanks, suggestion groups, safety groups, workshop involvement movements, productivity committees, management-by-objectives groups, and workshop talk groups. Regardless of what they are called, they have changed the meaning of "Made in Japan." Today, it equates with quality.

Study groups for practical action are a Japanese invention, as imbued in the country's culture as self-help groups are in the United States. While the attempt to directly transplant quality circles to the United States has not been all that successful, the United States does have an analogous cultural norm.

Small, voluntary groups dedicated to some highly localized purpose, whether in the workplace, neighborhood, or community, are very common in America. These valuable informal self-help networks just haven't been given a sexy name and much attention as a real, improvable form of organization.[12]

THE EXECUTIVE WASHROOM TEAM

The executive team is a notion that stretches the Western presumption that all hierarchies come to a point in one person.

The pressure toward more flexible, horizontal organizations—subtle but unrelenting—reaches into the executive suite, the very heart of the temple of hierarchy. At the pinnacle of corporate decision making is the ultimate cross-functional team: the top team. The question is: Are the people at the top a team or are they just a command-and-control system operating from on high?

In the West, people tend to believe true leadership points up to a single person. Traditionally, each Western hierarchy comes to a single, sharp point. Our deep cultural models are Egyptian pharaohs, Roman emperors, European kings, Catholic popes, American presidents, and CEOs, each one at a time, thank you.

The Japanese, however, with an ancient culture of a weak emperor and strong councils of local shoguns, typically have a *blunt* hierarchy, a small group of essentially peer decision makers at the top.

While many know about such celebrated instances of multiple top leadership as the Intel triad, including president Andrew Grove, few are aware how dramatic a trend there is toward teaming at the top in the United States. In the 20 years from 1964 to 1984, American executive team arrangements in large companies tripled from 8 percent to 25 percent.[13]

In the 1960s, the typical American company had a chief operating officer (COO) reporting to a chief executive officer (CEO), often also serving as chairman of the board. The heads of vertical functional and divisional line organizations reported to the COO. In the 1980s, a new form emerges: an executive team reporting to the CEO replaces the COO position. An executive team is "a group of people who collectively take on the role of providing strategic, operational, and institutional leadership for the organization. Each member is responsible for her or his own unit but also wears another 'hat,' that of corporate leadership," write David Nadler and Deborah Ancona.[14]

Corning, Inc.'s management committee, set up by CEO James Houghton, is an excellent example of a top team, which is so clearly beneficial in companies with complex and diverse businesses. ABB's 13-member executive committee headed by Percy Barnevik has the same mix of collective responsibility *and* strong central leadership.

The Synergy of the Large Organization

Economic Megagroup 5
Alliance 4
Enterprise 3
Large Organization 2   Sociotechnical Systems
Empowered Clusters
Cross-Functional Teams
Small Group 1

The small group is the first level at which teamnets occur; the large organization is the second. Here we see teamnets taking forms like cross-functional teams, cluster organizations, and high-performance work systems. Large organizations range in size from Conrail's Strategic Management Group with its 40 to 50 people (the typical size for an administratively self-sufficient business unit) to 200, the average size of Gore's factories and Asea Brown Boveri's companies (a typical size for a fully functional, cost-effective, autonomous business unit), to even larger departments and divisions.

In response to a crisis that clearly cuts across departments, companies pull together small groups of people into special-purpose teams that have a clear short-term mission. *Cross-functional teams* are a popular form of temporary group in big companies.

In response to the pace of change in the electronics industry in the 1960s and '70s, high-tech companies like TRW and Digital Equipment extend the cross-functional concept to semipermanent projects and programs. These multilevel groups often control a significant budget and head count.

Empowered clusters emphasize the administrative independence that is a hallmark of teamnets at this level. High-performance work groups, *sociotechnical systems*, exist in all different sizes, with very varying life spans, and radically varied access to resources. They can refer to a small high-value team or to an entire manufacturing facility, or even to a company as a whole.

TOYOTA'S QUALITY INVENTION: CROSS-FUNCTIONS

While cross-functional teams may be small groups, members often represent other groups who may be involved at some level. An engineer on a project negotiates resources and reviews progress with managers and other engineers attached to the function. A fully articulated cross-functional teamnet operates as a network of functional teams.

One $14 billion company hastily organizes a cross-functional team when it sees its biannual trade show fast approaching. Unfortunately, it has five competing internal groups, who, unless deterred, are about to present a horrifying picture of confusion to their customers. The cross-functional group buckles down to work, by everyone temporarily "throwing away"[15] his or her organizational affiliations and committing to work for the company as a whole. Within three weeks, a group of 60 people, represented by a core group of 15, presents its findings to seven of the company's top vice presidents: a plan to unify the competing products within 18 months and a common set of clear customer messages. For this cross-functional team, the trade show was a success as well as the end of the line for its work.

In the United States, horizontal coordination among cross-functional teams is typically a quick fix. Some companies are so entrenched in their ways that their functions take precedence over everything else. In a typical Japanese company, working across functions is a permanent part of the organization chart. It is a management process designed to encourage and support communication and cooperation throughout a company.

The corporate pioneer in cross-function management for quality is Toyota Motor Company, with 1992 revenues of $72 billion. In the early 1960s ferment of quality management, Toyota takes horizontal communication and coordination as its special problem to solve. It deliberately sets out to design a whole-cloth management process of horizontal woofs threading through vertical warps. Toyota uses Peter Drucker's divisionalized/functional classification of vertical management structures as a starting point to invent a new category of companywide *functions*. Dan Dimancescu, author of *The Seamless Enterprise*, likens this step beyond vertical organizations to Henry Ford's invention of the assembly line.[16]

Toyota manages its cross-functions with corporate teams headed by senior line managers. They are responsible for designing the lateral work processes that have impact on the whole system. Trying various cuts and combinations over 30 years, Toyota settles on 10 top management teams that attend to these horizontal functions:

Toyota's Top 10 Cross-Functions

Quality
Cost
Research
Production techniques
Safety and sanitation
Purchasing
Personnel
Training
Information systems
Total quality promotion

Not surprisingly, one American success story in cross-function management takes place at another automaker, Ford Motor Company. Ford's Team Taurus becomes a willing student of its Japanese partner Mazda. In just six years beginning in 1980, Team Taurus improves profits so much that Ford broadens the program across the company. It sets out to shorten development time under the slogan "Concept-to-Customer."

Hewlett-Packard (HP), a considerably younger Information Age company with just a sixth of Ford's sales ($14 billion), is another American success story with cross-functional management. Beginning in 1985, HP consciously develops an enterprisewide approach to horizontal coordination. It sets up a series of "companywide councils" to formalize lateral processes in areas such as procurement and productivity. In 1990, HP establishes the Product Generation Process Organization, a focal point for the councils, comprising cross-departmental line and staff members. In its Instruments Division, HP credits horizontal teaming with these results:

- Manufacturing cost reduced 45 percent.
- Development cycle reduced 35 percent.
- Field failure rates reduced 60 percent.
- Scrap and rework reduced 75 percent.[17]

EMPOWERED CLUSTERS

Teamnets are also at work in what Harvard Business School professor D. Quinn Mills calls posthierarchical *cluster organizations*.

"The main obstacle to the rebirth of the corporation is the hierarchy," he says.[18] One executive of a very large company tells him, "Hierarchy is dying. Everyone is sick of the rituals, delays, and inefficiencies. It's almost a corpse and soon will have to be buried." In its place, Mills proposes the cluster.

A common cluster size is 30 to 50 members, large enough to have internal administrative functions, yet small enough to be responsive. This is the "Profit Center" unit size of ABB's global teamnet structure. Typical types of clusters that make up an enterprise are:

- A core team, meaning top management;
- Business clusters with external customers;
- Staff clusters with internal customers;
- Alliance teams with external partners;
- Project teams; and
- Change teams.

Clusters draw people from different disciplines to work together on a semipermanent basis. "The cluster itself handles many administrative functions, thereby divorcing itself from an extensive managerial hierarchy. A cluster develops its own expertise, expresses a strong customer or client orientation, pushes decision making toward the point of action, shares information broadly, and accepts accountability for its business results," Quinn says.

Examples include British Petroleum's engineering organization, where 16 independent clusters of engineer-consultants are supported by three limited hierarchies that provide personnel, business, and R&D services. Another is General Electric Canada, where self-managing teams provide all the centralized services—financial, personnel, facilities, information systems. They have improved productivity and quality while cutting the workforce 40 percent. The GE Canada story also demonstrates that cluster organizations can be used for either centralized or decentralized solutions.[19]

While clusters can replace great chunks of bureaucracy and unproductive levels, an irreducible residual hierarchy remains within the enterprise. The big question with no easy answer: How much hierarchy is just enough?

MINING DIGS UP SOCIOTECH SYSTEMS

While Deming's work is percolating in Japan, British coal miners in Yorkshire provide clues for another approach. British researchers discover that new technology impacts performance in an unforeseen way. Productivity, they learn, is not a sole function of labor-saving technology. Rather, it's the goodness of fit between technology systems and human systems that enhances performance. The researchers release a simple prescription from the labs:

To be successful, design the technical system together with the social system.

By the mid-1970s, *sociotechnical systems* emerge as a major source of innovation in management practice. This proves to be especially relevant to the effective use of information and communications technology.[20]

"The high-performance work system . . . in its simplest form is an organizational architecture that brings together work, people, technology, and information in a manner that optimizes the congruences or 'fit' among them in order to produce high performance in . . . customer requirements and other environmental demands and opportunities," write David Nadler and Marc Gerstein.

Most American high-tech companies experiment to some degree with sociotech systems. Some, like Corning, blend sociotech with quality approaches in companywide programs. Another example is American Transtech, created by AT&T in 1983, to manage shareholder activity in the wake of the monopoly's breakup. American Transtech becomes a leader in work redesign in the United States when it reports productivity improvements of 100 to 300 percent with the company's self-directed team system, its flat three-level hierarchy, and its redesigned work processes. In the core stock transfer business, costs and staff are reduced by 50 percent.[21]

Over the last decade, there has been growing awareness on the part of the biggest consumers of information technology that they are not getting the promised vast benefits of productivity.[22] Many conclude that the biggest problem is organizational, not technological.

Information technology radically changes organizations. "People behave more empowered. Your ability to control is dramatically changed when you make it easier to move information from one person to another without a gate. When you put people on global networks, they send each other notes to accomplish a goal, but it might not be a goal anyone in the hierarchy had in mind,"[23] Judith Campbell of Xerox remarks at a conference examining the impact of information networking on the organization.

On the dark side to opening up communications systems, Wharton professor of management Michael Useem says, "The rapid distribution of information can also magnify errors."[24]

Many characteristics of today's teamnets are radically different than ever before, such as tools and techniques for communication and data handling.

> *The theme that sociotechnical systems emphasize—fit with technology—appears throughout the leading-edge examples of this concept at all levels and sizes.*

Technology networks may start small in work groups and departments, but eventually they spread to the enterprise as a whole and many interenterprise relations. It is to these "higher" levels that we turn in the next chapter, never forgetting the small groups whence we came.

Inside-Out Teamnets: Crossing Enterprise Boundaries Fortune 500–Style

Future survival for the Fortune 500 depends upon cooperating with competitors.

"Big company joint ventures, a business trend for the '90s, are springing up like mushrooms after rain," writes James Flanigan in the *Los Angeles Times*.[1] In the 1980s, acquisitions and mergers were the business deals of choice for Fortune 500 companies. Today, Fortune 500 companies breed boundary crossing teamnets as they announce hundreds of new corporate partnerships every week. Every alliance or joint venture causes people to work together across corporate borders.

Instead of creating jobs, big companies are eliminating them. From 1981 to 1991, Mobil cut 140,000, General Electric eliminated 120,000, ITT cut 122,000, USX and Union Carbide each cut about

100,000.[2] By 1991, the Fortune 500 employed just 12 million people, a drop of 3.6 million in ten years.[3] In the same period, the United States' small businesses created two out of three new jobs, employed half the country's workers, accounted for nearly 40 percent of national production, and developed most of the new products and technologies.

It's no surprise then that big companies are finding new ways to do business. Alliances with other firms allow companies to grow without having to bear all the costs. One familiar firm is now a pro at this: IBM.

Big Blue to Baby Blues?

Once the premier go-it-alone, we-do-it-all company, today IBM, beset by a $5 billion loss in 1992, finds it has to work with other companies. It has staggering numbers of strategic alliances. Since 1986, when its president Jack Kuehler first promoted the idea, IBM, for decades the world's computing behemoth—its $65 billion in revenues is still five times that of its closest competitor—has entered into *20,000* alliances. Only 2 percent of these, merely 400, involve equity investments.

To the astonishment of many, IBM now partners with arch rivals, including:

- The company that once advertised IBM as its enemy: Apple Computer—to produce a new computer operating system, code named Pink;
- Motorola, Groupe Bull, and, again, Apple to design a family of new micro-processors; and
- Siemens and Toshiba to develop new semiconductor technology, a 1992 deal that *Business Week* calls "the alliance of all alliances."

Clearly, this is not IBM's only change since 1986. In 1991, this bastion of centralized management stunned the business community with its reorganization announcement: 13 stand-alone divisions. Chairman John Akers, who resigned suddenly as CEO in 1993, described them as wholly owned but more or less autonomous companies in marketing, service, product development, and manufacturing. Each has its own financial report, Board of Directors, and responsibility for maximizing return on assets.[4]

The divisions in turn are being reorganized into profit centers and subunits. The 450-person Costa Mesa sales and support unit, for example, regrouped into boundary crossing teamnets of no more than 20 people. Each brings a specialty, contributing to rapid customization of products. In the first year, workstation sales soared 70 percent.

By 1992, IBM nearly doubled its revenue per employee from $129,000 to $210,000, while cutting 80,000 employees from its payroll, making *its* contribution to the 2 million lost Fortune 500 jobs. But the computer giant is still in trouble: 1993 will see an additional 25,000 to 40,000 job losses, even once-unimagined layoffs.

"What we're seeing is the beginning of the dismantling of IBM," said one securities analyst at the time. It is too early to tell how IBM will end up: Will the archetype of centralization successfully decentralize? From a teamnet perspective, IBM, a substantial player in the computer industry, is *dis*aggregating into smaller units and *re*aggregating into flexible alliances.

IBM is not alone in partnering. According to Decision Resources, the Burlington, Massachusetts, research firm, alliances among computer companies *quadrupled* between 1982 and 1992. The computer industry has no franchise on this trend, however. Boeing's new 777 development project, for example, involves 235 "design-build" teams, involving people inside and outside of Boeing. Industries as diverse as transportation, floor covering, textiles, aerospace, consumer electronics, communications, and pharmaceuticals all recognize the competitive value of cooperation. Collectively, they generate thousands of boundary crossing teamnets each year.

Whether inside or outside, teamnets offer competitive advantages that few people thought possible even a few years ago:

the power of scale and diversity in a world of limited resources. Many large companies, some on the brink of extinction just a few years ago, now depend upon boundary crossing teamnets, known by a variety of names. When people work across functions—in intracompany task forces, cross-functional teams, and interdepartmental management groups—they break allegiance to a single internal hierarchy. This presents new challenges to management, just as formidable as when people work with others outside their firms.

A powerful synergy occurs when internal boundary crossing reflects external partnership patterns, and vice versa. Because there is a common core to these teamnets, large and small, lessons learned in one arena can be applied in another. A shared set of values drives both renewal within and alliances without.

From small group and large organization teamnets, we move to enterprise, alliance, and economic megagroups on the Teamnet Organization Scale. One company that knows how to network across the range of levels—from small groups to multi-billion-dollar joint ventures—is based in the small town whose name it bears in upstate New York.

The "Global Network" Company: "A Work in Progress"

"In 1854, my great-great-great grandfather founded a small glass manufacturing business, the Union Glass Company. Today it is a global corporation known as Corning, Inc. . . . what we call a 'global network' . . . an interrelated group of businesses with a wide range of ownership structures. Although diverse, these businesses are closely linked."[5] So begins James ("Jamie") R. Houghton, the seventh, and probably last, Houghton to hold the reins of the now $3 billion specialty glass company, in "The Age of the Hierarchy Is Over," his 1989 *New York Times* article.

Through its global network, Corning produces much more than Corning Ware and Pyrex. It's in:

- Fiber optics, after 17 years of research and an investment of $100 million;
- Computing components, where "27 scientists in Corning's labs are poring over the glass used in liquid-crystal displays . . . found in laptops";[6]
- Environmental technology, with Cormetech, its joint venture with Mitsubishi Heavy Industries, established a decade before the big profits are expected. Corning supplies the ceramic-based technology to filter pollutants, while Mitsubishi Heavy Industries provides smokestack expertise; and, of course,
- Housewares, expanding its market considerably in 1991 by partnering with Mexico's giant glass manufacturer, Vitro. In Mexico, the company is Vitro Corning, owned 51 percent by Vitro; in the United States, the company is Corning Vitro, owned 51 percent by Corning.

Until controversy hits one of its partnerships in 1992, the company enjoys excellent press since 1983, when Jamie takes charge from his older brother, Amory, Jr. (who goes on to become a Republican U.S. congressman). *Business Week's* May 13, 1991, cover story is "Corning's Class Act: How Jamie Houghton Reinvented the Company."[7] The "reinvention" prompts not only good press, but also good results. Reversing three years of steady decline and a 70 percent dependence on slow-growth businesses, return on equity climbs from 7.3 percent in 1983 to 16.3 percent in 1990. Stock value of the company (incorporated just before the Civil War) increases 36 percent in the same period. Analysts predict earnings likely to grow 20 percent annually with good market share in strong growth businesses.

Corning's is not just a remarkable story of external adventures. It is also a tale of how a nearly 150-year-old company undertakes a 10-year internal effort to transform itself into a 21st-century corporation. It does so with boundary crossing teamnets.

CORNING'S INTERNAL DRIVE FOR QUALITY

Jamie Houghton recalls walking into a "dreary" Rochester, New York, hotel function room in October 1983, his first year of office. "Corning plans to spend $5 million on a 'total quality program,'" he tells his top managers. No one is interested. "It went over like a bomb. They thought it was the flavor of the month," he says later.[8] Undaunted, he barrels ahead with his vision to turn Corning into a quality enterprise. Houghton appoints Corning's first director of quality. As the new CEO, he goes on the road, carrying his vision to over 50 company and partner sites. Everyone is required to go through a two-day quality seminar.

At Corning, quality means "meeting and exceeding customer requirements." Delivering the keynote address (appropriately titled "Quality: Beyond the Corporate Walls") at the Economic Club of Detroit in October 1990, Houghton says, "Quality is more than a business process; it's an ethical behavior system. . . . Quality implies empowerment of all people at all levels in an organization. The old pyramid structure is flattening out with power spreading downward and outward through employee quality teams."

Houghton is not exaggerating:

- Corning people participate in quality circles, the small group management process that began on the shop floor in Japan in the early 1960s.
- Corning has hundreds of cross-functional teams in its factories and businesses, with people from many parts of the organization working together "spotting trouble and fixing it at the source."
- At its "Factory of the Future" in Blacksburg, Virginia, Corning runs 24 hours a day, 7 days a week, self-supervised by "high-performance work teams," with "mentor networks" guiding new hires.

Corning also partners with the labor unions. The company and the union jointly work to increase employee participation in worker teams. These teams determine job schedules and participate in factory design. When a molten-metal filter production plant moves from an older facility to Erwin, New York, union workers design the new plant with open spaces, sound-dampening ceilings, numerous windows, and a production line that keeps everyone on a team within earshot of one other. They redesign the organization, not only the technology: 47 job classifications fold into one, employees rotate jobs weekly, and salaries rise when people learn new skills. The defect rate dives from 10,000 per million to 3 per million, with virtually no customer returns. At Corning, quality works.

In 1987, Houghton launches a new crusade: he appoints two companywide teams to address workforce diversity. Corning, the tiny upstate New York town, also benefits. The company invests in the community, addressing economic, racial, and quality-of-life issues: it buys and rehabilitates properties; it builds a hotel, museum, and library; and it arranges for the local cable station to carry black-oriented programming. Corning understands the essence of quality: a focus on people.

CORNING AND ITS PARTNERS

Corning is not new to the joint venture business. It is 1924 when Corning first takes advantage of complementary product development with another company, making cartons for glass products. This practice of Corning and its partner each contributing its expertise will be echoed for the next 75 years in some 60 ventures. These partnerships, says Houghton, contribute about half of Corning's earnings, which he believes to be "unique among Fortune 500 companies." Some are really micro-joint ventures such as Corning's partnerships with Genentech in enzymes and tiny PCO, Inc., in optics.

Corning's partners include some newer ones—Siemens of Germany, Ciba of Switzerland, Samsung of South Korea—and some quite old—like Asahi Glass of Japan. Amazingly, even though the

Japanese partner and Corning did not communicate during World War II, Asahi Glass kept meticulous records and presented Corning with its earnings after the war was over.

During the same war, a handshake between Jamie Houghton's father and Dr. Willard Dow in 1941 established perhaps the most famous of the partnerships: Dow Corning to produce silicones. Dow Corning illustrates both the profits and the peril of partnerships. In 1991, Dow Corning's $2 billion in revenues contributes 25 percent of Corning's $316.8 million earnings.[9] In 1992, Dow Corning, which produces 5,000 specialty chemicals ranging from the sealants used on the O-rings of the space shuttle to Silly Putty, is on the front page because of silicone breast implants. Potential lawsuits could exceed $1 billion or more in liabilities.

In the long view, a vulnerable partnership will not deter Corning from its network strategy. In networks, the parts do not necessarily conform to the structure of the whole. Nor is Corning likely to alter its basic philosophy that respects the autonomy of both its partners and the joint venture spin-offs. Autonomous partners, for better or worse, comprise networks. Indeed, it is the real autonomy of Dow Corning from its founding parents that provides the break wall against the storm of suits that follows the ban on silicone implants.

Despite mistakes, Corning is extremely successful in its joint ventures. "Corning has the critical ability to treat its partners as true equals, to see their interests and respond to them," writes Jordan Lewis, author of *Partnerships for Profit*.[10]

As above, so below. The treatment of both corporate partners and employees as equals springs from the same culture and philosophy. "We have found that the successful operation of a global management network requires a new mind-set," Houghton writes. "A network is egalitarian . . . [with] no parent company. A corporate staff is no more or less important than a line organization group. . . . [B]eing part of a joint venture is just as important as working at the hub of the network."[11]

Houghton calls Corning "a work in progress." It is a rare long-term experiment in conscious transformation from a traditional

American hierarchy to a more networked form of management at every level. Is the Corning way right for every company? Probably not. Yet, other companies use these and similar ideas in different ways to improve their businesses.

Every business needs to adapt to change. By knowing what some companies have tried, you will get a clearer idea of what might work for you.

At the nexus of business boundaries, internal and external, is the enterprise.

Enterprising Teamnets

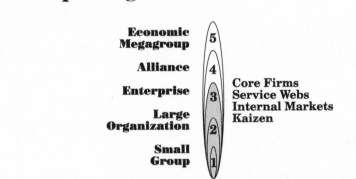

The process of transformation from a traditional organization into a modern teamnet structure takes a number of forms at the enterprise level. Teamnets appear in:

- *Kaizen* corporations. Although there is no such word in English, the Japanese have one for *ongoing improvement involving everyone*, which reaches from the shop floor to the company's external alliances.
- *Internal markets*, self-regulating mechanisms that serve the place of vast numbers of bureaucratic policies and procedures.
- *Service webs*, the classic flat distributed networks delivering everything from pizza to professional services.

- *Core firms*—with one foot on the enterprise level, and one on the alliance level—which use the external market to simplify their relations with a select number of suppliers and distributors.

KAIZEN: "ONGOING IMPROVEMENT INVOLVING EVERYONE"

Japan has built its powerhouse economy not on plentiful resources but on excellence in management. Excellence comes not from this or that technique. Rather, it is a pervading set of values. They give rise to a variety of quality management innovations, captured in the word "kaizen."

All sorts of teamnets arise under kaizen's umbrella:

- Total quality control;
- Customer orientation;
- Suggestion systems;
- Just-in-time inventories;
- Total productive maintenance;
- Zero defects;
- Productivity improvement; and
- New product development; as well as
- Quality circles; and
- Cross-function management.[12]

When people translate "kaizen" as "improvement," they lose its essence, which, according to Masaaki Imai, author of *Kaizen: The Key to Japan's Competitive Success*, means "ongoing improvement involving everyone." And it's been going on for a long time. As early as 1954, the Japanese were applying Deming's ideas beyond manufacturing to an overall management approach.[13]

At the enterprise level, kaizen is a process rather than results-oriented management approach. All the companies leading the quality movement in Japan—including NTT, Matsushita, Toyota, Nissan, and Komatsu—reflect this overall process orientation throughout their management layers, which other companies emulate and copy.

When the multinational Philips initiates its "company-wide quality improvement" program in October 1983, its then-president Dr. Wisse Dekker begins his statement, "The quality of products and services is of the utmost importance for the continuity of the company."[14] The first two of the 10 points of the Philips quality policy formalize the essence of kaizen:

1. Quality improvement is primarily a task and responsibility of management as a whole.
2. In order to involve everyone in the company in quality improvement, management must enable all employees—and not only employees in the factories—to participate in the preparation, implementation, and evaluation of activities.

INTERNAL MARKETS REPLACE BUREAUCRACY

Habitat for Humanity International builds houses for poor people all around the world. In India, one house owner could not make his small monthly mortgage payment. Instead, he brought an emaciated water buffalo as payment to the committee that oversaw loans. The committee, in turn, decided not to sell the water buffalo but instead to feed it, then to sell the milk it produced. This way, the man continued to make his mortgage payments and people had more milk. Instead of the man's losing his house because of regulations, the committee, close to its customers, realized the man had something to sell, if only someone would invest. Thus internal markets are born.

Markets can replace bureaucracy in many creative ways. The fall of Communism may be attributed to the extraordinary drag the bureaucratic apparatchiks put on Soviet economic development, performing functions that in the West are done by markets, such as the allocation of capital.

Asea Brown Boveri operates as an internal market with its 1,300 companies and 5,000 profit centers. These internal markets work in tandem with external markets, with internal units free to buy and sell outside the enterprise.

"The essential condition for free markets within an enterprise is that internal business units be allowed to purchase goods and services from external vendors."

So says Russell Ackoff, one of the great systems thinkers and a Wharton management guru, to a 1991 conference on internal markets. With speakers from Ford, Eastman Kodak, Armco, MCI, ALCOA, Dow Corning, Esso Petroleum (Canada), and Control Data, Ackoff opens the conference. He contrasts "free market policies" with traditional "monopolistic practices" inside most firms— i.e., manufacturing *has* to buy CAD services from the company's engineering organization.[15]

ALCOA Separations Technology has let free market forces loose in functions where costs have been getting out of control. While overall results are mixed, in some places, such as R&D, there is noteworthy success. The "old" R&D unit was costly, slow, and always "working on hare-brained ideas rather than getting the things done that would yield revenue sometime in this century." After instituting internal market mechanisms, R&D reorganizes and soon makes up more than 35 percent of its budget from external work. Internal customers also report significantly improved service.

Internal markets at ALCOA also work with manufacturing, pushing the idea to the factory floor. Members of work centers, as they call them, become excited about their jobs and "begin to see a direct link between their work, customer feedback, and the profitability of the unit . . . control was in their hands." In one work center, average lead time drops from 12 to 14 weeks to 2 to 5 days.

To be effective, internal markets must be populated with boundary crossing teamnets.

THE SPIDER'S WEB: HOW TEAMNETS DELIVER SERVICE

Whether they come off as sales presentations for Tupperware or "tax returns" for H&R Block, service webs find the smallest possible unit where production can be replicated to derive efficiencies, and combine the units to meet localized or individual customer needs.

Like a sponge for bureaucracy's excesses, the modern service organization naturally flattens the hierarchy. In some service businesses, the search for ever-smaller units of replicability has pushed beyond the sales counter and stockkeeping unit to measures of everything from "freshness" to "cleanliness." Information collection is so sophisticated among some large chains that headquarters instantly can detect problems in a decentralized unit, and often diagnose them.[16]

> *Organizationally, the basic replicable unit*
> *of service webs is the local operation*
> *(internal) or franchise (external).*

This model adapts equally well to very simple and very complex services.[17] Domino's Pizza represents one extreme, a "chain" of 4,500 "highly decentralized outlets" that encourages managers to regard themselves as "individual entrepreneurs." If Domino's were a "chain," it would break immediately. It works because it is a systematically applied network. A virtual science of pizza making eliminates much of the drudgery and ensures quality, while sophisticated information systems facilitate the bane of all managers' existence, paperwork. This frees managers to concentrate on customer service, a company hallmark, and for many people, the "fun stuff." Not incidentally, it provides an extremely effective centralized coordination system for management. Technology can so easily control or empower—here both happen at once.

Arthur Andersen and Company (AA&C) is another example of a service company with widely dispersed service locations or points of customer contact. Instead of pizza, AA&C delivers highly sophisticated customized information services through 40,000 professionals in virtually every country in the world. Like Domino's, Arthur Andersen "operates in a highly decentralized, real-time mode. Each local office is as independent as possible." Equally importantly, AA&C is a lead user of applying technology to professional services, generating a knowledge-based corporate resource that is the paragon of the much-heralded "knowledge company." Consulting is not alone. Investment banks, financial services, engineering, construction, research, health care, accounting, and advertising all use service webs.

Service webs are very information-sensitive. The key competitive advantage comes from a careful fit of management structures with the technology system.

When customers become the focus, companies flatten. According to James Brian Quinn and Penny Paquette, who have studied service webs extensively, the organization inverts to empower the employees closest to the customer. Toronto Dominion Bank's organization chart literally has the CEO at the bottom and customer on top. Federal Express, with 42,000 employees, has five levels of management and a staff complement that is one-fifth the industry average.

Because these replicable service forms tend to become "infinitely flat" organizations, Quinn and Paquette call them a "spider web because of the light but structured quality of its interconnections." They offer these conditions for "extremely wide reporting spans:"

- Localized interactive contact is very important.
- Each ultimate contact point or operations unit can operate independently from all others at its level.
- The critical relationship between decentralized units and the center is largely quantitative or informational.
- The majority of relationships with the information center can be routine or rules-based.

Flat service networks of common units represent one end of the network enterprise range of diversity. Chunky networks of core firms held together by complementary interests represent the other end of this range.

CORE FIRMS, NOT HOLLOW CORPORATIONS

"The Hollow Corporation will ultimately hurt the U.S. economy," thunders *Business Week* in March 1986.[18] The industrial sector provides productivity, innovation, and a rising standard of living, but there is a growing weakness, *Business Week* warns: outsourcing. "Outsourcing breaks down manufacturers' traditional vertical structure, in which they make virtually all critical parts, and replaces it with networks of small suppliers. Even such proud giants as IBM and GE are doing it to varying degrees. In the short run, the new system may be amazingly flexible and efficient. In the long run, however, some experts fear that such fragmented manufacturing operations will merely hasten the hollowing process."

In the 1990s, once-proud giants are scrambling to downsize and outsource, focusing on core competencies to survive into the next century. As the next two chapters illustrate, the "hollowing" of companies does not necessarily mean the loss of the manufacturing base. It does reflect an unstoppable trend as information-driven service technologies offer significant economies of scale coupled with flexibility and customer responsiveness.

In industry after industry, manufacturing is a shrinking part of the product cost. Only a fraction of a drug's value lies in manufacturing, while the great bulk of value-added costs derives from service functions such as R&D, legal and regulatory, clinical clearance, marketing, and distribution. Is Merck a manufacturer or is it really a service company?

Value chains that start with suppliers and end with customers segment work in firm-sized bites. For each staff function and for each service in the value chain, companies confront a series of "make or buy" decisions. Each such decision weaves another knot in the boundary crossing tapestry, giving internal (make) and external (buy) hues.

ADP can do your payroll; it can also track your banking, file taxes, and print messages with checks. Servicemaster is a $3 billion company that can do your maintenance function; it will also jointly invest in new equipment and share productivity gains with you.

Companies the world around are looking closely at what they do best. Cutting-edge management advice in the 1990s is to:

- Compare each function you perform with the best-in-class.
- Dominate those functions that are strategic and where you are or can become the best (core competencies).
- Outsource where you have no strategic advantage.

In 1964, Nike was a U.S. dealer for a Japanese shoe; in 1991, it is a $3 billion corporation. It got there by building an extremely effective core firm–supply network structure. It based its strategy on close relations with—but not dominance of—manufacturers in the resurgent East: Korea, Thailand, Indonesia, Taiwan, China. Nike expects its suppliers to sell to its competitors to remain competitive and not become too dependent on Nike. The core company maintains technical competence in R&D, quality processes, and even manufacturing in one U.S. facility that does leading-edge designs.[19]

Used strategically, outsourcing does not hollow out the corporation. "Instead, it decreases internal bureaucracies, flattens the organization, gives it a heightened strategic focus, and improves its competitive responsiveness," Quinn et al. assert, answering *Business Week*'s alarm.[20]

Teamnets in Alliance

Economic Megagroup — 5

Alliance — 4 — Flexible Business Networks

Enterprise — 3 — Strategic Alliances Joint Ventures

Large Organization — 2

Small Group — 1

When even the most rigid hierarchies organize to get something done together, teamnets naturally form. They use a variety of special-purpose vehicles that nonetheless all leave the participating firms reasonably independent.

So it seems unremarkable to call joint ventures and other intercorporate relationships "teamnets." Yet, for all the years companies have been forming strategic alliances, many clearly haven't done it very well. According to an oft-cited study of 880 cooperative arrangements among American firms, only 45 percent were deemed successful by all sponsors, only 60 percent have lasted more than four years, and only 14 percent have passed a 10th anniversary.[21] Mergers, the 1980s predecessor wave to the ally-making 1990s, have an even higher rate of failure—somewhere between half and two-thirds, according to some research.[22]

At the intercorporate level, enterprise boundaries can grow very fuzzy. For all the practice they've had creating them, distinctions are still something of a hodgepodge, as companies struggle to work together in spite of differences. The literature on new interenterprise forms is a lot skimpier than at the intraenterprise levels.

Joint ventures and *strategic alliances* are common to bigger companies. *Flexible business networks* show the power of teamnets now working for smaller businesses.

"TRUST ONE ANOTHER": THE KEY TO JOINT VENTURES

Joint ventures—the establishment by two or more partners of a separate business—is one distinctive form of strategic relationship. Its central lesson is this: The autonomy given to the new enterprise relates directly to the success of a joint venture.[23] According to Charles Raben, who has studied numerous alliances, joint ventures work when the partners:

- Trust one another, have compatible business philosophies and styles, and commit time to their relationship;
- Agree on venture autonomy, a process to resolve differences, on long-range goals, and on minimal direct involvement; and
- Each makes a contribution that the other respects, and each understands the business.

If the partners can't collaborate, then one partner should dominate. Some companies are widely recognized as having learned the secrets of external partnerships, like Corning in the United States and Olivetti in Europe. Olivetti's joint venture partners are worldwide and include Groupe Bull, Canon, Digital Equipment Corporation, and EDS, along with many other arrangements, such as strategic investments with AT&T and Toshiba.

PARTNERING AS A MATTER OF STRATEGY

How do you execute your corporate strategy when you lack critical core skills and components? Companies form alliances to meet specific business needs and to address opportunities that they cannot meet internally. To meet strategic goals, companies work together—in value-adding partnerships, precompetitive R&D contracts, corporate venturing, partial mergers, supply alliances,[24] large-small "winning combinations," and "virtual corporations." Each of these enterprise forms generates teamnets.

By Adding Value

When independent companies work closely together all along the value chain, they are participating in value-adding partnerships. McKesson Corporation, the $7 billion distributor of drugs, consumer, and health care products, is one example. Its network includes manufacturers, distributors, retailers, consumers, and even a third-party insurance supplier. To independent drugstores that retain local autonomy, it offers the benefits of scale, such as access to large computer systems that none could afford independently.[25]

Joint R&D Before the Competition

In the United States, Europe, and Japan, many companies collaborate in the early phases of new technologies. By cooperating, they lower the risk for discovery and pioneering. Then, they go their separate ways, competing to refine, produce, and market resulting products. Together, companies:

- Search for basic breakthroughs;
- Slog through the endless combinations required for applied research; and
- Do enough development to test the concept.

Precompetitive R&D has been popular in semiconductors, gene research, plastics, telecommunications—and every other major industry that depends on a stream of innovations.

Sometimes government and academia are involved; sometimes

not. Some research consortia include academic members; some don't. Japanese government-industry collaboration in new technologies is legendary, many led by MITI—from high-performance ceramics to fifth-generation computing to sea water desalinization. In the United States, the Microelectronics and Computer Technology Corporation (MCC) is one somewhat centralized example. Other collaborations set standards for emerging technologies. Among U.S. defense firms, cooperative teaming to produce a multi-billion-dollar prototype is the norm; then the companies split apart to compete for production contracts.

As transnational companies ally to do precompetitive R&D, national boundaries become fuzzy and government sponsorship lines grow murky. International transgovernmental sponsorship of basic research will be a big boundary crossing activity by the end of the 1990s.

Corporate Venturing

It may sound like a bit of an oxymoron, but "corporate venturing" has a specific meaning: it's when large companies take minority equity positions in young companies with good growth prospects.[26] For the big company, the purpose is not a direct return on investment. Rather, it needs to gain access to a new technology or market.

Olivetti, Europe's largest "local" information technology company, operates a globally diverse venture capital operation ($40 million in 1987) called Olivetti Partners. Some investments include European Silicon Structures (7 percent), Danish start-up Olicom (40 percent), Torus Systems of Cambridge, England (25 percent), and Yokohama-based Dixi Corporation (9 percent).

One interesting twist to this idea is targeted venture capital funds *that require the companies they invest in to foster cooperation.* Euroventures, founded in 1984 by a group including Asea, Fiat, 3M, Olivetti, Bosch, and Volvo, is goaled to encourage pan-European cooperation. To that end, it operates a "network of satellite funds throughout the European Community."[27]

A Step Short of the Altar

In the gray areas between mergers, ventures, and alliances, partial mergers sometimes appear as an intermediate stage. One Bayer merger took 17 years from start to finish. In 1964, Bayer merged its Agfa subsidiary with the Belgian firm Gevaert to form a photographic group owned 50 percent by each. Bayer raised its stake to 60 percent in 1980, when new capital was needed, and in 1981 completed a buyout. Honeywell-Bull represents the not necessarily successful tangle of relationships that have grown up as major players enter and leave the computer business. A 1960s alliance between the French government Machine Bull and GE—whose computer business was taken over in the 1970s by Honeywell (which at the same time bought up a number of small precision instrument firms)—and a 30-year relationship with Japan's NEC, all continue today in a triadic equity arrangement.

From Supplier to Partner

In 1971, when General Motors made its 34 percent strategic investment, it cemented relationships with Japan's Isuzu Motors, gained access to a needed component, and gained entry to a new market. This type of supplier partnership doesn't produce new enterprises, but it does require companies to work together. They increase strategic interdependence and generate significant boundary crossing activity. Manufacturers and their key component suppliers, companies doing contract R&D, OEM (original equipment manufacturing) customers, and key distributors are typical of vertical supply alliances.[28]

"Winning Combinations"

In the near future, "Goliaths"—large companies unable to muster the speed and take the risks to innovate continuously—will increasingly team with "Davids"—smaller companies quickly able to produce new products. To Davids, Goliaths bring financial resources and an ability to market and sell worldwide. Imagine the potential of allying the Fortune 500—the biggest of the big—with the Inc. 500—the best of the entrepreneurial small.

In *Winning Combinations*, James Botkin and Jana Matthews argue that "the innovation imperative" of the global market drives these types of alliances, enabling corporations to:

- Respond promptly, develop rapidly, and produce new products and services innovatively; and
- Take quick advantage of international marketing capabilities and distribution channels for new products and services.[29]

The "entrepreneurial partnership" combines the competitiveness of entrepreneurship, which is central to success in business networks, with the cooperation of partnership. "Collaborating to compete is an example of innovative management in action," writes George Kozmetsky in the foreword to their book.

The Virtual Corporation

In February, 1993, *Business Week* updated its 1986 concern about "hollow corporations" with cover text proclaiming: "Big, complex companies usually can't react fast enough. Small, nimble ones may not have the muscle. What's the answer? A new model that uses technology to link people, assets, and ideas in a temporary organization. After the business is done, it disbands. It's called the virtual corporation. Just another management fad—or a vision of the future?"[30]

Contrasting with its alarm at hollow corporations, *Business Week* clearly treats the virtual corporation as a wave of the future. Its definition of a virtual corporation is that of a teamnet: "a temporary network of independent companies—suppliers, customers, even erstwhile rivals—linked by information technology to share skills, costs, and access to one another's markets." Among those it lionizes for taking this approach are Jamie Houghton of Corning, John Sculley of Apple, and Andrew Grove of Intel.

Multiple company partnerships are not only a direction big, high-tech companies are taking. They are also the wave of the future in small businesses, even in traditional industries.

ON THE SMALL BUSINESS FRONTIER

In the 1990s, the really big news about interenterprise alliances is in small companies, not large ones. "Flexible manufacturing networks," with beginnings in northern Italy in the 1970s, are still in the early phases of their organizational ramp. This little-known but powerful grass-roots business movement promotes economic development: it creates jobs, improves productivity, and lowers costs. An important major new strategy for small business, it also improves the health of the economy as a whole.

The companies you meet in "Small Giants," chapter 6, are the harbingers of a new category—the Teamnet 500 for the 21st century.

Teamnets on a Grand Scale

Economic Megagroup	5	**SME Economic Development** **Voluntary Geographies** **Keiretsu**
Alliance	4	
Enterprise	3	
Large Organization	2	
Small Group	1	

Boundaries are fuzziest beyond the alliance level, when companies create such complex teamnets that they generate new *economic megagroups*:

- Perhaps the best known of these are the Japanese *keiretsu*— "societies of business," which dominate their country's and thus much of the world's economy. Keiretsu are precursors of vast business complexes and long-term alliances arising elsewhere.
- *Voluntary geographies* refers to large, lively concentrations of hundreds and thousands of companies in the same broad region or industry forming and re-forming business relationships.
- While individual flexible network successes are rewarding to the parties involved, real impact can come only when companies begin interorganizing on a massive scale. Network strategies for diverse multi-industry *small-medium enterprise (SME) economic development* have been demonstrated to work for regional and national economies.

KEIRETSU: NOT JUST JAPANESE

Japan's businesses use two general forms of keiretsu:

- Horizontal, bank-centered keiretsu, such as Sumitomo and Mitsubishi; and
- Vertical, supply keiretsu, such as Toyota and its vast penumbra of vendors.

Six bank keiretsu each comprise 20 to 45 major companies, generally one to an industry. NEC, for example, is Sumitomo's electronics company. Supply keiretsu control layers of subcontractors that extend to large numbers of tiny job shops and family firms, common in the auto, electronics, and machinery industries. These forms are mutually supporting: NEC is part of a bank group and is the principal firm in a supply keiretsu of electronics companies.

While the United States has for years been fighting keiretsu in trade negotiations, now many believe keiretsu are a necessity for the United States. Clear calls are coming that it is time to join them. "Unless we move in that direction, we don't stand a chance," says

TRW chairman Joseph Gorman, one of the CEOs who accompanied President George Bush on his ill-fated 1991 trip to Japan.[31] Others echo Gorman's view. "U.S. and European information technology companies face a stark choice: cooperate or become vassals of their Japanese competitors—hang together or hang separately," writes Charles Ferguson, a technology adviser to investment bankers, in "Computers and the Coming of the U.S. Keiretsu." He even goes so far as to propose a massive "Euro-American Keiretsu" anchored by IBM, Siemens, Philips, DEC, Xerox, and Motorola.[32]

In the late-1980s, Ford and Chrysler followed Toyota and other Japanese car makers in forming supply keiretsu by drastically reducing the components made in-house. In 1993, even giant GM is following suit.

Keiretsu create innumerable teamnets who, working together, generate an economic megaregion.

VOLUNTARY GEOGRAPHIES OF PLACES AND IDEAS

Until the 1970s, there was no such place as Silicon Valley. But since then, the Valley of Intel and Apple has been California's economic jewel. Stumbling in the mid-1980s in the face of Japanese competition, the Valley made a strong return in the early 1990s. The reason for the renaissance? "Small and medium-sized enterprises are pioneering a new Silicon Valley—one that fosters collaboration and reciprocal innovation among networks of specialist producers." Co-opetition provides the revitalizing dynamic, Anna Lee Saxenian finds. "Paradoxically, both cooperation and competition are intensifying as local firms organize themselves to learn with their customers, suppliers, and competitors about what to make next and how to make it,"[33] she writes.

These large-scale network economic conditions do not require physical proximity. The joining together of many smallish firms and professionals in endless combinations of temporary arrangements also characterizes a number of particularly fast-paced industries, some old, like publishing and the movie business, and some new, like electronics and biotechnology. Biotech, write Quinn, Doorley, and Paquette, "is becoming structured as a number of multiple-level consortia; each enterprise has its own network of contact and information relationships involving a variety of research, clinical, production, and marketing groups around the world."[34]

DEVELOPING ECONOMIES

Saxenian uses Silicon Valley's success to "underscore the importance of regional economies to industrial competitiveness and the need for local industrial policy in the 1990s." Jerry Nagel of the Red River Trade Corridor, Inc., expresses the idea simply, "If I think of myself as living in a rural town of 8,500, I'm pretty small. But if I think of Crookston, Minnesota, as part of a 1.5-million-person region that produces $20 billion a year, I'm pretty big." Nagel is thinking outside the geographic dots, connecting Manitoba, eastern North Dakota, and western Minnesota, running along the Red River. Their biggest trading partner? Brittany, France.

Italy's Emilia-Romagna region and Denmark's economic revitalization through small business networking provide evidence of the value of teamnets on the broadest scale, examples extensively explored in "Instead of Layoffs," chapter 7.

How Fast Is Your Environment?

As we hurtle through the early decades of the Information Age, new forms of organization such as the types described in this chapter and the last no longer just emerge; they erupt. Constant change and continuous globalization challenge all companies in all markets—from hidebound firms in backwater industries to speedster leaders in industries on the innovation bullet train.

*Teamnets are emerging as a response to
the pace of change, change driven above
all by technology.*

Turbulent environments once existed only in the province of high-tech companies, research facilities, and special-case industries like entertainment. The classic line about CNN is that they hold their meetings, lasting perhaps 30 seconds, in the hall. Today, fast-paced change is everywhere, pushing companies of all sizes in all industries into more flexible internal and external arrangements. You don't have much time for bureaucracy if you're making decisions every minute.

Can't keep up with the pace of change? Not surprising. While there are still important differences between the pace of change in semiconductors and television from the pace of change in machine shops and lumber mills, nevertheless:

*Everyone's pace is accelerating. Human
beings have never before had to cope with
such an accelerating rate of change as a
constant daily diet.*

Business, which strives for stability and predictability, is undergoing a major epochal shift. As the fundamentals move into new territory, dynamic balance and insightful anticipation are at a premium.

The speed of change is a powerful reality in our daily working lives. Companies need to adapt swiftly and flexibly. The old commands and controls don't work as the pace picks up. The fast-approaching 21st century appears to be dramatically different from the 20th. In the words of R. Buckminster Fuller, the designer of the geodesic dome, we must learn to "do more with less" in a world of shrinking resources and rising expectations.

PACE OF CHANGE AFFECTS ORGANIZATION

The here today, gone tomorrow, accelerating pace of change is the shorthand measure of many trends in technology, markets, and society. They affect organizations and people in every nook and cranny of commerce. Use the Pace of Change chart to assess how fast your business environment is moving.

Pace of Change

SPEED OF CHANGE	ENVIRONMENT	CONDITIONS
Slow.	Stable.	Predictable demand; unchanging competitors; gradual innovation; government policies set.
Medium.	Changing.	Demand fluctuates but is predictable over a few years; competitors enter and leave without major effects; innovation orderly and public policies changing predictably.
Fast.	Innovative.	Sudden, unpredictable demand and competitor shifts; innovation rapid; government struggling to make policy.

The pace of change has an environmental impact on the nature of organizations. Fifty years of research confirm that the more stable the environment, the more mechanistic and hierarchical the organization tends to be. Conversely, the more rapidly changing the environment, the more organic and networked the organization.[35] "Networks are designed to build the central competitive advantage of the 1990s—superior execution in a volatile environment," writes management consultant Ram Charan.[36]

Departments and other major components internal to an enterprise also organize according to the pace of change.[37] One Fortune 500 company organizes its fast-paced research and engineering groups as a network spread out over several dozen sites. Its purchasing department, though, where life is less chaotic, concentrates in a few places and functions as a typical bureaucracy. Thus, different parts of the same organization can have distinctly different cultures.

From Hierarchy to Network

Slow change	Fast change
HIERARCHY	**NETWORK**
Imposed control	Self-control
Specialized	Generalized
Dependence	Independence
Formal channels	Voluntary relations
Commands	Consultation
Appointed leaders	Natural leaders
Formal job descriptions	Loosely defined jobs
Vertical interaction	Lateral interaction
Rigid levels	Flexible levels

Professional cultural differences can erect internal boundaries so intense that people in the same company say, "We can't talk to each other." For example, innovators and designers often find it difficult to talk to producers and distributors, writers can't talk to engineers, sales people can't talk with accountants.

NOT ONLY FATHER KNOWS BEST

Doing more with less requires thinking differently about how to do business. Just as the old nuclear family of Mom, Dad, and the two kids no longer applies to everyone, the old nuclear work group of boss and bossed is now only one of many arrangements. The approach of "future managers . . . has to be less boss-ship and more participative," says Eugene E. Harris, general management and development manager for USS Fairless Works, a division of USX Corporation.[38]

Less bossy and more participatory teamnets are very scalable. Teamnet principles apply at all levels, from small groups to organizations to enterprises to groups of enterprises.

Empowered teams, study circles, and top teams all reflect different ways for small groups to function more flexibly and responsively. Cross-functional teams, empowered clusters, and sociotechnical systems are teamnet approaches for large organizations. Kaizen, internal markets, service webs, and core firms transform whole enterprises. Joint ventures, strategic alliances, and flexible business networks are boundary crossing teamnets at the alliance level. Keiretsu, voluntary geographies, and economic megagroups are examples of very large-scale teamnets.

———

Our focus now shifts to small companies in the next two chapters. As the biggest companies continue to retrench, the exciting new frontier for business development in the 1990s is in the multiplying power of small businesses.

Small Giants: How Grass-Roots Companies Compete with Global Corporations

When we look for new ideas on how to dig ourselves out of the economic pits, we may be gazing in the wrong direction if we fixate only on Japan and the Pacific Rim. Quietly, in such unlikely venues as Denmark and Italy, profitable new economic forces are at work that already have their parallels in the United States.

"Flexible business networks"[1] is the phrase coined to describe the banding together of small firms to achieve global competitiveness. Here, networking doesn't mean the much-maligned business card exchanges of the 1980s, where people sought contacts for jobs. Rather, it means the creation of jobs as coalitions of small firms develop the economic muscle to do the work of giants. Just as the large firms are forming alliances, so are the small ones.

In 1988, Denmark, with a population comparable to Massachusetts's, was the economic mirror image of that state in the early 1990s: high unemployment, mounting trade debt, low corporate investment, and considerable difficulty funding public services.

With its 5 million people in a land mass the size of Massachusetts and New Hampshire, Denmark also faces the onslaught of the new European Community trade bloc, completely changing the rules at the end of 1992.

"Size is the problem," McKinsey & Company, the consulting firm, says in a government-funded report. Denmark's manufacturing companies are too small, too independent, and too diversified to compete in the global market. According to McKinsey, Denmark needs to reorganize and develop a few "industrial locomotives." "Critical mass" in financing, access to new technology, marketing, and management experience will create these multinational companies. To achieve critical mass, McKinsey recommends mergers.

Instead, in 1989, Denmark embarks on what becomes over time a $50 million program to support its small and medium-sized firms by developing flexible business networks. Denmark's plan is inspired by the notable economic success of the industrial networks of northern Italy, a vibrant source of that country's 1980s economic renaissance. In the Emilia-Romagna region, the networking movement began in the 1970s in the then depressed but now flourishing textile industry.

Danish results also come quickly. After only 18 months, "more than 3,500 firms, including many manufacturing companies, are actively involved in networks," according to Niels Christian Nielsen of the Danish Technological Institute. For the first time in its history, Denmark posts a positive trade balance with Germany, the *only* European country that can make such a claim in 1991.[2] The "country consensus," according to Nielsen, is that networking "enhanced the competitiveness of small companies." Small business networks get credit as "key players" in achieving the positive trade balance.

Denmark is remarkable. A small country saves its economy by creating networks among its little firms. Can it happen elsewhere?

How a Bolt Maker "Did a Denmark"

It's fine to talk about creating networks when it's a trend sweeping a whole country. But what about the individual company? Can one company do what Denmark did—just because it's the best way to do business?

Erie Bolt Corporation did. Today, the Erie, Pennsylvania, maker of metal parts and components is a healthy company with a bright future—an example for small manufacturing firms in the United States and elsewhere.

It wasn't always so. In 1985, Erie Bolt is close to bankruptcy. Harry Brown arrives from a 15-year career at Bethlehem Steel Corporation to find Erie Bolt losing at least $100,000 annually. "Morale [was] so low you couldn't measure it; quality control had been eliminated to cut costs, the pension fund was underfunded, and payables were overdue."[3] He persuades the board to sell him a majority interest in the company through a leveraged buyout.

"We looked like a mini-GM," he says. The company employed 63 people "with five management layers separating the president from the shop floor." (Federal Express with its 45,000 people has only five layers of management.)

To stop the hemorrhaging, Brown applies standard turnaround tactics: layoffs of about 20 percent, flattening the management structure, and cutting deals with creditors, all of which "bought . . . some time." Then he goes after the basic question: What business is Erie Bolt in? Erie Bolt is not just a specific "product maker." It is "a company with certain capabilities . . . it could forge, heat-treat, machine and perform other metalworking functions," Brown says. Regarding it this way gives "it entry to lots of different and growing markets for precision metal parts." This is the path Brown follows:

- To become a multifunctional shop, workers need cross-training on at least three machines. Brown cuts a deal with the unions, begins training immediately, and watches productivity improve dramatically.

- To be able to specialize even more, he strikes deals with competitors who can make certain parts more cheaply. One such arrangement cuts 28 percent from the cost of producing an electrical motor part.
- To simplify purchasing for customers, Erie Bolt advertises itself as "The One Source for Outsourcing," representing arrangements with numerous vendors, including 12 local artisans.

That's not all. "Brown worked closely with suppliers to improve production processes by sharing information, allowing them to use gauges and instruments (including the firm's CAD—computer aided design—system), and even lending them his engineers," Gregg Lichtenstein, who studied Erie Bolt and many other such flexible businesses, writes.[4] As a result, companies now share:

- A common gauge room;
- A library of manufacturing specifications; and
- A video library on technical subjects.

Within two years, Erie Bolt's sales grow 35 percent and the customer base quadruples to 420. In 1991, sales top $6 million. Eighty-three people now work for the company, an increase of 30 people since the downsizing. All layoffs have been rehired along with some new employees.

What lessons can be learned from Erie Bolt?

Working with other companies, sharing costs, and pooling talents create business, which creates jobs.

"When business is not good firms are willing to try anything. There will always be one or two people who will try to steal an account, but customers come back. They want fair treatment and the benefits a network of firms can provide. People are reluctant to sign forms.

When you keep a network informal, you can do almost anything. Creating relationships is a slow process," Lichtenstein writes.[5]

It's an unusual success, and Erie Bolt is not alone. Although Harry Brown acted without knowledge of the flexible business networks bubbling elsewhere in the United States and Europe, he intuitively used its principles to save his business.

Business Networking in Small Towns and Big

"Networking Comes to America," reads the Spring 1991 headline of the *Entrepreneurial Economy Review*, almost a trade journal for the flexible business network world. Although Europe leads the United States in benefiting from flexible business networks, many small American companies already are involved.

They are found in neighborhoods—like the East New York neighborhood of Brooklyn, with its 450 small manufacturing and warehousing companies. In a single square mile, there are 150 metalworking shops and suppliers, so many, "we could make a car," says Kart Joerger, owner of Woodhaven Telesis Corporation, which does metal stamping.[6] In one industrial park, nearly one-third of 66 companies are metalworkers. Now there's an East Brooklyn Metalworking Industry Network. Its first product is a directory of names, products, and technical resources, step one in building a collaborative network of business relationships.

For all we hear about the very big companies and the success or failure of the economy, it is myriad small companies that produce nearly half of America's industrial output. This is the heart of flexible business networks—micro-industrial centers, engaged in commerce at the grass roots. Little shops employing a few people— like Roberts Printing down the street from us, concentrated in a small industrial enclave in Newton, Massachusetts, that includes the remnants of a once-thriving garment industry.[7]

Across America are pockets of flexible business activity. They are the core of the bedrock producers. Often, these pockets operate next to each other—90 percent of Boeing Helicopter's small metalworking suppliers are situated in one contiguous area near Philadelphia. Assembled, they are the Metalworking Initiative, designed to bring Total Quality Management practices to the member firms. Boeing now requires this quality capability from its suppliers. Separately, they cannot afford to retrain all their workers in quality methods; together they can.

In just a few years, "at least 50 nascent networks of firms" have appeared, operating in at least 14 states and involving "more than 1,500 small firms," according to the Corporation for Enterprise Development (CFED), the Washington, D.C.-based association of state economic development organizations.[8] This core group, identified by CFED, is unusually successful—and it is evidence of the larger trend among enterprises to join flexible networks. The number takes on gargantuan proportions when you fold in all the informal alliances that businesses create on the fly. One state with innovative activities is in the Midwest:

- In the Appalachians of Ohio, ACEnet, a network of 30 firms across an 11-county area, produces accessible housing retrofit products, aimed at a niche market of the disabled and elderly population.
- In the Southern Ohio Wood Industry Consortium, 22 companies—most of them sawmills—cooperate in training, finance, R&D, and product innovation.
- Twenty Ohio forging companies belong to the Heat Treaters Network, providing process technology and diffusion of new ideas.

One-at-a-time network formation is often a painfully long process. It took two years for the Heat Treaters Network to get off the ground. "Intensely competitive, the small heat treating companies that came to form the Heat Treaters Network chafed at the cooperative bit. [They] would not have participated if there had been any reasonable hope that they could save themselves individually," explains Dennis Giancola, the marketing consultant who facilitates HTN.[9] Elsewhere:

- In Michigan, 70 machine-tool manufacturers combine forces to pursue vital R&D in basic technologies as the Michigan Manufacturing Technology Association; 21 firms establish the Independent Parts Suppliers as a cooperative for marketing, quality standards, and training; and nine firms—four companies employing between 100 and 350 people and five employing up to 20 people—belong to the Northern Michigan Furniture Manufacturers Network to share training in continuous improvement.
- In Massachusetts, the Metalforming Network, five metalworking firms, each with 50 to 100 employees and annual sales of $2 to $4 million, are jointly developing environmentally sound technology for reducing use of solvents in parts cleaning. Alone, they couldn't afford the R&D costs; together, they can. To undertake the project, they received a $30,000 grant from the Massachusetts Office of Toxic Use Reduction and $10,000 from the Bay State Center for Applied Technology. Each firm's $5,000 investment leverages the whole: $65,000.
- The Oregon Wood Products Competitiveness Corporation encourages secondary wood products businesses to find joint solutions to common problems: exports, product development, marketing, and publicity. State legislation—Oregon passed two bills in its 1991 session that support flexible business networks—set up the agency to assist its 1,200 firms employing 20,000 people to become "the finest, most competitive value-added producer in the world."
- In a rare three-way arrangement involving business, government, and labor, the Garment Industry Development Corporation (GIDC) is a nonprofit service center for New York City's $12 billion apparel industry that directly employs 110,000 workers in 4,500 factories. Besides offering vocational training programs and marketing and technology assistance, in 1992 GIDC initiated Fashion Exports/New York, aimed at expanding the city's apparel exports.

New Ideas in the Old South

BORN IN ATLANTA

At a large March 1988 meeting in Atlanta, Georgia, southern business leaders and public policy makers gather to discuss the health—or lack thereof—of the region's manufacturers. According to the findings of the Southern Technology Council (STC), a regional consortium of states, the South had missed the glory days of the mid-1980s as it struggled to overcome the recession at the beginning of the decade. With many jobs lost, existing plants, with their aging technology and shrinking skilled workforce, couldn't compete. Public economic development policy had been reduced to fierce local competitions for the few new branch plants offered by national firms.

In retrospect, this meeting is a turning point in public sector endorsement of flexible business networks in the United States. A critical mass of the key actors in flexible networks on both the world and national scene convenes at the conference in the hopes of adapting the Italian lessons elsewhere: Italian economists Sebastiano Brusco and Danielle Mazzonis, firsthand witnesses to the revival in northern Italy; MIT professor Charles Sabel, whose 1984 book, *The Second Great Industrial Divide*, written with Michael Piore, focused attention on Italy; and C. Richard Hatch, a major policy adviser to Denmark, among others.

In his address to the meeting, Stuart Rosenfeld, then executive director of STC, offers a compelling case for improving the region's manufacturing base by helping small business:

- Though vital to the region's economy, small and medium-sized firms, who often can't meet standards required by corporate suppliers, are at risk.
- As large firms downsize, they rely more on small suppliers, whose quality and quickness become key factors in overall competitiveness.

- Governments—who do precious little for small firms—cannot possibly help companies on a one-by-one basis.[10]

Rosenfeld proposes interaction among firms to share the costs and risks associated with innovation and modernization: "flexible manufacturing networks," described as "new forms of interfirm collaboration." The group endorses the idea, setting in motion what would become dozens of pilot programs throughout the South. STC describes seven of its North Carolina pilots in a January 1992 newsletter:

- They span the state geographically.
- They involve diverse technologies: joint development of a production monitoring system, just-in-time manufacturing, vendor quality certification, environmental marketing, and R&D.
- *Companies match the average network grant of $10,000 on a scale from 50 percent to 100 percent.*[11]

The STC report also does a roundup of other flexible network activities in the South:

- The Florida High Technology Council wants to duplicate the remarkably successful Technology Coast Manufacturing and Engineering Network in other sectors: pharmaceuticals, laser optics, tool and die, software, environmental firms, and minority defense contractors.
- Alabama—with four target sectors: apparel, electronics, metals, and wood products—sponsors a certified metalworking apprenticeship program through a community college.
- In South Carolina, Enterprise Development, Inc., is "leveraging resources at the University of South Carolina, Spartanburg, the State Technical Education System, the Southeast Manufacturing Technology Center, and the Spartanburg

Chamber of Commerce." It's launching a network challenge grant program with seed money from the Appalachian Regional Commission.

- Kentucky has pilot projects in biotechnology and wood products, including the 20 members of the Kentucky Wood Manufacturers Network who will do joint market development and training.
- Maryland's Office of Technology Development funds six Regional Technology Centers and sponsors a network broker program, the people who facilitate flexible business networks.
- In Virginia, a public-private task force, partly funded through the state's Economic Development Department, plans two pilots, focused on the wood products and furniture industries in Southside, Virginia, and defense contractors in the north. And, of course,
- Arkansas, in this issue reporting on the Arkansas Industrial Network Project, which trains network brokers.

A SYMBOL OF HOPE IN ARKANSAS

Commemorative Wood, Inc., designs, produces, and distributes "A Symbol of Hope"—literally. The five-company firm sells a special product by that name: a solid oak plaque with photo, political highlights, and the signature of native son Bill Clinton, commemorating his election as 42nd president of the United States.

But Commemorative Wood, born just two weeks after the 1992 presidential election, is not just a plaque producer; it is an excellent example of a small, flexible business network that comes together to exploit a particular market opportunity. Alone, none can produce the final product; together, they can. A wood shop in Arkansas's Delta glues together previously discarded scrap pieces of oak to form a blank. Another shop cuts the edges. In central Arkansas, a printer prints the artwork that a manufacturer in the western part of the state applies and finishes. Commemorative Wood in Little Rock is the distributor.

The tie-in to Clinton is not gratuitous. He had been briefed on Emilia-Romagna by Rosenfeld; Richard Hatch; and Mary Houghton, president, and Ron Grzywinski, chair, of the Executive Committee, Shore Bank Corporation in Chicago, the most successful economic development bank in the United States. (Houghton and Grzywinski were already working with Clinton in setting up the Southern Development Bank Corporation in Arkadelphia.) In the late 1980s, as governor, Clinton took time on a trip to Europe to spend two days in northern Italy, and saw Emilia-Romagna's success for himself. He also had a long-standing interest in manufacturing issues, participating in numerous conferences and seminars. In 1987, Rosenfeld, as executive director of the Southern Technology Council, had invited Clinton to be the opening speaker at the Southern Legislative Conference Annual Meeting, which featured manufacturing policy issues.

When Hatch traveled to Magnolia in southwest Arkansas to talk with metalworkers about starting a network, he was joined by John Ahlen, the president of Arkansas's Science and Technology Authority (ASTA).[12] Clinton asked Ahlen to go on the trip. A grant to the Southern Technology Council from Winthrop Rockefeller Foundation helped ASTA play its public sector role. Between November 1990 and March 1991, ASTA, in conjunction with the Southern Technology Council, sponsored three two-day "Seminars in Manufacturing Networking," training sessions attended by 30 potential network brokers. By early 1992, it had awarded six network challenge grants—the companies put up the other half of the money—in the wood products, metals, and chemical industries.

One cornerstone of Arkansas's flexible business activity is the Metalworking Connection, a joint venture involving 67 companies, with an average of 11 employees each, and three universities located in an 18-county area in a 100-mile radius. Two directors of economic development at Southern Arkansas University, one in Magnolia and one in Henderson, sparked the network, after meeting Rosenfeld and Hatch. "Clayton [Franklin, the other director] and I were going to a meeting in northeast Arkansas. We drove together for a few hours and talked and connived and started hallucinating until we

146

The TeamNet Factor

said, 'Let's do it,' so we did," says Bob Graham, the Magnolia campus economic development executive director.

Among the Metalworking Connection's achievements is a Youth Apprenticeship Training Program (Clinton attended the kick-off dinner) that addresses Arkansas's urgent skills problem. By the year 2000, 83 percent of the state's tool and die makers will be gone. To counter this trend, the program provides high school students with academic credit while they work on the shop floor. The Metalworking Connection also:

- Shares a process capability information system, which profiles exactly what machine and worker capability exists in the state's metalworking industry;
- Has undertaken a group assessment of collective purchase of all insurance with savings estimated at 25 to 30 percent, and already collectively buys health insurance; and
- Has begun implementation of a Just-in-Time Supplier program, linking major buyers in the network.

Clarksville's Gerald Stokes, president of Arkansas Technology, Inc., applies the network idea internally. As part of his new production organization, he includes firms that plug holes in his company capabilities. "This has allowed Stokes to concentrate his firm's effort on what it does best—design, engineering, and marketing, to produce the very best product," writes Rosenfeld.[13] "The new network of eight firms has renamed itself the Arkansas Technology Manufacturing Network."

In Phillips County, eight companies, including two chemical companies and two food producers, name themselves Delta Safety Network to jointly provide their workers with safety training. In Arkadelphia, Brian Kelley of the Arkansas Enterprise Group is the spark plug for a cooperative network for small forest products firms in south Arkansas, which eventually folds in with the Arkansas Wood Products Trade Group. The Trade Group draws from Arkansas's 700 companies in the secondary wood products industry, employing more than 17,000 people.

Sandra Miller of Winrock International, the foundation that helped get the trade group off the ground through the Arkansas Rural Enterprise Center[14], was amazed at the results of the group's first survey of its members. "I never would have guessed in a million years that worker's compensation is the number-one issue for the secondary wood products industry in Arkansas," she says. Thirty-eight of the firms have started a task force to assess alternatives, including self-insurance, and evaluate proposed legislative reforms.

In Little Rock, the Woodworkers Manufacturing Network, seven minority-owned firms—design, marketing, engineering, and cabinet building—are in a joint venture to build a high-tech router. CNC (computer numerically controlled) devices are the core high technology for many machine-based industries: they provide precision, which is what high-skilled labor is all about. The goal is to produce the router at a cost in the $30,000-to-$70,000 range, considerably less than the $200,000 turnkey system currently on the market. The technology will provide access to a new market and a new product line: the 32-mm cabinet industry for which the network will supply components. They're even considering selling the router technology itself to other firms like their own.[15]

The really good news is that Arkansas is not alone in its efforts.

NORTH CAROLINA'S SUCCESSFUL PILOTS

The combination of Rosenfeld's unusual commitment and talent and the economics of North Carolina's industries has produced an unusually rich set of flexible business networks. North Carolina produces 60 percent of U.S. hosiery products, grossing $1.5 billion in annual shipments. Of the state total of 11,000 firms, 82 percent employ 100 or fewer people. More than half of the hosiery firms are based in North Carolina's Catawba Valley. In other words, small companies produce most of the U.S. domestic hosiery output. So the hosiery industry is a logical target industry for one of the pilots Rosenfeld proposes at the 1988 Atlanta meeting.

After a series of disappointing starts, the program begins to move when some company owners assume leadership roles in the fledgling networks.

Bill Wyatt, a retired apparel firm owner with 35 years' experience, is a good example. He offers to be the North Carolina Sewn Products Network's unpaid broker or coordinator. "I had been involved in networking before by subcontracting with a company that had a series of mills that worked for them," Wyatt recalls. "I saw [that] it ... built business. It took business that one firm couldn't handle, like a big order, [and gave it to] a network that could handle [it]."

In the next five months, the network coalesces. A critical mass of firm leaders, a committed broker, and a clear project all come together. They decide to offer their services through a *Capabilities Directory*, which combines their collective resources for prospective large customers. The directory also facilitates the network's ability to subcontract between one another. The directory is introduced at the September 1991 Bobbin Show in Atlanta, *the* annual industry event.

The Sewn Products Network is not the only one to form out of Rosenfeld's initiative. Randall Williams, president of Advanced Fabrication Technology, Inc., is the spark plug for the North Carolina Precision Metal Fabricators Association (NCPMFA). In a February 1989 presentation, U.S. Amada, a major supplier of equipment to the industry, warns that the region is becoming "technologically unqualified." In response, Williams calls a meeting of sheet metal fabricators and educators to launch the NCPMFA. Its initial objective is joint training. It takes a few months' time, but in November of that year, North Carolina's first state-of-the-art training facility opens, using equipment donated by U.S. Amada. Two years later, a major training center for the sheet metal industry is complete, rivaled by only three other facilities in the United States.

Not all the pilots are successful, however. The Composites Industry Network, a coalition in the eastern North Carolina boat industry, still struggles to crystallize a year after a November 1990 symposium introduced 77 firms to the idea. The Component Manufacturers Network, another group, seems destined to succeed when it begins with what looks like an ideal set of initial conditions, but eventually founders when members are unable to agree upon a clear business need.

AN ASSOCIATION BECOMES A NETWORK

Perhaps the most successful pilot is the Catawba Valley Hosiery Association (CVHA), a 30-year-old trade association that transforms itself into a flexible manufacturing network. By creating a network within a network, it marries high-tech competitive-edge technology with its low-tech industry.

Although the CVHA as a whole is big—it has 275 members, including 115 hosiery mills and 160 industry suppliers—each member is quite small. "The typical CVHA mill is small, has no industrial engineer on staff, and is often unable to afford in-plant training."[16] This makes the network ripe for its first initiative: an industrial engineering and employee training assistance center. Since this word-of-mouth industry documents very little, in-plant training curricula become a high priority. Next, the network tackles costs: reducing telephone and health care costs through pooled buying. In another counter-intuitive but cost-effective move, CVHA chooses a self-funded plan, managed by a third party, which yields the members 30 to 40 percent savings on health insurance.

The third initiative is the most daring—and the most potentially lucrative. It solves the "10-day delivery problem," which most U.S. hosiery customers now demand of their suppliers. The supplier no longer controls the supply; the customer does by refusing to warehouse inventory, and by insisting on buying virtually on demand. To even process orders requires EDI, meaning that people can submit their orders electronically and that order status is trackable at all times.

The 1950s and 1960s machinery used in these North Carolina firms indicates the depth of the problem. Machines now worth $1,200 to $1,500 have to compete with $35,000-to-$40,000 state-of-the-art models. These Italian and Japanese engineering marvels are worth it: they triple production and reduce pattern change time from hours to minutes. The promise of quick response opens up new possibilities for manufacturing capacity sharing. This leads to TEEMS, software produced by a flexible business network within the CVHA network.

A TEAMNET IN A TEAMNET

TEEMS (Textile Efficiency Engineering Monitoring Software) is a "production monitoring system which can be installed in hosiery mills utilizing old and/or state-of-the-art hosiery knitting machines." It "allow[s] the introduction of state-of-the-art technology in hosiery mills one step at a time." With a target price of $6,000, the software will be much more in the range of CVHA members than the currently available $30,000 products.

TEEMS is a joint venture of Digital Eyes Company, a systems integration firm, CVHA, and STC. Digital Eyes president Stephen Cowan is the spark plug. He convinces CVHA and STC of the value of his idea when they realize that the technology can benefit all knitting firms—large and small. Cowan works closely with Dan St. Louis, the CVHA staff member who developed the in-plant training curricula, and with CVHA's 24-member Knitting Technology Committee. Together, they design, develop, manufacture, install, and market TEEMS.[17]

"Steve Cowan . . . realized he did not have the capability to complete the TEEMS project for CVHA on his own," write William Meade and Ray Daffner.[18] "He lacked the programming expertise required to develop the full range of software and the electrical engineering skills to develop the data collection devices. . . . [So he] decided to use a network to create TEEMS, identifying firms with unique and complementary skills. These partners required minimal initial investment to participate."

Computer Strategies, a local four-person software engineering firm, develops the TEEMS software platform in exchange for future revenues. For a small retainer, Eridani, a local two-person electrical engineering firm specializing in design, puts together a proprietary data collection product. It keeps the exclusive manufacturing rights in exchange for Digital Eyes's having the exclusive marketing rights. As a result, an estimated $100,000 software development project requires just $40,000 in actual cash. And it is quick. It takes just a year from the product concept to the first installation. The target price is more than met: CVHA members can license the program for $1,000; nonmembers can license it for $2,500. First-year revenues are estimated at $500,000, quite a healthy return on the investment. According to CVHA members, most mills will initially install TEEMS on 20 to 30 machines, gradually moving it to all their machines.

The next project is to set up the Manufacturers' Bulletin Board, proposed by Paul Fogleman, CVHA's executive director: "It is not unusual for a large hosiery mill operator to walk into the plant on Monday morning and find a message from a major retail customer inquiring about the ability to complete a potential order of 50,000 dozen socks within 10 days. . . . The system we propose will enable a greige goods mill [the first in the value chain which knits product from raw yarn] to notify all CVHA members . . . to determine their available production capacity . . . and offer it."

AN ENCYCLOPEDIA OF FLEXIBLE NETWORKS— IN HYPERTEXT

Northwest Policy Center publishes as close to an encyclopedia of basic information about U.S. manufacturing networks as we've seen: it's upbeat, informative, and thought-provoking, and it's available only in hypertext![19] It includes a directory of the key players in the flexible manufacturing network world and such wisdom as this:

- The competitive *disadvantages* of small firms "provide the most powerful rationale" for flexible networks. When you're small, you have no time to think about new markets and product development; limited access to new technology; and low productivity.

- The "three sine qua nons" of networks: (1) network brokers, the spark plugs who guide the networks into existence; (2) "challenge grants," small amounts (usually $10,000) of public sector money that companies match; and (3) a "goal definition process" by which the companies in the network commit to a mutually beneficial purpose.
- The private sector, not government, drives these networks, which ultimately limits public sector involvement.
- Not every country's experience with networks has been an unqualified success. The Australian clothing industry, with its labor-intensive history of small firms serving as subcontractors, raises serious questions about "severe exploitation of the home-based workforce."

The 1992 *Catalog of U.S. Manufacturing Networks*,[20] compiled by Gregg Lichtenstein and published by the National Institute of Standards and Technology (NIST), is an excellent, thorough source of examples. These models are changing the face of America's small businesses. What makes them work?

Five Principles of Flexible Business Networks

Flexible business networks combine *independence* with *interdependence*. They pool resources and capabilities to obtain the benefits of scale and diversity. By cooperating, small firms can play effectively in the global market. Their flexibility and swift responsiveness to change provide a global competitive advantage. Network flexibility comes from many small entrepreneurs able to make quick decisions and to act immediately to accommodate change. These benefits apply not only to manufacturing networks, but also to business networks of all descriptions, whether product-based or service-oriented.

In *Flexible Manufacturing Networks: Cooperation for Competi-*

tiveness in a Global Economy, a prescient 1988 pamphlet, Richard Hatch describes the phenomenon this way:

> A flexible manufacturing network is a group of firms that cooperate in order to compete—that collaborates to achieve together what each cannot alone.[21]

Every flexible business network definition we've seen contains the cooperation/competition duality in some form. "A network is the cooperation and the mechanisms of cooperation that allow a small company to compete successfully with the best of the large," Denmark's legislation reads.

1. UNITED BY THE COMPETITIVE PURPOSE

Flexible business networks must have a clear, common purpose that all participants ascribe to, the first critical success factor. "Joint solutions to common problems" is a popular slogan in the movement, and an apt one for this critical catalytic element of teamnets: purpose. Regardless of the specific reasons why competitors cooperate for common benefit, which vary as widely as the types of business, *some* particular purpose represents the core of every network.

Broadly speaking, business networks tend to organize either vertically or horizontally. Vertical networks integrate the parts of a process, product, or product line, like ACEnet. Horizontal networks gain benefits of scale and flexibility, such as the Metalworking Initiative. Networks-of-a-kind are especially common among smaller businesses, while larger firms typically look for product and process complements.

Networks may satisfy more than one business need. The most common purposes for networks are:

- Joint marketing;
- Industry-specific training programs;
- Technology transfer;

- Sharing expensive equipment; and
- Bulk buying.

The chart provides a more detailed list of reasons why business networks come together.

Business Reasons to Network

Marketing	• Co-marketing/pool selling • Market research • Common needs assessment • Common brand • Export services/international offices
Training	• Specialized and expert trade skills • Basic trade/professional skills • General skills
Resources	• Purchasing/pool buying • Common stock/warehouse • Vendor coordination • Specialized equipment • Professional services
R&D	• Joint product/service development • Joint process development • Shared research and innovation • Technology transfer and diffusion
Quality	• Joint quality program • Benchmarking • Shared internal standards • International standards certification

2. INDEPENDENT SOVEREIGN COMPANIES

Network members must be independent, the second critical success factor. Networks thrive in the challenging dynamic of co-opetition. The basic units of networks are independently incorporated firms, whether small craft shops in Italy or woodworkers who partner to build a state-of-the-art spray painting facility in Bemidji, Minnesota.

"Networking is *not* about giving up independence. The small company in a network is still an independent sovereign company," says Nielsen emphatically.[22] Small businesses, wherever they are, highly value independence. This is a source of great strength in networks, and is also, of course, a source of great weakness. When there are not strong countervailing cooperative forces, competition can split networks apart.

Enterprises are classic components of networks: they have a life separate and apart from the network. They are self-reliant. Like a PC, when the network goes down, local work still gets done. However, independence is only part of what leads people to see a network. When "independents" link "interdependently," they generate a viable flexible form.

3. LINKING SOVEREIGNS

Networks must have many channels of communications and rich relationships among members, the third critical success factor. While purpose motivates, connections between members put the network into motion on a day-to-day basis.

Many people associate "networking" only with people-to-people connections. A rich set of personal interconnections is a sine qua non of successful business networks. In the computer world, "networking" means the physical methods of electronically connecting distributed places of work. This underscores an important attribute of networks: the existence of real channels of communication between members. In networks, communication is essential, and time-consuming. Technology connections are critical, whether low or high tech. (Even a telephone tree is a technology strategy, albeit a low-tech one today.) Facilitating effective and efficient interaction is of critical practical importance.

Biological metaphors suit networks well, even better than mechanical ones. Networks naturally start small and grow over time.

They grow through communications, diverse interactions around common concerns, and the deepening of relationships, person to person and firm to firm. Different people and different cultures communicate differently. Yet, all communicate. Information, like oxygen, is in the lifeblood of every network, coursing between its members.

4. MULTIPLE LEADERS, PRIVATE AND PUBLIC

Networks must have more than one leader, the fourth critical success factor. By its nature, a flexible manufacturing network has many leaders. First, there are the business people who represent the firm members, individuals who sit at the top of their own firm's totem pole, whatever its size. Then, there are the network brokers, technical consultants, government agency representatives, and retired industry leaders who help a network through some of its growth pains to self-motivating cooperation.

Private sector leadership is critical to network success, according to people who have successfully catalyzed networks as well as those who have failed. Without direct business leadership, networking programs, whether publicly or privately stimulated, always fail. Yet, without some outside support, it is often difficult for a private group to establish the requisite common ground that leads to a viable network. So, besides multiple individual business leaders in a network, networks also often involve brokers, consultants, and other public, nonprofit, and educational leaders.

5. PLUGGING IN AT MANY LEVELS

Successful networks must hook in at a variety of levels within the larger economic system. In flexible manufacturing networks, the fundamental commandment is to respect the integrity of every member firm. At the next level, the network as a whole must function as a coherent system. Finally, at the level of many networks functioning in a region, the whole set of networks becomes an economic strategy. Large-scale dynamics can help networks flourish or leave them to wither and die. Systemic integration across levels depends upon respect for the systems involved.

We remember vividly the excitement of Jean-Pierre Pellegrin, the French economic development official who came to the John F. Kennedy School of Government at Harvard for a few months to study American manufacturing networks. He sat in our Networking Institute office in the fall of 1991, marveling at the wider world of networks beyond the boundaries of flexible manufacturing networks that we have been researching and reporting on since the late 1970s. We, in turn, have him to thank for deepening our knowledge of the international flexible manufacturing network community, which we see as the most dramatic business networking development of the last decade.

Watching a Paradigm Shift

In the broad view, the flexible manufacturing movement is a spontaneous development in the world economy. It exemplifies the larger trend to networks at all levels. We catch a rare detailed view of just how a new paradigm emerges as we trace the multilevel threads of the story.

It begins in Emilia-Romagna in the 1970s. Inspired by the Italian success, Denmark in the late 1980s designs a plan to catalyze "spontaneous" networking. Denmark's success in adapting the Italian model in turn leads to adoption of the idea in other parts of Europe and the United States.

In 1984, MIT economist Michael Piore collaborates with political scientist Charles Sabel to produce *The Second Industrial Divide*, where they provide an economic context for the phenomenon and coin a new term:

"Flexible specialization"—the emergence of loosely connected small economic units in the emerging wave of economic activity.

C. Richard Hatch is a catalytic node in the flexible manufacturing network world. Because of his love of race car driving, Hatch, director of the Manufacturing Network Project at New Jersey Institute of Technology, happens to be living in Italy when the "Third Italy" begins to bloom. Also a motorcycle enthusiast, Hatch runs a specialized metalworking company in Modena, Emilia-Romagna, that is part of a flexible manufacturing network. Hatch lives the experience, understands the phenomenon he is observing, and soon exports his knowledge.

After returning to the United States, Hatch leads the first U.S. study tour to Emilia-Romagna, sponsored by the German Marshall Fund, and does the seminal 1988 study of the Emilia-Romagna networks for the Corporation for Enterprise Development. Hatch is also instrumental in conveying the Italian lessons to the Danish government, and the Danes are subsequently helpful to the state of Oregon and other networking efforts in the United States. In 1992, Hatch designs Oregon's Network Broker Training Program and completes a NIST-sponsored manual on broker training.[23]

If people mention Hatch's name in the first breath of the U.S. flexible manufacturing network movement's "Who's Who," then Stuart Rosenfeld's is the second. "He's the leader of the movement from a convening sense," says Anne Heald, a key node in the network and an expert in the transfer of learning internationally. She describes Rosenfeld as a "prolific, prodigious worker who connects everyone nationally while doing fieldwork."

Before starting her Center for Learning and Competitiveness,[24] Heald was at the German Marshall Fund, where she sponsored a number of seminal projects. The Fund had a longtime intellectual interest in the Italian "miracle" because of the foundation's director of programs, Peter Weitz, who had done his dissertation research in Italy. Like Hatch, Weitz had studied the Emilia-Romagna renaissance.

In 1986, Heald funded Hatch's proposal to bring a delegation of

Italian experts to the United States. The meeting, held at New York Port Authority, brought together many early leaders in the already bubbling network in the United States, and was followed by five regional seminars that firmly planted the idea around the United States.

A year later, Heald funded Hatch's proposal to lead a group of Americans interested in manufacturing on a study tour of Emilia-Romagna. That trip proved to be catalytic in spreading the idea to the United States. It included: Mary Houghton and Ron Grzywinski of the South Shore Bank in Chicago, who carried the idea back to Clinton; Bob Friedman, now chair of the Corporation for Enterprise Development and an early convenor of the movement; Bob Coy, who under then Pennsylvania secretary of labor Harris Wofford developed the Manufacturing and Innovation Network that enabled firms in four diverse industries in the state to assess their global competitiveness; and Brian Bosworth, a public policy expert on interfirm cooperation, who has worked on nearly every major network project in the United States.

Oregon's legislative initiatives are direct outcomes of that trip. In its 1991 session, the state legislature passed two bills that mandate formation of business networks, one under the leadership of Senator Wayne Fawbush, and the other under then Speaker of the House and now Portland mayor Vera Katz. Sparked in part by the crisis in the timber industry, known nationally through its famous northern spotted owl controversy, both bills encourage the creation of networks of firms and authorize funding of network broker training.

Big changes often appear "suddenly" because processes of many little changes reach some critical mass. The new economic order is being built one team, one company, one network at a time. Individually, these are often slow processes, sometimes painfully so. As more boundary crossing teamnets assemble, the simultaneity of many slow processes begins to show rather rapid large-scale change. Feedback from the larger environment in the form of examples of success and failure helps new networks form faster. It is this whole system that develops over time into a new, healthier, more flexible economy.

Instead of Layoffs: Saving, Improving, and Creating Jobs

As a new century dawns, people, skills, and knowledge are the basis of real wealth, not raw materials. Japan is one country that capably demonstrates this, as does Denmark. When regions combine innovative cooperative leadership with resources in knowledge, diverse industries, and a good infrastructure, they become leaders in the new world markets.

Getting involved with government is not most small business people's highest priority. In the area of enabling companies to become more competitive by cooperating, some governments already play a low-cost, high-leverage role.

In place of huge tax breaks for a few favored companies, some implement a "doing more with less" strategy. They use scarce taxpayer dollars in small amounts to leverage large private sector results. The key to success is simple: business people not government officials lead the effort.

Communities can't wait for global and national recovery to trickle down years from now, if ever. Localities need to position their regions as healthy competitors in the new global economy where networks are increasingly the organizational norm.

What About Jobs?

At century's end, jobs are the central issue world around. Some jobs go elsewhere. Some jobs go nowhere. Jobs are about survival, security, independence, and prosperity in very personal terms.

There is more to the job news than additional layoffs at big companies. To see the good news requires a shift of focus. Future prosperity depends upon the cumulative effect of a few jobs at many small firms. Here, job growth trickles up.

Since the beginning of the Industrial Era, ever-bigger companies have created most new jobs—but no longer. Around 1970, small business employment began to climb after almost a century's decline, according to a 1990 International Labor Organization study.[1] Even more remarkably, the study noted, the trend reversal appeared all around the world in widely varying economies in roughly the same amount at approximately the same time.

> *In capitalist, socialist, and communist countries, 1970 was the unheralded takeoff point for small business employment growth.*

While governments can do little to directly affect jobs with big companies, except through huge public expenditures and tax write-offs, they can have great impact on the health and prosperity of small companies. With very small dollar expenditures, governments can help small companies survive, compete, and innovate.

Three Aspects to Jobs

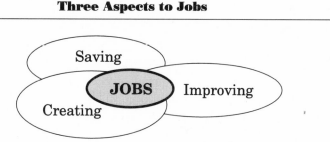

"Jobs" is a complex little word that has several important aspects. While attention usually focuses on new jobs, a community's first struggle is often to maintain existing jobs. And all new jobs are not necessarily of equal value. Replacing good lost jobs with low-skill, low-wage opportunities is a long-term prescription for a lousy place to live and work.

Most business networks originally spring from the need to stay alive. "I know I can't do business the way my father and grandfather did. Something has to change, so I'm willing to try anything," says one member of Arkansas's Metalworking Connection at an early meeting.

The most common joint programs are marketing, training, and bulk buying. Once they meet survival needs, networks move on to goals of enhanced competitiveness and growth.

SAVING JOBS

The only way to maintain jobs is to compete and survive in the global economy. Joint marketing efforts, whether shared lines, market research, trade shows, or trade missions, lead to global marketing clout. Purchasing together lowers costs and helps local businesses survive. Investment in education, training, and skills makes for a superior workforce, allowing productivity gains to offset lower wages available elsewhere. Governments can encourage these activities, and amplify their messages. The province of

Ontario, Canada, is a good example. Its Ministry of Industry, Trade, and Technology has outposts in 15 cities around the world, including Paris, London, Milan, Frankfurt, Hong Kong, Seoul, Tokyo, and Boston (where commercial officer Catharine Arnston invited us to attend the International Software Alliance Symposium, co-sponsored by the Ontario government and the Commonwealth of Massachusetts). The symposium introduces Ontario software companies to the New England computer community.

IMPROVING JOBS

It is not enough to maintain commodity jobs, or work that can be done almost anywhere.

> *The best jobs with the highest satisfaction, most freedom, and greatest reward are those that sell expertise.*

Value-added jobs, based on specialized and customized work, serve high-end markets. Technology transfer, rapid product development, and quality programs enable networks to offer higher value-added products and services. For a region to offer the world's best jobs, competitiveness—striving for excellence—needs to be Job Number 1 for everyone. Some places already have this as a goal: the state of Oregon's 1989 strategic plan calls for a workforce "equal to any in the world by 2010," a rather large challenge.

CREATING JOBS

New, high-value jobs are ultimately a function of innovation and risk taking. Basic science, R&D, education, incentives, and smart people are all part of the brew. To stimulate creativity—

fundamentally where high-value jobs come from—few cookie-cutter approaches guarantee success. As with companies that strive to be learning organizations, visionary localities can strive to create large-scale learning environments—where key strategic information is widely available and quickly circulated.

To maintain jobs, networks form for marketing reasons, to target training, and to develop purchasing power. To improve jobs, networks engage in joint product development, technology transfer, and quality programs. To create new good jobs, networks seek cooperative R&D arrangements and participation in mutual learning opportunities, wellsprings of innovation.

Economic development based on a small business networking strategy is not pie-in-the-sky. It is a proven path to economic vigor.

Small Business on a Large Scale

THE NEW ITALIAN RENAISSANCE

In 1970, Italy, a country known for its constantly changing, confusing bureaucracy, organizes itself into 21 administrative regions that never existed before. (After all, we are talking about the country that gave birth to the West's first highly centralized government, the Roman Empire, 2,000 years earlier.) Emilia-Romagna, an old, historic, moderately rural but highly industrialized region with Bologna as its capital, is the fourth poorest—and in decline.[2]

Just 15 years later, Emilia-Romagna looks entirely different. By 1985, Emilia-Romagna is Italy's second wealthiest region. It has raised its income level from 10 percent below the national average to 25 percent above. In the mid-1970s, unemployment is 20 percent. Ten years later, it is 0. At the end of the 1980s, it is cited as the seventh most prosperous region in the Economic Community. Fairly impressive statistics if recession is your problem. Bologna is forecast to have the most rapidly improving standard of living in

Italy in the 1990s, according to a 1992 Cambridge University study.[3]

While Emilia-Romagna always was home to numerous small businesses, in 15 years, the number explodes. By the late 1980s, there are 325,000 firms in this region of 4 million people—an incredible one firm for every 12 people—90,000 of them manufacturing firms alone. Propelled in part by Emilia-Romagna, Italy passes France as the world's fourth largest manufacturing economy. The area is thriving so much that people want to invest there. In late 1991, the Dutch bank ABN/Amro capitalized its "Enter Italy" fund with $77 million, targeted specifically at investments in small and medium-sized firms in central and northern Italy. Bank deposits reflect another measure of the region's economic success: in 1991, the group of 45 small rural and artisan savings banks showed a 20 percent increase in deposits, a 21 percent increase in loans, against only a 2.9 percent default rate.[4] *The Economist* attributes Emilia-Romagna's remarkable growth to a "large number of very small interlinked enterprises."

How did this happen?[5] In one of its first acts after the 1970 national administrative reorganization, the Bologna regional government establishes an economic development program based on its strong foundation of small firms. Beginning in 1976, the government sponsors a variety of programs intended to stimulate collaboration, such as grants to attend trade shows, buy equipment, or even build factories. These benefits are generally *available only to groups of firms acting in concert.*

> *This notion of a "grant to a group" is the essence of the new approach to economic development in a time of scarce resources.*

Like many rural and semirural communities around the world, Emilia-Romagna has a history of small business cooperatives. CAMA is a good example. Established in 1945, this association of

300 small woodworking firms is a large cooperative for buying and warehousing lumber and veneer. CAMA is itself an affiliate of an even larger network, Confederazione Nazionale dell'Artigianato (CNA), the artisans' confederation, the premier trade association in Emilia-Romagna. CNA provides services to more than 140,000 member firms—accounting, payroll, tax preparation, financial advice, and training. Most have fewer than 25 employees. These trade associations provide a safe, rich environment for business networking.

Technical service centers—another critical success factor of these new industrial networks—enable the collaboratives to compete globally. In 1974, the Emilia-Romagna government set up the Regional Board for Economic Development (ERVET), a semi-autonomous joint stock company. ERVET, in turn, opened 10 service centers, each with a different focus. Some address specific cross-industry needs, like ASTER for advanced science and technology, and SVEX for export assistance; others target specific industries—such as CERMET for mechanical industries and Centro Ceramica for ceramics and CITAR for the garment industry. Among other services, CITAR maintains state-of-the-art marketing and design information about fashion worldwide.

Although public funding initiated the service centers, today many are independent. CITAR, for example, is now completely self-supporting through private member fees. CERMET, by contrast, is still entirely government-supported, while Centro Ceramica moved from 85 percent public funding initially to 85 percent industry funding a decade later.

In this conducive incentive brew, networking developed spontaneously and grew rapidly among the region's myriad small firms. While the Italian experiment was clearly successful, it was not clear how transferable the experience was.

Were medieval artisan communities the hidden secret ingredient in Emilia-Romagna's success? For example, the ceramics center, an area southwest of Modena, has ancient origins stemming from the Middle Ages when a tile-making artisan tradition developed in the area. Around the small cities of Sassuolo and Fiorano, more than 100 ceramics firms and many hundreds more collateral firms—e.g., design, tool making, and distribution companies—flourish.

The answer seems to be that business networks can indeed happen elsewhere under different circumstances. Denmark shows how.

INTO THE LAND OF LEGO: DENMARK'S STORY

In the early 1990s, Denmark should be an economic disaster, what with the new 1993 European market, the dominance of Germany, and the imperatives of scale. Instead, Denmark is a boom economy, with the lowest inflation in the European Community (EC).

In 1988, however, Denmark, one of the smallest nations in the EC, a mere 1.5 percent of its 320 million population, is in crisis. According to McKinsey & Company's diagnosis, the Danes' declining economy is attributable to terminal "smallness." Almost all their industries are "traditional": textiles, wood and furniture, food processing, along with the usual assortment of tool, metalworking, and service industries. Most companies have 10 to 30 employees; there are few even semilarge firms in Denmark. The only really well-known large company is the Danish maker of very small things: Lego.

Although some indicators look good—GNP in the world's Top Ten and social services in the Top Three—the Danes can nevertheless see the danger signs in their economy, and all the trends are going the wrong way. Moreover, the recommended merger strategy is not working. Small business people hate giving up their independence. Then, when small companies do merge, all they manage to create are not-very-big (i.e., still small) companies compared with the multinational giants that populate Europe's successful economic machines.

Long one of the world's richest people, the Danes can see, and feel, disaster staring them in the face. Smallness puts them at a disadvantage in what seems to be an economy of giants. The challenges they face include:

- Marketing at an international level;
- Keeping up with innovation globally;
- Utilizing full production capacity;
- Fading ability to compete with high value-added; and
- Home markets threatened by international competition.

Until recently, experts prescribed mergers, mergers, and more mergers as the one basic economic development cure for the disease of smallness. While mergers are sometimes the right thing to do, the general prescription does not sit well with the Danes.

In the midst of the merger debate comes an emissary from Italy—ironically, an American. C. Richard Hatch had lived the Emilia-Romagna experience firsthand as the manager of a metal-working firm. In a seminar for a group of Danish manufacturers, Hatch draws on the Italian experience: "It's not size that counts but competence. If individual small firms are weak and vulnerable, networks give them strength. Networks are, quite simply, collaborative efforts to escape from the limitations of size."[6]

Hatch's seminar sets other wheels in motion. Niels Christian Nielsen, then at the Jutland Technological Institute (JTI) and now Director of Corporate Strategy at the Danish Technological Institute, suggests that a letter be sent to the new Minister of Industry, Niels Wilhjelm, proposing a program to encourage cooperation among Denmark's small businesses. It meets with some hesitation because no one seems to believe it will work. "The basic attitude in the country was that there was no way to make a small company owner cooperate. He [stet] is fiercely independent. He created his own business to be able to make his own decisions. He is going to make his stand on independence till he dies. . . . And even talking about building next steps in the national economy on cooperation among small companies was made quite a laughing stock," Nielsen later tells a group of Oregon legislators.

But the Nielsen-Hatch letter convinces Minister Wilhjelm. He, in turn, sets up an industry steering committee to oversee the network project. The Ministry hires JTI to develop the program, and JTI hires Hatch to develop broker training. In March 1989, the

Danish Ministry of Trade and Industry announces "Strategy '92," the network plan. The government passes a bill in the spring, and by August, the program is rolling. Within a year, networks involve 1,554 firms, and just six months after that, 3,500 of Denmark's firms belong to networks, according to Nielsen's Oregon testimony.

How did the Danes accomplish this feat in such a short amount of time?

HOW CONTROVERSY RAISES THE VOLUME

Upon its announcement, Strategy '92 has a great good fortune. It unleashes a storm of opposition, sometimes the best thing that can happen with a new idea, better than being ignored. "By luck, the whole thing became quite controversial and that meant that the media coverage was free," says Nielsen. While national trade associations oppose the idea, smaller sector trade associations support it, as does the Federation of Crafts and Small Industries, one major group. These controversies keep the issue on the front page and TV news for two months, not the usual fate of economic development initiatives. Nor does Minister Wilhjelm shy away from the controversy. Rather, he works to see that the government approves legislation, with a three-year limit put on the experiment.

At the heart of the program is the feasibility study, what Nielsen later called the "tiny element that set the whole thing going at a large scale." The conditions are simple:

- Any group of three or more companies with an idea for a network can apply for a $10,000 grant to investigate its feasibility.
- The application form is only two pages.
- Response time is usually less than a month.
- The answer is almost always "Yes."

Instead of requiring companies to call or write for application forms, the program distributes them in places where business people naturally go: banks, post offices, insurance offices. Banks, which have been losing money on small businesses, become among the strongest advocates of networks. Eventually, forms are available in most banks in the country.

Another key part of the program is the multiplier effect provided by broker training. If grants are not highly competitive, broker training is. The Ministry sets high qualification levels and selects 40 from numerous applications, then charges $4,500 for seven two-day training sessions given six weeks apart.

The Ministry also finances lawyers to work up standard contracts for networks and to work out some of the product liability issues. Accountants and tax consultants work through other financial issues so each new network will not have to reinvent the cooperative wheel. Importantly, an evaluation process enables program administrators to learn quickly from their mistakes and take advantage of opportunities.

Denmark's initial program consists of:

- $22 million in development grants, including $3 million for feasibility studies, $5 million for detailed planning grants, and $14 million in operating awards to the networks; and
- $3 million for creating the overall environment for networking, including promotion, technical support, evaluation, and broker training.

The $10,000 micro-grants, known as Phase 1, leverage great potential. There are enough of them—hundreds, each involving at least three companies—to create critical mass. They encourage companies to talk and to take the critical step of coming up with an explicit idea for what a network can achieve.

It is the process, not the idea, that is important. "Of course, two-thirds of all the ideas that people came up with were miserable and unsound. But then in the process of paying someone to work on that idea, give them feedback, give them suggestions, and so on, 10 new ideas would come up and eventually they ended up coming up with networks. Often, not the same networks that they started out with, but networks anyway," Nielsen says.

Phase 2 grants, which offer up to 50 percent of detailed planning costs, require participating firms to come up with matching investment. Here, grants are not virtually automatic, but the application process provides additional direction for successful networks. In Phase 3, grants cover up to 50 percent of the first-year costs of establishing the network and up to 30 percent of the second year's costs. This start-up operating capital is critical, an innovative way to provide venture funds to groups of businesses.

MADE IN DENMARK

To those involved with Denmark's economy, this abrupt success story is no accident. It came about because of a deliberate attempt to revitalize small business in the country by establishing networks of small firms in a variety of industries—and being creative about the business they do together.

Garments—Sewing Together a Line

CD (Corporate Design) Line, one of a number of Danish successes in the clothing industry, is the 14-company textile manufacturing network aimed at the job wear market, i.e., uniforms. Each company produces part of a complete collection: shirts, suits, skirts, women's knitwear, men's knitwear, ties and scarves, leather, and so on. Marketing an entire collection benefits all the firms. Together, they hire a quality manager, then set up sales agents in their two most promising markets—Sweden and Germany. They jointly contract with famous clothing designers, bringing success and name identification in the upper end of the market. Then the network moves into new markets previously closed to small firms. Contracts with major customers, like Volkswagen, now require "EDI," but network members don't know what it means. After solving the mystery—it means "electronic data interchange"—one member firm with this capability provides it to the network on a cost-sharing basis. Through this and other lucky matches, CD Line now competes with very large companies. Jointly, they employ 900 people; 45 percent of sales are exports.

Danish Furniture—Made in Taiwan

In the 1950s and 1960s, Denmark's furniture industry enjoys a reputation for fine design and exceptional quality. Then, it goes into decline. Foreign competitors, particularly the Taiwanese, begin turning out superior "Danish" furniture. In Denmark, the industry myth is that they lost U.S. market share to big companies. In fact, Danish companies had lost the desired high-price end of the market to Italian companies even smaller than themselves. The important difference was that the Italian companies organized themselves in networks. So, Danish producers quickly assemble into "spectacularly creative networks," according to Nielsen. Together, they buy advanced equipment, hire design firms, fund export marketing, and jointly develop work processes.

In one case, when five firms get together to brainstorm other value-added options, a former contractor helps them spot a new business opportunity: subcontracting the interior furnishing of a major new facility—like a conference center, hotel, or government agency. Usually a madhouse of hundreds of individual subcontractors, they map out the whole job, noting requisite skills and products, and recruit the lamp, carpet, curtain, and, of course, furniture firms that allow them to bid on projects worldwide. They hire the best Danish designers and architects to give the network's products a common coherent look—and they name themselves Alphabetica.

Landscaping, Golf Courses, and—Cemeteries!

New buildings mean work for landscapers; conversely, when construction is down, so is landscaping. With Denmark's weak economy and the building industry in decline, five landscapers get together to see what they can do. When a golf lover among them complains about the busloads of Swedes "invading" Denmark's courses, a light goes on. What about exporting golf courses? Which they proceed to do.

First, they research the best courses and construction practices, found in the world's only golf course industry—in the United States. Then, they sponsor a U.S. tour, sign contracts with U.S. course builders, import specialized equipment, and hire salespeople with reputations in the golf world. Within the first year, they have four golf courses under construction in Sweden. Then, someone has the bright idea to contact the Polish minister of tourism with this suggestion: "If you want to attract rich German tourists, you have to have golf courses." Presto! A contract for 15 courses in Poland.

There's an eerie twist to this lush story. Noticing how beautiful Danish graveyards are, one of the group's U.S. partners spots a market opportunity going the other way. Soon the U.S. firm begins to import Danish graveyard know-how. So the Danish golf course consortium eventually pays for its American knowledge of greens and fairways with graveyard beautification expertise.

A Special Ability in Disability Aids

Denmark's national health system has given rise to a craft industry that produces high-quality aids for the disability device market. To remain in the forefront, the industry needs to embed electronics in its products. By falling behind the technology curve, the industry descends into crisis. Small firms can neither afford to develop electronics expertise in-house nor subcontract with the best engineering firms. It isn't only the money. Larger electronic producers just cannot be bothered with small specialized disability device manufacturers with a yearly output of 18 units. However, when a network of 36 producers contacts the best electronics companies, it finds itself in a bidding war as the companies seek the network's business. Combined with international marketing and quality programs, this industry reestablishes its reputation for leadership in the field.

Even Lawyers

As small Danish firms in a wide range of businesses begin to form networks, the small-town lawyers and accountants have to respond. Used to local manufacturers serving nearby markets, the professional services community suddenly faces complex new situations involving a much higher degree of international activity. So the lawyers face a crisis. Unless they can expand their resources, they will lose their business to the large Copenhagen law firms. Their response? To form networks themselves, combining expertise in international law with knowledge of patents and experience in specific sectors as different client situations require.

Not to Mention Big Business

Even Denmark's most famous large firm, Lego Systems, Inc., is intimately involved in the effort. Networks of small toy producers sell their products globally under the Lego name. In 1992, Lego launches its high-quality, attractive children's clothing line, developed out of Denmark's excellent network of small garment producers who put the Lego logo on their products.

RESULTS TO THE NATIONAL BOTTOM LINE

It doesn't take long for results to show. First, the evidence comes from within, the rapid spread of networks throughout Denmark. Then comes the impressive evidence from without.

Germany provides the test of excellence in European exports. It is a major magnet for Danish industry, concentrated as it is at the western edge of the country on Germany's border. Germany is always a difficult market to enter, and the economy seems to favor larger companies. In November 1989, shortly after the August launch of Denmark's network grants program, the Berlin Wall comes down and the two Germanys hurtle toward reunification.

Businesses all over Europe race to adapt to the changed, greatly enlarged, reunified German market that appears almost overnight. Denmark speeds across the finish line.

With the first returns in on the new market, Denmark's positive trade balance with Germany shows a remarkable performance, particularly since no other European country can say the same. The result is a first for Denmark.

The rest is an impressive array of statistics. "We have the highest per capita trade balance surplus of any country in the world. After 30 consecutive years, we reversed a negative balance of trade with Germany in 1991—the only country in Europe to do so," Nielsen says.[7]

Not surprisingly, a number of studies are undertaken to assess why Denmark did so well. One study finds that "smaller companies cooperating in networks had quite a penetration into the German market and contributed significantly to these new exports."

The Danish government shows its faith in the practical results of networking by launching a second stage to the program. Already, the first $25 million had been appropriated against the tide, as the government was simultaneously abolishing all industry subsidies. A second $25 million extends the original grant program through 1992 to complete applications in process, targets tourism for network development, and supports export networks, including international subcontracting.

SMALL CAN'T DO THE JOB ALONE

Denmark's "midterm evaluation" of its networking initiative, which interviewed 70 networks, reveals that:

- All increased employment;
- All reduced costs in one or more important areas;
- Forty percent introduced new products or new product ideas;
- Sixty percent entered new markets; and

- Ninety percent planned to continue regardless of government funding.

Even with all these positive indicators, Nielsen can point to "no real trend, yet, to our solving the problem of unemployment." Not even small businesses can keep up with the pace at which big businesses and other institutions in Denmark are reducing jobs.

"Denmark has 15,000 new companies every year adding 25,000 jobs; 8,000 die in the first five years, taking with them 25,000 jobs," Nielsen says. "Small firms in networks have a slightly higher growth and survival rate: 57 percent to 52 percent. Those five percentage points are very dramatic. They contribute 10,000 jobs, but the individual never sees this."

On the U.S. scale, Denmark is a state-size economy of small firms naturally pursuing a small business networking strategy to compete globally. The U.S. economy as a whole is the world's largest and is a relatively even mix of small businesses and large. America's strategy for dealing with unrelenting change needs to address all levels, sizes, and types of business.

AND ELSEWHERE IN EUROPE

In the early 1990s, Denmark's other Scandinavian neighbors begin to experiment—regions of Sweden and Norway, and the government of Iceland, an island economy 75 percent dependent upon raw fish exports. In Spain, several regions now have networks. In Germany, 56 Chambers of Small Industries and Crafts undertake a major networking effort: *three-quarters of a million small firms employing 4.7 million people have jointly trained 500,000 apprentices.*

"Portugal will surpass networking anywhere because of the readiness there. Everything is much more adolescent. They're enthusiastic and ready to conquer the world," Nielsen predicts.

Nielsen is an adviser to Albertino Jose Santana, manager of

PEDIP—the European Community–funded program to increase Portugal's competitiveness and raise its GDP to the level of other European countries. Jointly appointed by Portugal's president and minister of industry, Mr. Santana keeps a "very lean staff, just eight people who network. They spend money on people who can do it locally": $4 billion over three years in industrial modernization in a country with just 4.5 million people.

Nielsen's first encounter with Santana was not all that auspicious. "The first time I met him was a Saturday morning in Copenhagen after a big company party. Let's just say I needed sleep, but at noon, I had to leave for Tanzania and he was on his way to Asia. So we walked in the sunshine together and agreed to do something.

"The next thing I knew I was at my laptop computer looking at Kilimanjaro, writing about what a network project could be in Portugal, and faxing it to him in India. Then I flew to Oregon to testify before a state committee, where Mr. Santana called and asked me to fly to Lisbon. So I arrived the next Sunday and we spent the morning together. Unfortunately, I had spilled orange juice on my shirt on the plane, so I felt a little silly. But we sat on the banks of the Tejo River in Lisbon and looked at the monuments to Portugal's explorers."

OREGON'S NETWORKING "LAWS"

As we catch the early history of the worldwide movement unfolding in the United States, Oregon leads the way at the state legislative level. As Denmark was inspired by Emilia-Romagna, so has Oregon been inspired by Denmark.

Denmark proves that centuries-old concentrations of small firms are not required for networking to begin. In Emilia-Romagna, there is one company for every 44 inhabitants, a phenomenal figure. Denmark's one manufacturing firm for every 684 people, however, is more like the U.S. average, based on 365,000 American manufacturers nationwide.

Oregon's 7,000 manufacturing companies about match Denmark's number. Oregon's 2.8 million people give it a higher per capita concentration of firms, however—one for every 400 people. Major sectors of Oregon's economy include agriculture, forestry, fisheries, metals, tourism, and electronics.

The world increase in small business employment becomes a fact of life in Oregon in the 1980s. Among Oregon's manufacturing firms, "small firms created all of the net new jobs, while large firms were actually losing employment," according to *Small Is Bountiful*, the Joint Legislative Committee on Trade and Economic Development's 1988 report. In a more extensive study of the whole economy, the state's Economic Development Department found that "firms with fewer than 20 employees have been the source of most new jobs since 1981. This finding holds for every major industry group, including manufacturing, distributive services, producer services, social services, and personal services."[8]

Like Denmark, Oregon in the late 1980s faces a crisis in its economy. Providing almost one-fifth of U.S. softwoods, Oregon's timber industry accounts for 36 percent of the state's manufacturing jobs. More than half of the harvested timber comes from federal lands. Environmental pressures to preserve the fast-disappearing old-growth forests explode with the fight to save the habitat of the northern spotted owl.

Although some paint the owl as the villain in destroying logging jobs, other forces are also at work. Changes in U.S. Forest Service land use management plans and the quality of second-growth timber point to a long-term decline in the raw resource lumber business. In five years, it is estimated that over 11,000 jobs will be permanently lost.

In addition, Oregon is in the midst of a statewide renewal of its vision and goals. In May 1989, then governor Neil Goldschmidt issues *Oregon Shines: An Economic Strategy for the Pacific Century* with three key initiatives:

- A superior workforce that is "measurably the most competent in America by the year 2000, and equal to any in the world by 2010";

- An "attractive quality of life that . . . will drive an advanced economy"; and
- An "international frame of mind that . . . distinguishes Oregonians as unusually adept in global commerce."

Against this backdrop, in September 1989, the Northwest Policy Center leads a five-country European tour for 11 government officials and business people. Sponsored by the German Marshall Fund, the group looks at how the European experience applies to small business problems of the Pacific Northwest economy.

One of the participants is Joseph Cortright, executive officer of Oregon's Joint Legislative Committee on Trade and Economic Development (including both the president of the Senate and the Speaker of the House), that later sponsors Senate Bill 997, one of two laws passed in the 1991 session that encourage networks. Cortright's report to the committee, *Old World, New Ideas: Business Assistance Lessons from Europe*, brilliantly applies the European networking lessons to American soil, and articulates the policy implications of these lessons for states.

At the heart of Oregon's Senate bill are two key ingredients adopted directly from Denmark. First, the state's Economic Development Department is to "promote the concept of flexible networks and provide network feasibility grants" of up to $10,000 for groups of three or more firms. Second, a network broker training program is set up "to provide persons with the necessary knowledge, skills and abilities to assist private firms in the formation of flexible networks."

The bill also encourages other activities in support of key industries that directly empower networks:

- Focus groups to identify key issues and members;
- Support for the formation of industry associations, such as publication of directories;
- Help in establishing research consortia;
- Joint industry training and education programs;
- Cooperative market development activities;

- Analysis of the need for certification services; and
- Providing methods for electronic communication and information dissemination to facilitate network activity.[9]

Finally, the bill mandates an award program to encourage and recognize firms and groups of firms that employ "high performance manufacturing practices." Remarkably, the statute defines such practices as "methods for organizing work that devolve greater decision-making responsibility onto front-line workers." It sounds like a teamnet.

How is Oregon funding this unusual program? With money from the state's lottery and its Strategic Reserve Fund.

AUNTIE TRUST

The specter of large companies' working together can also suggest price fixing, collusion, and other not-so-aboveboard business practices. To date, there is no clear answer as to where companies cross into antitrust territory.

"Whenever competitors cooperate, it always raises the issue of antitrust," says Ron Katz, a partner with Coudert Brothers and former prosecutor at the U.S. Justice Department's Antitrust Division. "Antitrust is very fact-intensive. Everything is situational, so it's hard to make any general statements."

Rick Berenson, an attorney and former McKinsey & Company consultant, concurs. "Antitrust is entirely a matter of Justice Department policy. This is a leading-edge antitrust area and it's not that well litigated."

No-Frills Government Strategies

If alliances make good business sense from the point of view of an enterprise, eventually results will show up on the bottom line of each company. While that's great for the companies involved, from a global view, the success of a few small company alliances causes not a ripple in a regional economy. The success of many networks of many small firms can have dramatic impact on a national or regional bottom line.

How can we develop successful strategies on a large scale? Combine practice and theory, examples of what works with concepts of networks. Combine forces in the private and public sector. Five suggestions follow based on Teamnet Principles for how to start successful regional networks:

THE BUSINESS JUSTIFICATION: MEET THE NEED

Rule 1. Target markets.

Business networks work because they meet specific needs of specific sets of people. To identify the critical "specifics," look to the markets. Firms identify with a specific industry—in policy parlance, an economic sector. So, target markets. This European lesson tracks with common sense. "Businesses in a single sector of the economy have common problems and opportunities, speak a common technical language, and have a base of affiliations that can promote effective teamwork. Sectors define network programs along the logic of the market instead of the logic of the bureaucrat," Cortright writes.[10]

Europe shows how targeting some traditional industries can leverage great economic effect. The older industries that benefit most quickly from networks are those where:

- The economies of scale and economies of vertical integration are limited; and
- The market requires flexibility and rapid response to changing needs.

Textiles, garments, metalworking, and woodworking—some of the most common foundation industries—fit this description.

Within an industry, the reasons why networks form and flourish vary from group to group. However, everybody needs to look for their own leverage points. A regional industry may have general needs that solved once can serve many, such as:

- The need to identify and adopt new technologies; and
- The ability to pinpoint markets globally, certify quality, and provide industry-specific training.

By targeting markets, that is, clarifying their purposes, large economic communities can focus their business development strategies.

TREATING MANY FIRMS AS ONE

Rule 2. Offer inducements to groups of firms.

To help jump a high early hurdle in regional networking strategy, Denmark and Oregon provide incentives to participation.

"Fiercely independent small entrepreneurs" top Cortright's list of similarities between Europe and America. On the European policy tour, participants repeatedly ask about small business people: "How independence-minded are they?" "Are they 'joiners'?" "What do they think of government interference?" Repeatedly, the Europeans assure them that small business people everywhere feel the same as American entrepreneurs.

Showing the benefits of cooperation to fiercely independent firms is a great hurdle no matter where networking works. The inevitable question is "Can it be done here?"

At the regional level, networks include agencies—both public and private. Trade associations, businesses providing services to multiple networks, and motivated individuals all belong to regional networks. Prophetic local leaders, spark plugs for an industry, multiclient brokers, and other voices add texture and variety to the regional economic orchestra. The broader view from the regional perspective sees the overall system affecting the quality and quantity of jobs in the larger community, enabling everyone to take smarter actions.

Governments can boost a general economy by supporting an environment within which networks form and re-form easily. Groups of firms—alliances—are the units of network activity in a region or nation. Hundreds and then thousands of business alliances leverage the effect of flexible boundary crossing teamnets on a massive scale.

LINK AND LEARN

Rule 3. Facilitate communications and capture the learning.

What happens when not just a person or a company but a whole region learns? When firms jointly apply for services, they must interact: they communicate; personal relationships flourish; and businesses generate ongoing arrangements. By working with many interrelated groups, public dollars benefit the competitiveness of an industry as a whole, rather than simply bringing advantages to a few favored firms. European evidence shows that when governments work with groups of firms, they reduce costs. It "minimizes the considerable burdens of communication, marketing and administration, and in particularly successful instances harnesses firms to be one another's advisors."[11]

Just as there is advantage to individual firms banding together in networks, there is a higher-level competitive advantage to all from an environment rich in networks. Richly connected competitive firms greatly facilitate the spread of new information—whether exposure to technology innovations or news of sudden market shifts. While individual firms and networks scramble to make use of the information and search for the next advantage to differentiate themselves, the regional industry as a whole pushes to higher levels of competitive excellence compared to distant global competitors.

As the physical channels of communication are a high practical concern for all boundary crossing teamnets, so are communications infrastructures a basic regional competitive advantage. There is a natural synergy between business networks and technology networks. In networks of all kinds, people exchange information. New technologies—ranging from the simple fax to local cable systems to far-flung computer networks—greatly aid the rapid communication of large amounts of complex information. Through international data highways, regions can export their brainpower and skills without having to build more airports to accommodate the ceaseless travel of international expertise. Technology networks are key drivers of the dynamics of global change and one of the major forces breaking down isolated hierarchical management structures.

STRANGE BEDFELLOWS

Rule 4a. Industry leadership is essential.

A fourth rule of regional strategies is to involve industry people. Let us be even more blunt. Industry needs to lead government, not the other way around. Specific business networks require business expertise. Business leadership is also needed at the government level. Easier said than done. By sheer luck in Denmark, the minister of industry at the time was a business person rather than a politician. Sometimes people take quite creative means to ensure that businesses control the networking process and find it useful.

"Industry leadership is mandatory for success," says Ray Daffner of the Oregon Wood Products Competitiveness Corporation, a state-funded organization whose Board of Directors comprises seven industry leaders with companies averaging sales of $5 million. Daffner's group doesn't even use the word "network," preferring terms that are "more familiar to business people, like joint ventures, alliances, and strategic collaborations."[12]

While industry leadership is assiduously sought, European experience also provides a corollary to Rule 4, a role for public leadership:

Rule 4b. Provide the catalytic margin for success.

Small business networks, a way to acquire competitive advantages available to larger companies, face a daunting "chicken-and-egg" problem. Where do small companies find the marginal time and resources to explore cooperative alternatives that might eventually provide competitive advantages? Once a business network starts to generate tangible benefits, it becomes a self-sustaining economic activity. Small companies often need start-up help in multifirm collaborative arrangements. Big companies also can offer this help.

Without spending huge sums, public agencies can help create awareness about collaborative opportunities and processes, establish incentive programs to seed networks, provide staged support during formative phases, and encourage the development of brokers and other catalysts.

The catalytic margin is particularly acute in the early phases of network development. To establish credibility, new ideas cost money. The public sector plays an excellent role in showing how the idea has been successful elsewhere and what the problems are. Often, people need to be brought together to get up and over the cultural barriers to cooperation before they can get down to work on their own joint solutions to common problems. Here, the public sector can play an all-important convener and facilitator role. In later stages of regional network development, the need for a catalytic margin recedes: the evidence of network success is all around.

It doesn't have to cost much. When the state of Montana balked at the idea of a $1 million network program, Bob Friedman, chair of the Corporation for Enterprise Development, proposed a low-cost alternative. "Why not sponsor a free lunch program? If four or more firms want to discuss a common opportunity, the state says, 'We'll buy lunch.' At $5 a lunch, that's $20 a cluster," he jokes. "It's a little tongue-in-cheek, but we need enough of a kick to get people out of doing business as usual."

ALWAYS BEGIN WITH PEOPLE

Rule 5. Seek to enhance the skills, experience, and creativity of people.

The food chain of levels of organization starts with people. Small businesses are enterprises, and they are also small groups. They bring us closer to the true source of wealth in the future economy— the skills and knowledge of individuals.

Networking releases people potential.

A comprehensive economic networking strategy stimulates boundary crossing teamnets in all industries. They offer flexibility and speed in response to change. Flexible business networks are but one type of boundary crossing teamnet transforming the business world. They show that alliances are vital to small companies as well as large. In many ways, they complete the puzzle, also showing that the network advantage is available to a very wide range of companies, applicable to traditional industries as well as high-tech.

"The key is to figure out how to get to the threshold of momentum and publicity," Friedman says. "It won't take that much—in small states, perhaps several hundred networks; in large states, perhaps 1,000, but not 10,000 or 30,000."

Harnessing the Power of Teamnets

In section I, we focus on "what is." Here, in section II, we focus on "how-to":

- Develop teams with network characteristics;
- Design the work of larger and more complex teamnets;
- Leverage tools to help make planning as effective and painless as possible; and
- Avoid failure.

In the spirit of a time when all the traditional forms of media hurtle toward one another into one digital mass, we use a computer metaphor to help shape our presentation of a teamnet how-to.

TEAMNET Version 1.0: The Application Program

Think of the structured ideas in this book as computerless software.[1] The Teamnet Principles in "Seeing the Obvious," chapter 2, the Teamnet Phases of Growth in "Quick Start," chapter 8, and the

189

Target Method in chapter 9, "Launching Teamnets," function like an application program. Just as spreadsheet or word processor designers provide general-purpose capabilities to handle information, we as software designers provide generic tools. You provide the content, and you use these tools to manage your specific information in your way.

Software applications help people do things they define as necessary to do. With each new application, the computer provides a new set of tools. By contrast, most mechanical devices are specialized; they do one thing well for as long as they last.

Cultures develop new metaphors as new technologies become dominant. The metaphors from the Bureaucracy Era are based on precision industrial machines, the mind-set that still pertains in traditional business cultures:

The mechanistic ideal is an organization
that runs like a well-oiled machine,
preferably with steering wheel,
accelerator, and brakes.

New metaphors emerge with the rise of information technology:

The 1990s organization is an open system
with inputs, value-added outputs, and
feedback loops.

In this book, we offer TEAMNET Version 1.0. Tomorrow, we hope Version 2.0 will reflect the experience of countless users of the original.

How the TEAMNET 1.0 Manual Is Organized

The TEAMNET 1.0 manual is organized in the same way as any good software manual. It starts simply and offers progressively more detail.

Chapter 8 is the "Quick Start" section:

- Use TEAMNET 1.0 right out of the box through the "Teamnet Checklist." Remove the shrink wrap, open the box, get out the "Quick Start" booklet, and begin.
- Apply the "Teamnet How-to" tutorial with sample problems to your situation. It introduces the application of the Teamnet Principles to process along with some basic facts of teamnet life.
- Use the Teamnet Phases of Growth (start-up, launch, perform, test, deliver) to do a quick planning run-through.

The basic "User Manual" begins in "Seeing the Obvious," chapter 2, and "Linoleum, Furniture, and Electrical Systems," chapter 3:

- The Five Teamnet Principles (purpose, members, links, leaders, levels) are the first thing to learn; they help you describe and navigate diverse organizational forms.
- The Co-opetition Dynamic (cooperation/competition) is intrinsic to every teamnet; don't leave home without it.
- The Teamnet Organization Scale (small group, large organization, enterprise, alliance, economic megagroup) is the basic pocket tool for applying the teamnet idea in your work group, your company, and your economic region.

"Launching Teamnets," chapter 9, gives you the workhorse techniques you need to get your teamnet off the ground:

- To scope the whole process that your teamnet must tackle, take your first pass at answering the five W's (who?, what?, when?, where?, why?) using the Target Method.

- To launch your teamnet, develop the five T's (targets, tasks, team, time, territories) to drive a second planning pass.

"Those That Do, Plan," chapter 10, is for the power user:

- Gain access to the rigor and discipline of the method, using data to plan, manage, and capture the learning of your teamnet.
- Put the teamnet conceptual tools together with a supporting set of existing software applications.
- Learn ancillary methods to improve meetings and increase communication.

"Rascals in Paradise: How Teamnets Fail," chapter 11, provides an in-depth look at some of the difficulties in networking:

- Spot some of the weak spots in teamnets and learn tips to avoid them; and
- See how much agreement there is on the basic pitfalls.

The Reference Section is the "advanced stuff" at the back of the manual. Designed for the serious programmer, not the casual user, here you find the equivalent of call routines, code interfaces, and translation tables.

- Relate traditional bureaucratic forms to teamnet types to help develop transition paths from traditional to 21st-century organizations.
- Make use of some core TEAMNET code and access the underlying systems philosophy of the program. Use them to build your own extensions to the TEAMNET platform.

It's easier than you think. You already are likely doing many of the approaches we suggest. The value we're adding is some order and missing parts to provide a new context for many capabilities you already have.

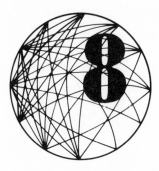

Quick Start: Getting Your Teamnet to Click

How long does it take to build a house? If you go by the name of its videotape, the Building Industry Association of San Diego says there is such a thing as a *Four Hour House*.[1] However, if you watch the tape, actually a competition between two teams to see who could build their house faster, you find out the answer is actually 2 hours and 53 minutes. With extensive planning and a practice run, a 350-person team transforms a bare plot into a 1,500-square-foot, three-bedroom, two-bath, fully landscaped house with a fireplace, family room, and two-car garage in the time it takes to qualify for the Boston Marathon, under three hours.

The "Four Hour House" is a superb example of a teamnet, involving more than 140 firms, and excels at demonstrating the value of up-front planning. "We literally spent thousands of hours planning these houses. And that is not an exaggeration," says Randy Muelhein, a construction supervisor for one of the houses from J. H. Hedrick.[2]

For six months before the competition, the Building Industry Association (BIA) met every Thursday to coordinate the project. They also met with supervisors and city building officials. "What is important here is that we're cooperating on a project with the inspectors before the fact. It is something that can be done in the future to speed up the whole process," says then BIA president Ray Jessen.[3] Instead of the inspectors coming in when construction is complete to point out errors, they consult with the builders in advance to avoid costly rework.

Cooperation on the team is also noteworthy. "I've never seen the trades work together better. Normally, they're throwing hammers at each other. This time they're helping each other," says Nicholas Haluskey, senior building inspector.

Amazing as the Four Hour House is, even more remarkable is that a group of volunteers, working with knowledgeable trades people, can achieve the same results. On one of its "blitz builds," Habitat for Humanity,[4] the nonprofit organization that builds low-cost, affordable housing, builds 10 houses in five days. Calculated according to an eight-hour day, these, too, are four-hour houses.

Like the people in San Diego, Habitat builders plan extensively beforehand, including construction of a test house on five prior consecutive Saturdays. They also publish an extensive manual that details all aspects of the blitz build, including floorplans, day-by-day construction supply lists, Gantt charts with hour-by-hour schedules, and strict quality criteria. Volunteers each receive a color code—red for highly skilled, orange for semiskilled, and yellow for unskilled—and a category assignment—ranging from crew leaders and runners to specialists and painting coordinators.

"To build a frame house in the United States, 20 people work on each shift. There's one supervisor who's in charge who's not hammering or nailing. Five highly skilled crew chiefs each have teams of four semiskilled and unskilled people working with them. When there's something difficult to do, they bring the crews together and ask for volunteers," explains Tilly Grey of Habitat for Humanity International.

Habitat has little problem getting volunteers for its projects. "They get such a high building a house. It's just magical to see a house go up before your eyes," she says. The program is so popular that Elderhostel offers Habitat house building as one of its courses for older people.

Teamnets spring up all the time. They spontaneously erupt when something terrible happens, like a natural disaster.[5] People and organizations flock together to do something about it. When crisis intervention teams spend a few up-front moments defining objectives and modifying contingency plans, they work considerably better. When this doesn't happen, groups pay dearly for their lack of planning. The Four Hour House team proves that for the boundary crossing group, planning is the ultimate way to achieve goals. Without certain basic ingredients, you don't have a boundary crossing group. Check your teamnet against these criteria:

- The members of the group *cross traditional boundaries*.
- Members cooperate for *mutual benefit* in at least one area.
- Members can survive *independently* in business, sometimes competing against one another.

First look at the people who make up the group. Are they from different organizations, or does every one simply work for you? If you're just looking at the same people who appear on your traditional organization chart, then you're not looking at a teamnet. When your new chart starts to look a little messy, then you know you're on your way to *crossing traditional boundaries*. Scary as this may seem at first, messiness just happens to be a fact of life in teamnets.

Does the group that you have in mind have reason to cooperate? Is there some shared purpose to which everyone involved aspires? If so, there is a basis for cooperation for *mutual benefit* (although there are no guarantees).

Is the group made up of members who can manage on their own? When members leave the team, do they have some place to go or can they marshal the resources to continue? If so, they are *independent*, which may include competing with one another in other situations.

The Teamnet Checklist

"Okay. Go ahead. Do it." Have you ever fought hard to get approval for an idea, only to dread the final "Yes"? The difficult work of getting something off the ground kills many a great idea. "What now?" you gasp, when the germ of an idea must come to life. Exciting and exhilarating as beginnings of projects are, they are also tough.

> *The unknown can seem personally overwhelming. Mixing in other people and groups "some distance away" across boundaries only adds to the nervousness about the potential for success. They represent more help, of course, but getting more people involved brings its own problems. Then there's your unique problem to solve with a unique set of constraints and resources. And you don't want to reinvent any wheels. Whew!*

"I often dread the final go-ahead because I feel like I've had to sell my soul to get there, promising to do the impossible with the impoverished," says one senior engineering manager whose large high-tech company is downsizing like crazy.

We offer guidelines, not prescriptions. Each situation is different. The players, place, and motivation are unique for any specific group that needs to cross boundaries. You bring the details and we provide a program in this section of the book so you can be more effective.

Think it through. If you do nothing else, take the time to look at your overall problem. This is an excellent way to *get started.* For teamnets, "beginning with the end in mind"[6] is not an optional exercise. It is an essential one. Discipline and control can come only from commonly held agreements and clear understanding of what the group needs to do. The next essential lesson is to *think it through more than once*. Iterate, iterate. Further flesh out the plan with each repetition. To make the iterations truly productive, consider as many potential downside risks as possible. More than one great project has died because its members have not been willing to think the unthinkable.

The key points to remember about teamnets number only a handful. Use these five questions as a checklist for assessing the teamnet potential of your group:

COMMON VIEW?

Does your organization have a clear purpose?

Define your *purpose*. It is at the top of the agenda for teamnets to work. If your organization or project has a clear purpose, you are well on your way to success. If you don't, this is the first hurdle to cross. Until the players agree on the purpose, they have no other work to do. Once you've agreed on a common purpose, you're on your way to knowing the tasks required to complete it.

COLLEAGUES?

Are there other people besides you working toward the purpose?

If you're not the sole champion of an idea and others work with you, then your group has *members*. These are the people who cross the boundaries. People identify with groups, and groups identify with people. Either way, a group takes off when a critical mass of people, each with an idea of the role he or she will play, becomes involved.

CONNECTIONS?

Do you have sufficient communication and relationships among you to effectively achieve the purpose?

For a group to accomplish any goal requires interaction—meetings, phone calls, memos, letters, agreements, and the like. To interact, people need *links*—both the technology kinds (phones, paper, computers) and the people kinds (relationships and roles). When a group makes it to the point where people have multiple voluntary relationships among them and numerous, often used communication channels, it can get work done.

VOICES?

Is there more than one leader in the group?

Contrary to popular belief, in the case of teamnets, two heads—or more—are better than one. If only one person plays a leadership role, then the group is no different from a traditional organization. *Leaders* become known through the process of defining purpose and figuring out who's going to do what. Leaders are also followers.

INCLUSION?

Can you "look up" and see that your organization is a part of a larger one? Can you "look down" and see the smaller parts that make up yours?

If the group intends to effect long-term change, it must interact at multiple *levels* with other parts of the business environment. A teamnet needs relationships with larger systems of which it is a natural part. It also needs to recognize its own subgroup components.

Remember to keep a light touch while trying this out. It is very easy to fall into the trap of thinking that exhaustive attention to every detail in the process will ensure success. It won't, but it will wear people out. Beware overdoing it.

The Teamnet How-to

As your organization, under pressure of change, migrates from a mechanistic hierarchy to an organic network, the future grows fuzzier. You lose the reductionist promise of prediction, but, through planning, gain the ability to *anticipate* the future.

In the real world of teamnet work, many things happen at once. A group process also plays out in something of a logical, relatively straightforward step-by-step sequence that develops over time. The Teamnet Checklist translates into a recipe, a plan to launch your group across boundaries. Take your group through these five steps:

> **Step 1.** *Clarify purpose* by agreeing on mission and goals.
> **Step 2.** *Identify members* by defining who will be involved.
> **Step 3.** *Create links* by connecting people to one another in as many ways as necessary.
> **Step 4.** *Multiply leadership* to maximize the responsiveness of the group.
> **Step 5.** *Integrate levels* to maintain dynamic balance within and without the group.

STEP 1. CLARIFY PURPOSE

When producers at WGBH, Boston's public television station, get together to develop a new idea for a show, they call such exercises "retreats." Digital Equipment Corporation calls its planning sessions "Woods Meetings," because the original ones took place at founder Ken Olsen's New Hampshire home. One of the United States' last family-owned metropolitan newspapers calls them "think tanks." One consulting company calls them "summits." Many companies simply call them "offsites."

Regardless of what name they have, such meetings encourage people to step out of their everyday routines. Together, they go through some sort of process to arrive at a shared view of the work to be done. Clear purpose is the secret of successful boundary crossing. All teamnets need to take this step, whether a joint venture, a new television project, a new self-help group, or a burgeoning political campaign.

Untouchable and invisible, purpose is sometimes hellishly hard to express. Rarely completely defined to everyone's satisfaction, it is nevertheless the bond that makes the impossible possible.

Deep commitment to a few basic tenets inspires groups. Statements of visions, core values, ideologies, missions, goals, objectives, and joint interests all point to the intangible "center" of a network, its defining characteristic. Common belief binds disparate people into a goal-oriented social organism.

Groups cohere through shared purpose.

Purpose throws an anchor into the future. It sets forth the endpoint of the journey and is the internal source of motivation that brings a group alive. Ironically, because a shared purpose can never be completely captured, it needs continuous and varied expression to be kept vital.

Purposes are processes.

Boundary crossing teamnets "get a life" by carrying out their purposes. If purpose remains static and unrenewed, goals die and eventually so does the project.

People fail to realize that purpose is the vital ingredient that links investments to real business goals. To bring purpose to life, consider these possibilities:

- Hold a "project launch" meeting just to focus on purpose. The only agenda item is to clarify the purpose. Begin by brainstorming a list of key words that expresses your purpose. Group them by category, separate nouns and verbs, then write a sentence. Move on when you accomplish this mission.
- Come to the meeting prepared. Beforehand, gather all the existing renditions of the purpose: slogans, symbols, and mission statements already hanging on the wall. Send out a call to everyone for vision statements. Display them all on the walls. One firm quickly collected 39.
- Interview three active members of the group. Ask each to tell you the group's core beliefs. This standard consultant interviewing practice reveals the basic viability of the group. If people have the same basic picture, then the group is ready for takeoff. Three conflicting answers indicate trouble. We spent one day interviewing seven training directors in a 13,000-person technical organization, asking them to assess their shared purpose. Four aligned in one camp, two in another, and one stood in between. With irreconcilable objectives, the group was not able to move.
- Write down your group's lingo. This is your tribe's "language," the frequent phrases, acronyms, and nicknames, which are clues to what's really important. One new product development team produced T-shirts for each of its 20 members. Printed on the front was each person's favorite phrase. Before delivery to

its recipient, the group played "name the shirt," as people tried to figure out whom it belonged to.

• Clarifying the purpose doesn't have to take forever, and can usually be completed in a few meetings. Regardless of how long it takes, this step is crucial before proceeding.

STEP 2. IDENTIFY MEMBERS

A teamnet gets off the ground because a certain group of people makes a personal commitment to an idea. They tie abstract purposes to their flesh-and-blood actions and decisions. Identity is the basis of autonomy. It's a fundamental tenet of good psychology and of good business. It's the clear set of people—the members of a boundary crossing teamnet—that makes it happen. This is true whether you are undertaking an ad hoc project or putting into place a major multi-million-dollar development program that will permanently alter the future of your company.

The inspiration to create a teamnet usually results from the vision of a "spark plug" or two, people with a deep personal conviction. We first learned the term "spark plug" in the mid-1970s, when we worked with the U.S. Department of Commerce to develop a national fire prevention education program, the first of its kind in the United States. There we met Larry Paretta and Lonnie Jackson of Arlington Heights, Illinois, two of the United States' earliest fire prevention "networkers." As a fire fighter, Paretta had carried a dead two-year-old child out of a burning building. He knew the death would never have happened if people understood the fundamentals of fire prevention. Paretta became a crusader, along with Jackson, for fire prevention, traveling all over the country and advising the Commerce Department in its efforts. Everywhere Paretta went he told what he called his "sacred story," which moved people to action.

Often, a few spark plugs have an idea at the same time and find each other. However it happens, people begin to identify with one another and before you know it, a group has jelled. In other situations, corporate strategy calls for a project or program that can be done only by crossing boundaries, as in the case of Conrail's Strategy Management Group.

There is a "proof" test for whether the members of your teamnet cross boundaries or just occupy another seat on the bureaucratic bus. Imagine mentally removing the head of the group. Do the parts survive? If the members also can stand alone, they're crossing boundaries. If removal of the control mechanism brings everything to a grinding halt, then bureaucracy most likely interlocks the parts.

- To identify members, name the key players. This is the hub of your group. Make a sketch of your group on a piece of paper. Put people's names near one another if they're in particularly close communication. Then draw the picture of whom the people in your teamnet connect to; whom do they communicate with?
- Call a membership meeting, specifically to create a directory. Include everyone who identifies with the group, then add the names of the other people they need to be in touch with. Don't just list individuals; include the names of groups, too. Publish as much contact information as possible as frequently as necessary.
- Remember that *not everyone* needs to be involved in everything. Research shows that in order for people to feel involved in something, they don't actually need to participate. They only have to feel that they can participate if they want to. Too much participation is just as costly as not enough. "An easy way to allow more people to participate is to make them part of the review process," says John Manzo, a senior engineering manager at Digital Equipment Corporation.
- Organizations need a variety of types of people to be successful. A group of all visionaries won't get any further than a group of solid tacticians. The best groups have people with skills in vision, theory, method, and communication.

STEP 3. CREATE LINKS

The next step is to establish links. Begin with the physical connections. Then notice the actual use of the connections, the interaction traffic among the players. Over time, interactions carve a pattern deep enough to forge relationships, the lifeblood of teamnets.

Personal relationships are the threads that bind the network. Many people's jobs consist primarily of networking—passing information, making connections (both personal and conceptual), staying in communication with the vested interests. This is the special "networker" role, the person who focuses on the linking function. Such people can be found setting up information systems, serving as "switching centers" of connections, facilitating relationships, and encouraging a trusting environment.

Every successful boundary crossing teamnet has many internal pathways and multiple connections. Many teams get off the ground quickly if people already know one another. This is not at all a prerequisite; teams only need to account for it when their members do not know one another. Regardless of their familiarity with one another, people thrive on their connections, the more the better.

So leave plenty of space, time, and support for links. Without them, your teamnet is going nowhere, which is precisely what happens if a boundary crossing group lacks purpose.

- Take your membership sketch and add the key relationships in the group. Where are the strongest links? Where are the missing links?
- Because everyone cannot be together all the time, you need to solve the distance problem. Hold a brainstorming meeting to figure out what technology is available to people, what kind of communication system you would like to have, and then tally up the inevitable cost in dollars. Adjust if necessary. Remember that time is key to effective boundary crossing groups.
- No matter how much technology you introduce, make sure you

also meet face-to-face periodically. Face-to-face meetings are where people learn to trust each other.

- Develop a joint presentation that captures the purpose, mission, goals, and plans of the group. Use this to recruit new members and marshal resources.
- Develop a simple handbook of key shared information, and a glossary to capture common vocabulary. Include the membership directory as a section in it. It doesn't need to be fancy to be very helpful.

STEP 4. MULTIPLY LEADERS

Of the many myths about successful groups, the most confused are about leadership. There is a popular misconception that networks are leaderless.

On the contrary, they are leader*ful*. Teamnets need many leaders to express common themes from different points of view. Since teamnets cross boundaries, members bring different needed contributions to the table. In our experience, most successful groups have multiple leaders.

This idea is a lot easier to write about than it is to put into practice. Because we've all been brought up in the old hierarchical style, with single teachers, religious leaders, and authority figures, we naturally tend to buy into the sole person-at-the-top as the only way to go. Put that model aside for the moment.

The most effective way to run a boundary crossing teamnet is with many leaders.

Successful teamnets substitute this new approach to leadership for the old one. Everyone involved has a contribution to make toward a shared purpose. Individual expertise plays a critical role in boundary crossing. One software project team that we worked with for two years had five team leaders, each responsible for a different module of the overall system. The project was highly successful even though the original appointed leader resigned after about four months, and the newly appointed "acting" leader rarely came to meetings or even paid much attention to the project. So long as things were going well and the team met deadlines, he had no concerns, even if he frustrated the team with his lack of involvement. The team was effective, as each of its leaders stayed in close communication and shared the same overall goal.

"Team leadership enhances the possibility that different leadership skills can be brought to bear simultaneously. One member of the team may be a visionary, another may be gifted in conceptualizing a course of action, and so on. No one knows enough to perform all the complex functions of contemporary leadership. Yet most—almost all—discussions of leadership deal with it as though it were a solo performance," John Gardner told the Annual Membership Meeting and Assembly of the Independent Sector in 1984.[7]

The technical term for multiple leadership doesn't exactly roll off the tongue: "polycephalous." Once you learn its simple definition—many = poly, headed = cephalous—you'll never forget it. Astute anthropologists invented the word to replace one that didn't explain a certain phenomenon they were observing.[8] Until they came up with a new term, they described tribes with more than one leader as "acephalous" (without a head). Most indigenous social systems do not have a single chief (monocephalous). Rather, there is a chief warrior, chief midwife, chief hunter, chief herbalist, and other leading experts. The tribe distributes its leadership among the handful of functions vital to survival and prosperity. A particular leader comes to the fore depending on the nature of the crisis facing the group—an enemy, a food shortage, an epidemic. Everyone is first among equals.

Not only networks, but hierarchies also, can have multiple leaders. The Japanese have perfected the form of the "blunt" hierarchy: a small group of powerful representatives makes final decisions. The West usually regards hierarchy as "single-pointed," a pyramid with a single chair at the top. Still, great differences remain between hierarchical and network leadership. Hierarchies minimize positions of power and changes in leadership. Networks maximize leadership and rapid turnover in response to change.

Whether the external hierarchy appoints or anoints leaders, natural leaders always emerge from within a group based on its own dynamics. Appointed and natural leaders can coincide, complement, or conflict.

Leadership ability includes knowing how closely to entwine leadership with followership. Distributed leadership is regarded as necessary for the successful functioning of a distributed process.

- Does your group have multiple leaders? The test is simple: Can you hear several voices or only one? Is dissent encouraged or discouraged?
- Multiple leadership requires facilitation. Although this role can rotate and its title can vary—facilitator, coordinator, or even chair—someone needs to be responsible for overall facilitation at all times.
- As you plan, think about the roles each person will play and how that endows them with leadership. Make a list of what each person contributes to the group. This is his or her area of leadership.
- Call a leadership meeting. Talk through who is responsible for what, then write it down. Include this information in your "Teamnet Handbook."
- Discuss who else fulfills each responsibility. This exercise indicates where leaders are also followers. The ability to move between these two roles is itself a sign of leadership.
- Think of the different leadership roles at different stages of development: visionaries, communicators, facilitators, practitioners, theoreticians, challengers, collaborators, and contributors all have their moments as the team process unfolds.

These activities are extremely useful: they serve to winnow out which people are truly committed to the task. They also help define who your liaisons will be to other organizations. People connect at all different levels, and in complex loops.

STEP 5. INTEGRATE LEVELS

The more "connected in" any new initiative is to a larger universe, the more successful it will be. The more isolated it is, the more difficult it is to obtain resources and accomplish goals.

Consultants work at multiple levels in organizations. Foreigners "with a pass" (often physical badges) have the privilege of being outside the companies' hierarchies. Without going out of bounds, they talk to the CEO, the executive team, middle managers, secretaries, and people on the shop floor. This access gives them the ability to connect at many levels of the organization simultaneously. The more levels they interact with, the more complete their view of the organization. To connect in at many levels of the organization, teamnet members need to take on a consultant viewpoint.

When it comes to levels, there are two directions in which to look: to the context bigger than yourself, and your components that are smaller. The Center for Quality Management (CQM), a consortium of 35 companies working together to learn new quality techniques, connects to something bigger and to something smaller. It is part of the bigger Total Quality Management movement, which involves thousands of companies, with numerous cross-company and cross-industry trade associations. Smaller, CQM comprises all its member companies, each of which is a whole enterprise unto itself. CQM is successful because it both connects with the outer world, and works closely with its member companies.

The same principle holds for a teamnet within a company that works across internal boundaries. It needs to connect up into the higher levels of the whole company as well as down into the specific functions that its members come from.

- Call a meeting to talk about the levels. Use a white board and markers to draw a common picture of how your teamnet connects in. What boundaries does it cross? When you agree on the picture, enlarge it and hang it on the wall of your regular meeting room. Add a notebook-size version to your "Teamnet Handbook."
- Play "Targets and Arrows." Whom do you need to influence? These people are your "targets." If you lack connections at certain levels, figure out who the "arrows" are: the people you know who know the targets. Who can make things happen? Who can stop them? Who can influence the stoppers? Who are the silent supporters?
- It is a misconception that successful groups are "flat." They are not. They are lumpy, clustered, multileveled organizational forms. Form as many subgroups as are practical, corresponding to the work at hand. Each subgroup chooses a leader. This leadership group gives the network sufficient latitude to do its work quickly, without having to consult everyone on every decision.

Thinking About Teamnets

One piece of good news about teamnets is that you already know much of what you need to know to be successful. Successful boundary crossing groups have many of the characteristics of any healthy team. They employ many of the same methods as any good quality effort, and they follow the basic principles of any good change process. Apply the well-known fundamentals in these areas, and you will meet with success—whether you do so unconsciously, accidentally, or by design.

Now beware. Most how-to resources on teams—tacitly or explicitly—assume that the people co-locate, that the group shares a common workspace, and that they depend on regular face-to-face meetings.

> *By definition, boundary crossing
> teamnets are rarely located in the same
> place.*

This makes the teamnet contribution clear: adding the boundary crossing dimension of distance and difference—across space, time, and function—introduces an entirely new slant. By incorporating existing knowledge of teams, quality, and process, we add the "teamnet dimension."

Small groups are the basis for larger groups. The world works because small groups of people eventually sit down together and make decisions. When multinational companies negotiate global alliances that affect measurable proportions of the planet's resources, they do so in small groups. No more than a few handfuls of people sit down with one another to explore options. At the other end of the scale, when small manufacturers sit down to discuss a flexible business network, they represent companies that are themselves small groups. When a new project gets going, a small group sits down in a conference room to figure out what to do next.

When people come together in small boundary crossing groups, they automatically seek to perform as a teamnet. Networks of any greater size comprise clusters, groups, and teams of people as well as free-floating individuals. If you examine large groups in close, fine detail, you inevitably see small groups interacting with other small groups.

You have been gaining knowledge of small group behavior since the day you were born into your family. You already have an understanding of the dynamics of small groups—perhaps you've even taken a course, read an article or book, or attended a lecture. Basic knowledge about small groups is an essential prerequisite for effective participation in networks of all sizes and scope.

Today, companies urge managers to:

- Get closer to the customer;
- Solve local problems locally;
- Create small business units;
- Push down decision making; and
- Decentralize.

All these prescriptions and trends lead naturally to more empowered small groups and more networked organizations.

The best networks start as teams and grow into teams of teams.

Teams and quality go hand in hand. Companies form teams to consider whether to do a quality program, then to design and implement programs. Within the program, teams form to tackle specific quality issues. Companies that implement quality programs tend to become more team-based organizations. One consequence of business process redesign is often a permanent team approach to a work process.[9]

Quality programs focus on people as the sources of solutions. Participation is a key value. Good ideas can come from anyone and are most likely to come from people closest to the problem.

You have been part of groups that work, and groups that haven't worked. On more than one occasion, you probably have asked yourself, "How can such smart people be so dumb?" If you're lucky, you also probably have experience as part of an exceptional team—a "dream team," where everything clicks. The group that clicks does so because it pays attention to some fundamental ideas.

> ### Think Teamnets
>
> - Mission and goals
> - Customer satisfaction
> - Players and stakeholders
> - Leaders and decisions
> - Group dynamics
> - Stages of growth

BE EXPLICIT: MISSION AND GOALS

Teams form around outcomes and serve customers with needs. Where work is a natural chunk of purposeful, needed results, teams with a common alignment of diverse capabilities form in powerful *synergy*. Where teams form around poorly related activities and unclear outcomes, an equally powerful energy *sink* sucks the life from all people trapped in such a system. Following a merger of two airlines, the new company puts groups with the same names from each of the old companies together in the same organization. With entirely different work processes and strikingly different goals, the merged group becomes a war zone, accomplishing nothing.

Take out any how-to book about teams, no matter what decade it was written,[10] and you'll receive your first assignment, something like: "Write a mission statement." Goal setting is usually the first chapter in these what-to-do books. It's very, very basic and particularly important for the boundary crossing distributed sort of team.

Every teamnet needs a sharp, concise expression of motivation. While you do not have to produce a mission statement in any formal sense, you do have to know what your group is about. Regardless of how the group articulates the mission in the beginning, it is the spark of life itself for the still-forming group. Nor do you necessarily have to write it down. A picture, image, diagram, or chart may clearly convey the needs that drive the group. A few spoken words of intention, or even the napkin that everyone signs at a "commitment" dinner, are heartfelt expressions of the group's fundamental beliefs. One of the most successful vision statements we've seen was the front page of a newspaper set five years in the future. The group manager drew her view of where the project would be with headlines and "photos" with captions.

What is the single most important thing that teamnets must do? Be explicit.

Unless people can externalize the purpose and make it tangible, teamnets cannot fully form. Explicitness of purpose needs to reach some minimal level. Otherwise, there is no basis for common cause. Few actions are as powerful as a teamnet all signing its joint statement of purpose, and hanging it on the wall of its regular meeting room for all to see.

Myriad team training manuals provide a wealth of tools and techniques for helping a group divine and define its vision and goals. However, buyer beware. There are no guarantees that any specific group of people can arrive at a shared purpose using any particular technique.

While difficult for any newly forming group, developing purpose is even more challenging for boundary crossing groups. The problems of distance, time, and diversity aggravate the situation. Unless your distributed group comes to a common picture when together, you'll all go home and go your own way. A shared outcome becomes the potential adhesive for the group.

YOUR CUSTOMER'S CUSTOMER IS YOUR CUSTOMER

Wondering where to start? Quality provides a specific direction to look for purpose.

If the quality movement has done nothing else for modern business, it has brought the "voice of the customer" to everyone's attention. Quality practice begins with the end in mind—the customer of an organization's work. For an accounts receivable group, your customer is not just your company's customers; it is also the people in your company who have to do business with the customer. The customer provides the enterprise with its external goals. The essence of the quality approach is to satisfy or exceed customer needs.

In the search for purpose, the quality view provides direction.

> *Look to the consumers of your organization's output: they are the ultimate judges of the value you add. They vote with their preferences.*

Quality processes build in a feedback loop. Customer focus ascertains needs and dictates where the change process begins. At the end of the process, the organization offers its output to customers, who make their marketplace statement as to whether their needs have been met on time and at an affordable price.

Stumped on how to quickly gather information on customer needs, one short-term strategy development group set up a two-day-long event. Since they couldn't bring in customers on such short notice, they brought in the major sales account managers, and interviewed them extensively about *their* customers' needs.

In many situations, customer needs stand for shared goals. They serve as the "higher authority" driving your teamnet's work and providing the context for decision making. Focus on customer needs as an easy way for your boundary crossing teamnet to arrive at shared goals. With a common customer view, your group can work side by side and from afar. To fully understand your customers, you need to understand their customers, expanding the view of who is in the loop.

WHO'S IN THE GAME? PLAYERS AND STAKEHOLDERS

Your mission points to your essential membership. While the quick impulse is to involve everyone you can think of in the network, it is better to at first think small. Ask the question, "Who are the key people who need to be involved to accomplish the purpose?"

Each person brings energy, change, and differences to the purpose. As your group expands from its founders, it needs to reevaluate and reaffirm its commitment to the common purpose. Over time, there is natural feedback between the players and the purpose. The best approach is iterative, shaping these factors together.

Begin with an idea. Get some of the obvious people together. Discuss the idea and decide who needs to be involved. Talk with these people. Incorporate their ideas or debate the issues. Get agreement on a common plan. Go to it . . . whoops! the unexpected. Things happen. Things don't happen. People come, people go. Goals shift and are adjusted. The plan is modified. People affirm revised targets, and continue working.

Within the constraints of purpose and the ever-present limits of resources and time, you need variety in your teamnet membership. The specific purpose determines one type of membership variety: the experience, skills, and commitments required to accomplish the goal. The more complex your goal or context, the more diverse the mix of skills and knowledge required.

Another type of variety required is general and related to team dynamics over time. This is not another set of people. In a network, everyone is part of the process. In a network, the pattern of interactions and the realization of a common output are what is truly "real."

People do not play a single process role in a group. Over time, they play multiple process roles. New steps along a group's journey require different capabilities and skills. Generally speaking, there are four general styles of team members:

- Collaborators,
- Communicators,
- Contributors, and
- Challengers[11]

To see the need for multiple styles, just imagine a team composed of all one type: the vision-no-action group of collaborators, the interminable talkfest of communicators, the isolated confusion of contributors only, or the endless bickering of a collection of challengers.

LEADERS AND DECISIONS

Are leaders born? Is there a unique leadership type, style, or personality? Is leadership learned? Is it earned? Is it Nature or Nurture?

Leadership is the most ubiquitous role in human groups. Every group has leaders because groups need leaders. They create leadership roles that members fill. While in some groups leaders also are appointed, every group develops natural leaders. Sometimes these leaders coincide; sometimes they collide. In teamnets, leaders are not only born; the group itself makes them.

To see leaders in your boundary crossing teamnet, shift your focus from individuals to the group system. The system as a whole has leadership needs that permeate the entire group.

In a teamnet, there is no single person on top all the time.

One or more members take and shift responsibility to represent the group at different times. Every task offers an opportunity for leadership. "Leadership involves conducting, coaching, and mentoring: A conductor brings forth the best talents of an orchestra; a coach builds capabilities and confidence, and a mentor shapes talent. Knowledge-era enterprises are a composite of orchestras, basketball teams, and jazz combos," writes Charles Savage, an expert on "knowledge networking organizations."[12]

Leadership invests purpose with particular people. People make purpose tangible by propounding a position. Different people argue for a need, take responsibility, enlist support, take action, resolve conflicts, move things along, know when to get out. Different people become leaders in varying situations.

Recalling one successful teamnet experience of 15 people from diverse internal organizations in the United States, Canada, and Europe, a manager remarked, "When we needed a technical expert, Joe was the leader. When we needed a marketing expert, Steve was the leader. When we needed a product development perspective, Celeste was the leader. When we had to talk to the vice presidents, I was the leader."

Hierarchies minimize leadership. Teamnets maximize it.

Do not confuse leadership in teamnets with decision making. Leadership without portfolio, pocketbook, or power is typical in successful networks. Each group's decision-making needs are different. Individuals handle some decisions, smaller subgroups handle some, and the group as a whole handles some. Deciding for the whole used to be the job of the top dog; in a teamnet, it can be many people's jobs, depending on what decision needs to be made. When four vice presidents acting as co-sponsors of a major business change process could not come to agreement, they jointly took the decision to the CEO, who was able to frame the question in strategic terms, and make a decision.

The first principle of teamnet decision making is to know what level the decision calls for. Keep the list of big decisions short. The second principle is to develop and cull options iteratively, avoiding "winner-take-all" votes.

Teamnets usually make big decisions by consensus. This does not mean one-member, one-vote where everyone agrees unanimously. This is a potentially deadly practice. Nor does it mean a majority vote with an unhappy minority. In practice, a consensus decision is one without significant opposition, one members can support, or at least tolerate. In hindsight, people seem to make many decisions by virtue of having stopped talking about alternatives.

When a decision calls for some level of formality, try the multivote:

- Generate a list of options, as many as possible, perhaps through brainstorming.
- Combine those that everyone agrees are the same.
- Give each person multiple votes—equal to about one-third of the number of options—to indicate preferences. For example, if there are 15 options, everyone gets five votes.
- Vote. Then reduce the list by dropping items with the fewest votes. Discuss and revise the list as necessary.
- Multivote again. Repeat as necessary until a clear favorite emerges or everyone agrees the next vote is final.

REMEMBER THE T-GROUP: ATTEND TO GROUP DYNAMICS

In the real world, goals are not always clear. Membership is cloudy. Leaders tangle. Time marches on. Meanwhile, groups have their own dynamics, some thousands of years in the making; some in the making now.

There is no shortage of tools and techniques for dealing with the nitty-gritty of team life. For each stage of maturity, from vision to decision making to action to testing to realization, there are multiple approaches already canned and "on the shelf." Resolving conflict, for example, is an ancient team problem. Principles of negotiation, conflict resolution, and constructive feedback codify some of these timeworn best practices. Availing yourself of these resources is well worth the effort.

Today's teamnets are creatures of the Information Age. The modern world of information recasts the ancient scene of a group of people all in one place together.

Information has displaced place as the central organizing principle of human groups.

Information connects people. It explains why a group can spread out and still accomplish work together. Information makes distributed work possible. Distributed work, in turn, requires more explicit communication and information. More information begets more distributed work that begets more distributed teams needing more information, and so on.

In contrast to the use of decreasing physical resources, information tends to increase with use. Too much of a good thing brings its own problems; too much communication may end up choking the system. People and groups need new ways of coping with and assimilating more information faster with less effort.

Team how-to handbooks can barely keep up with technology. Some of the new modules required are:

- How to use new communication systems that connect all of people's channels;
- Adaptation of all the standard face-to-face prescriptions—such

as goal setting, brainstorming, or decision making—to diverse communication media; and

- New methods for coping with information overload.

Design in face-to-face time for your boundary crossing teamnets. It's hard to ever get enough of it from a traditional process point of view. Spread-out work creates teams in which not all members can meet frequently. Teamnet life is a dynamic of people being together and being apart in various configurations at various times. We need to learn a whole host of new techniques for working with exceptionally distributed groups.

CONSIDER THE LIFE CYCLE: THE TEAM STAGES

Teams take time to grow. While each team's life is unique, teams are just like people: they go through general stages of maturity. Some groups go through the stages very rapidly, some slowly. Many get stuck at a stage, perhaps fatally.

Team handbooks usually offer a whole section on group passages, with a chapter devoted to each stage of growth, or stage of maturity, or phase of development, of a group's life cycle. "Forming, Storming, Norming, and Performing" is one easy-to-remember and popular team growth process.[13]

Teams form and perform in stages that combine general maturity phases with particular steps rooted in the purpose of the group. Thinking it through requires looking ahead, anticipating what's next, keeping all the right balls in the air. Since everything can't be done all at once, it is necessary to lay out a scheme for what happens when. To do that, you need to chunk time. Group activities into simple phases:

- Things to do right away,
- Things to do next, and
- Finally, the last things to do.

Without strain, you have defined the beginning, middle, and end of a three-step process. Clustering activities into steps is a powerful tool. Used consciously, you can integrate natural group development phases with the steps required to achieve the desired outcome. You can anticipate, generate, and monitor the future.

Phases to Growing Your Teamnet

No matter how you cut it, every project has a beginning, middle, and end. Companies cut the process and name each of these stages differently. Some have formal processes for getting from here to there, while others grope their way along the life cycle.

Regardless of names, boundary crossing teamnets go through five general phases. Each phase represents a set of activities and objectives. While the phases overlap, with some tasks carried out in parallel, there are clear differences between them. Progressing through the phases, the group moves through the life cycle of the project.

PHASE 1. START-UP: SIZING UP THE OPPORTUNITY

This is the just-a-glimmer-in-the-eye stage. That doesn't mean there's no work to do. There is plenty, as the idea goes from vague conception to something that people can act on. "Start-up" means gathering information and arguments, assessing the situation, finding allies, sizing it up, quantifying and qualifying it. It's the early beginning, the concept stage. It may last a very long time, or be brief. It's before things really get started but after the idea's Big Bang.

PHASE 2. LAUNCH: GETTING IT OFF THE GROUND

Fasten your seat belt. You can expect to encounter significant turbulence here. Pressure mounts. Time is short. Things begin to get
really rocky and you'd like to hear a reassuring announcement from
the captain. Unfortunately, none is forthcoming as the group must
make choices and take responsibility. Differences appear, tempers
flare, people drop out, others want in, promised resources become
scarce, risk takers dare. It begins to feel like the worst thing you've
ever been involved in when suddenly things begin to click into place.
David Ryder, a consultant at CSC Index, calls this ATAMO—"And
Then A Miracle Occurs." Then don't be surprised if things go bad
again, relieved by new spurts of progress. "Two steps forward, one
back" typifies the zigzag pattern of this phase.

PHASE 3. PERFORM: MAKING THINGS WORK
IN REAL TIME

If you make it through the critical Launch Phase, you sail into the
Perform Phase with the momentum of pent-up energy, newly re-
leased with someplace to go. For some people, this is the stage
they've been awaiting impatiently. It's the time to put the plan into
action, get the work done, and produce results. Often the longest
phase, it is less rocky than the previous one, with many signs of
progress. Things look good, but watch out! Keep your seat belt
securely fastened. More turbulence is expected just ahead.

PHASE 4. TEST: SHAKING OUT THE RESULTS

Here is where the quality of the early phases is really tested. As
completion nears, the team faces the limits of time and money, as it
stares at the prospect of delivering the results to its customers.
Sometimes the turbulence here is so bad that oxygen masks drop

from the ceiling: massive rework, designs that don't work, planes that don't fly, prototypes that are impossible to manufacture, products that can't be repaired. Benchmarking, testing, qualification, and verification are all ways to evaluate the interim success of a team's work. As the Test Phase causes decision making, unforeseen winds come up suddenly and shake the group from side to side. Many a team has stalled and crashed here, perhaps with a perfect product in hand, but no customers willing to buy.

PHASE 5. DELIVER: HANDING IT OFF TO THE CUSTOMER

At long last, the project reaches completion. After successfully undertaking the Test Phase, there is something to deliver to the customer. Issues shift from development to how to support the results over time. If the original mission was to develop and implement change, here the process stabilizes, and the change becomes operational or routine. Of course, time doesn't stand still. Things happen and new ideas lead to new opportunities. Newly dominant processes contain the seeds of their successors, and the cycle begins again. Today's last stage is tomorrow's first stage.

While all the stages of a team's life cycle are important, we focus especially on the critical second phase, Launch, in the next chapter.

Launching Teamnets: Taking Off by Thinking It Through

The most difficult transition that any group makes is the first one: going from a vague idea to putting it into action. Projects need sufficient momentum, commitment, and critical mass to take off. Many fail because they just can't get up to speed. Let's explore Phase 2: Launch—how to get your teamnet off the ground.

On the Wings of a Big Bid

April 24, 1991, is a big day at Digital Equipment Corporation. On that date, McDonnell Douglas chooses Digital as one of two final bidders to become the computer systems integrator for its new commercial jumbo jet, the MD-12. To respond to this highly complex bid, Digital's core team of nine will need to expand to about 50 people—technical experts from across the company representing several dozen disciplines. To win, Digital has to rapidly create and make operational a team that crosses traditional boundaries.

A few days after Digital's selection as a finalist, the core team meets to plan its next steps in Digital's Irvine, California, facility. Irvine is just a short ride south on Route 405 from Douglas Aircraft's (St. Louis–based McDonnell Douglas's commercial division) Long Beach headquarters. The planning meeting is a "raucous event," according to one participant. With phones ringing, and people coming and going, the group still manages to churn out some of the essentials: a mission statement, a list of broad goals, a "key concepts" graphic, and the invitation list for the second meeting a week later.

The group statement of purpose—*to win the MD-12 bid and prepare Digital to deliver on the contract*—expresses why the group wants to cooperate for mutual benefit.

Two weeks later, the "MD-12 team" now numbers 30. It meets in Irvine again to integrate new people and repeat the process the core group went through. The team reviews the purpose, translates it into a clear set of goals, and begins to assign tasks. Ten days after that, a third planning meeting takes place, this time in Massachusetts, near Digital's home base on the East Coast. This time, 50 people attend, representing engineering, manufacturing, and services. They iterate—go over all the aspects of—the plan again, subdividing into seven distinct "Goal Teams." Each addresses a separate objective, each has its own leader, and each depends on people working together from different functions. Tasks are designed and assigned for each component part of the proposal to Douglas. Each Goal Team competes for management attention, organizational support, and allocation of overall resources, both within the team and with other parts of the corporation.

Digital's MD-12 program fits the criteria of a boundary crossing teamnet:

- Purposes cross traditional boundaries.
- Members cooperate for mutual benefit.
- It and its members have independence.

BEING ASKED TO DANCE

A "close to the customer" salesman brings Digital the MD-12 project. As a longtime vendor to Douglas, he invests in personal relationships and chance encounters at the customer site. Eventually, he detects the early signs of a new program that in time will need a systems integrator. *Systems integrators* tie together the disparate parts of an organization's computer installations. Since most companies have bought their computer systems without much planning, it's a huge market.

Douglas does not list Digital as one of the original companies invited to bid on the program, which includes IBM, Hewlett-Packard, Andersen Consulting, Computer Sciences Corporation, and Electronic Data Systems. Digital wins its spot when a few of its people, including a very senior, experienced executive, participate in Douglas's six-week MD-12 brainstorming session in summer 1990.

During that session, Digital positions itself as understanding the *process* of product development. The building of the MD-12, with its complex partner/investor arrangement—each major "supplier" will invest its portion of the plane, including the engines, the wings, and the fuselage—is less an engineering and manufacturing issue than it is a process one. Digital's central message to Douglas is simple: "Integrate process and product," which Digital holds to through the down select and its final bid.

Why does Digital make the final bid round, when it doesn't even qualify for the first round? It sponsors a key customer event. In mid-March 1991, Digital facilitates and hosts a three-day meeting for the senior Douglas MD-12 executives in Digital's Irvine facilities. Under preparation for months, and delayed several times, the MD-12 general managers' meeting finally takes place just as Douglas names a new MD-12 program manager. The meeting includes his boss, the vice president charged with new product development. In this ideal, though intense, session, the importance of attention to process demonstrates its power in the team's development. Our role at this event and in the resulting MD-12 project is that of process consultants.

THE THREE-DAY PLANE PLAN

The executive conference room is packed. There are 10 general managers from Douglas and six people from Digital, along with some portable computers, an electronic white board, a poster maker, and numerous dignitaries floating in and out.

With more than 200 years of plane-building experience in the room, the group devotes the first day to establishing its purpose. They agree on a mission statement, strategies, key concepts, and common assumptions. Here, preparation has been critical. For several months prior, a Digital management consultant worked these elements in interviews with the Douglas managers and their staffs. The two weeks before the meeting have been particularly intense and the group experiences considerable success in this part of the process.

During the next day and a half, the group sketches out two plans: one for the next four months, and the other for the next five years. They define phases, list tasks, rough out the logic, and estimate times, some in detail. The Digital team captures all this information in real time, both with traditional notes, flip charts, and copy board, as well as directly into word processing on a portable computer and into other computer modeling tools. The software tools not only capture the data, but process them, too, generating several views, including a schedule.

Because of the fast turnaround time, the group has its first view of the data within hours. It is able to revise its assumptions, enabling participants to see the effects of their changes. In 36 hours, they complete three iterations—run-throughs—of the short- and long-term MD-12 plans. By the end of the third day, the group begins to make key decisions as certain things become obvious even at the coarse level of detail.

This meeting reinforces Digital's message about the importance of process. While demonstrating its capabilities, it also obtains invaluable insight into the program. Significant personal relationships strengthen among people in the two companies, while Douglas benefits from a genuine service.

Six weeks later, Douglas selects Digital as one of two finalists. The other is EDS.

THE THREE-WEEK BID PLAN

Douglas forms technical evaluation teams to review the proposals. It assigns an official liaison person to the Digital team, whom Digital in turn invites to its team planning meetings. Douglas provides security badges and makes offices available to all members of the Digital team; Digital then shifts its base of operations from Irvine to Long Beach. The aircraft company assures access to its people so that Digital can obtain the information it needs to propose solutions and make its bid. It sponsors tours of the MD-11 production facilities, its current flagship plane. EDS enjoys the same privileges.

At Digital, a handful of people suddenly find themselves riding atop a very big project, a systems integration bid two orders of magnitude greater than the average business in the area.

One day during the project, an MD-12 team member says, seemingly out of the blue, "One hundred fifty-eight." His partner starts to laugh. We are all standing in the Irvine hallway as a Digital employee from the United Kingdom walks by.

"One hundred fifty-eight?" we say quizzically.

They interrupt each other to explain that they've been keeping track of the number of people involved, and the British fellow who just walked by is the 158th person to be associated with the MD-12 project.

In a few weeks, the Digital team grows from an ad hoc, mostly part-time, group of fewer than 10 to a funded, functioning program of 50, with as many more active at any one time, drawing on and reporting to several hundred more.

To plan its work and get up to speed, Digital uses the same process it used with Douglas. The company holds a series of three planning meetings over the next several weeks. In these meetings, the Digital team designs the organization that will guide it for the next four months until proposal delivery at the end of August. We call these meetings Work Process Design (WPD) sessions.

The first iteration of the Digital team's own WPD is the raucous two-day event at the beginning of May. By the second WPD session, the group has grown to 30 or so, people who have much of the experience and life cycle diversity (e.g., engineering, manufacturing, and product support) required to develop a comprehensive proposal. The packed conference room looks much like the MD-12 general managers' meeting held just across the hall eight weeks earlier.

Over the next two days, the group clarifies its purpose, defines its goals, and forms "goal teams." Materials developed in the first WPD session seed these tasks, which speeds things up. With attention paid to leaving enough time for "bio breaks," meals, and schmoozing, each goal team brainstorms its lists of tasks, then reconvenes with the other goal teams to knit together the overall logic. In the large group, people identify who will own each task, define cross-functional relationships, and estimate how long each task will take.

With the same simple set of tools used in the March Douglas meeting, the team captures, displays, revises, and redisplays its planning data quickly enough to iterate it twice. People leave with a 30-page handout of their joint work, including a directory of participants, a schedule, and a cross-functional chart of milestones and deliverables.

While the team accomplishes a great deal in a short time, it is still in its very early shake-out period. Clearly, the group needs more time to complete sufficient planning, while the usual politics and power problems erupt. Some gaps open up, and the team realizes it needs to involve other people. In the next few days, the team reforms and heads east for one more two-day planning meeting the following week.

For the third meeting, each team member receives a personalized "MD-12 Program Handbook," containing basic information, key documents, the WPD results to date, and their names printed on the cover and the spine. Directories, task lists, models, schedules, and the like all have their places in the three-ring binder, designed for updates of more current material.

With some new blood and a chance to absorb the experience of the previous week, the team runs through the process again. The goal teams, which now have formal status in the group, break out tasks by specific deliverables, schedule key meetings, and define where they will have to make major decisions. They work on the task logic, resolving vague and overcomplicated areas. People review their commitments, including the cross-functional ones. They estimate resources and generate rough budgets. The meeting far exceeds most people's expectations and Digital's MD-12 team is launched.

THE THREE-MONTH PLANE PLAN

During the third session, an ad hoc group forms—including people from several goal teams—to look at the whole life cycle of the MD-12 plane-building process. Digital has won down select on its process promise. Now the task is to produce a plausible high-level process view of the plane as a whole. Digital will tie its technology solutions to the work described in that view.

A self-initiated work process design team pulls together the available information and begins the process of synthesizing an initial picture of the MD-12 development life cycle. Three weeks later, Digital invites key Douglas general managers and their staffs to a presentation of its initial findings.

It's the ribbon cutting for Digital's "MD-12 Process Room"—the first of several process rooms at both Douglas and Digital. The odd-shaped room (12 by 20 by 15 feet at its largest) contains graphics of the vision, theory, and method of Digital's approach. Information covers the walls, gleaned from the March MD-12 executive meeting, formal briefings, and from responses to recent information requests. The first draft of the MD-12 Work Process Framework occupies the "power spot" on the wall: it has the phases of the plane along one axis and the functions along the other.

The MD-12 Process Room opening is a success, the most important measure being Douglas's instant willingness to cooperate with Digital to flesh out the Framework and to develop multiple process views.

Within hours, Digital hosts the first of 10 meetings over the next two months with various cross-functional mixtures of Douglas staff. New information replaces obsolete information, blanks get filled in, concepts jell, and new graphics capture the shifts. All this information shows up on the walls of the Process Room, now moved to a Douglas building at Long Beach, with a window overlooking the runway, where MD-11s are running their test flights.

As the picture of the MD-12 process stabilizes, the Digital team tests its various solutions against the long-term view of the work required. In numerous technical meetings with Douglas organizations and experts, Digital's view gradually shifts from getting requirements to demonstrating increasingly better solutions. By the time Digital submits its proposal at the end of August, it ties all technology solutions to the required work according to the plane's life cycle framework.

Planning Is Doing

Each of the three scales of planning described in the MD-12 story used a similar methodology—the three-day meeting for 10 people, the series of three meetings for 50 people, and the three-month distributed planning process for a five-year effort. Once you are comfortable using a basic set of planning elements, you can easily scale their application to the situation at hand.

The remainder of this chapter and the next provide you with a methodology and supporting set of tools to apply to your situation, whether small and simple, or large and complex.

INVEST IN BEGINNINGS

Get it right early and often.

Investments in good beginnings reap big rewards in later stages and final outcomes. This big lesson from the corporate trenches translates into a team that jells around a purpose, lays out a sensible plan, and launches itself on a path to success with high expectations.

Planning is hard work. A critical mass of the people involved in carrying out the work must do the planning. Although good templates that incorporate past experience greatly enhance and accelerate a new planning process, planning in absentia does not work. When was the last time you put together a dynamite plan, then handed it over to someone else to carry it out successfully? Planning and doing go hand in hand; it's the reason work process design is so important, and why it works.

Using a river as a metaphor to represent processes, early activities are "upstream." They set parameters and determine big choices. Performance is "downstream," where rework and redesign caused by poor initial planning take effect. Suppliers are upstream; customers are downstream. Value chains of suppliers and customers inside and outside the enterprise are processes within processes. They run downstream from customer to customer.

Beware the lure of the downstream fix. It is always cheaper and better to fix something upstream. The trick is finding the right fix early.

A rule of thumb in the software industry is that a bug found in the early stages that would cost $1 to fix could cost as much as $1,000 to fix when found after the product is deployed. Most of today's major business improvement movements emphasize the long-term payoff for early efforts, stressing concepts like the motto "Begin with the end in mind." The goal of good planning is to get the shared mind of the group to see the same end.

"Concurrent engineering" is one of a number of product development approaches that bridge conventional boundaries. It brings downstream players into upstream activities. In reality, this means something quite practical, like inviting manufacturing and service representatives to early engineering design meetings, or inviting customers to new product development brainstorming sessions. Experience indicates that these cross-functional teams produce designs with far fewer changes later for manufacturing and product support. Hence, they yield products that have higher quality, cost less to produce, and reach the market sooner.

CALS is a U.S. Department of Defense initiative similar to concurrent engineering.[1] It puts the quality viewpoint to work for the government as the customer of defense contractors. CALS takes the far downstream activities of logistics and product support as the starting point for requirements. Engineering and manufacturing need to conform to product support requirements, rather than the other way around. Data show that planning for product support reaps great value for the customer, propelling the CALS initiative far beyond the defense market to many of America's biggest businesses. Its benefits are convincing, showing up in such simple things as clutches in cars designed for easy repair without having to dismount the engine to reach them.

MD-12 is an example of a very large, very long life cycle, new product program. Big project or small, plan early and involve all the players. These are the secrets to success. Every moment spent planning is an investment in a streamlined, sensible process.

WHERE JOURNALISM COMES IN HANDY: THE FIVE QUESTIONS

Sound complicated? It's not. There is a relatively easy way to plan— to develop a work process design. It only requires taking a page from the reporter's notebook. To plan, you first need to understand the story. The first thing every reporter learns is that to get the story, you have to answer the five W's:

- *Why?*
- *What?*
- *When?*
- *Who?*
- *Where?*

Good managers intuitively ask themselves these questions in the present and future tense. Why are we doing this? What do we need to do? When will this happen? Who is involved? Where is everyone located?

- *Why* is the starting point. It expresses the driving need, the mission, the vision of the future that galvanizes the group. It provides the ultimately unifying fabric.
- *What* transforms purpose into work. It is the specific set of activities people need to accomplish to achieve their goals.
- *When* takes the discrete activities and turns them into a dynamic process that unfolds over time.
- *Who* is the team, the network of people and organizations that is going to accomplish the work.
- *Where* names the locations in which the team and its work reside, bounding the physical universe that must be accommodated.

The key to success is rapid iteration of answers to these questions involving key people in the group. Convene "work process design sessions" to answer the five questions in sequence. Consider face-to-face meetings as expensive, precious resources.[2] The most effective ones are well thought out and well designed. False starts are very costly. Follow up on action items and decisions in meetings. Once initiated, you must nourish your process. Maintain momentum—it's critical.

Honesty and trust are basic values for any successful group. Ask questions. This is an ancient and honorable method of learning the truth. Honesty with oneself and others is a prerequisite to understanding. The five W's make it easy to take the first steps on this path.

THE PROCESS OF DOING THE DESIGN

It takes time and patience to ask and answer basic questions about goals and work. They require gathering information from different people with multiple perspectives. People don't just give out information without some idea of how it will be used. What are the benefits of deriving the information? This situation holds the potential both for creativity and for conflict. Use an orderly process to mitigate the normal problems of planning.

Work process design is a people-intensive process, requiring the right players in the same room at the same time focused on the same task. You can sketch out a high-level rough plan in a morning. You can lay out a somewhat more thorough, though still preliminary, set of detailed plans in a three-day working session. You can support very long, very complex processes of cross-functional collaboration in a three-month project.

Gain the power of WPD from *iteration*. Iteration is to planning what early blocking sessions and rehearsals are to stage performances. They allow you to see the whole and expose the problems while it's still easy to address them. Think about the whole thing. Rethink it early and review it often until the plan stabilizes. Hold a session that corresponds to the level of detail that you need. Ask your group to consider these questions:

> *Why are we doing this project? What do*
> *we know? Where are the obvious holes?*
> *What are the downsides? What are the*
> *major parts? Whom do we need to*
> *involve? When are the key milestones?*
> *How much will it cost?*

By defining the purpose, you can specify tasks. Defining objectives leads back to purpose. When new people and organizations engage, they inevitably cause the group to loop back and revise the "why" and recut the "what." Time and cost estimates cause a rethinking of goals. And so it goes. These factors are, of course, interrelated, and cannot be determined in isolation. Yet human nature—differences in function, responsibilities, or style—usually leads people to look at one or two factors and miss the dynamic whole. "Don't get blocked by the problems and apparent showstoppers. Go on and come back to them when you know more," says Roy Rezac, director of R&D at Protocol, a division of Zycad Corporation.

The *experience* of iteration in a condensed period of time conveys the power of WPD. By capturing planning in real time and rapidly processing changes, the participants have constant feedback to their ideas. With experience and working with others, you will be able to undertake a highly complex face-to-face WPD for a highly distributed process.

The First Run-through

It's time to begin planning and you have all the players in the room—one way or another. Those who can't be there in person can attend by speaker phone; and for the truly technologically wealthy, by video conference. Essential equipment is all very low-tech: flip charts, overhead projectors, white boards, a telephone, a box of new markers (perhaps the most scarce resource in any conference room), and a pot of coffee. An electronic white board, at a premium in most companies, is a superb tool for planning if you can commandeer one. Encourage people to bring their laptops and arrange to have a printer available for real-time output. Consider this picture of physical readiness as a metaphor for thinking about what's really important: people going through the process of developing a successful teamnet by addressing some very basic questions.

WHY?

- *Find the source.*
- *Express the needs.*
- *Determine readiness.*
- *Broadcast benefits.*

Why is the starting point. Ask this question to drive your group's early sporadic process. Pieces of the answer can come from anyone anywhere. It may emerge very slowly. It may seem to appear from many places at once. The information you need is not necessarily in the room. Be creative in gathering information from many unlikely quarters.

Customer needs are a good place to start when asking "why." You may recognize needs inconspicuously from a casual customer comment, or have them burst forth to you in a blinding flash of insight. Customer needs usually lead you to ask another fundamental question, "Who is the customer?" Typically, the "why" question clarifies itself at a face-to-face meeting among a critical number of team members. Use one of numerous organization development techniques to help your group discover its core mission—or to discover that it has none. Use all the materials in the room to express the mission.

Are you making progress toward your explicit purpose? This is the first measure of a group's readiness to undertake real work. Nothing in business gets started and keeps going unless it brings benefits. When people question why they are doing something, they usually are asking, "What's in it for me?" Unless the benefits are large and obvious, most people will not sign up for the frustration involved in trying to get something going. Sometimes negative benefits provoke people to act. The threat of dire consequences if the old ways continue much longer or the crisis of traditional systems collapsing gives birth to many an organizational change.

WHAT?

- *Scope the work.*
- *Sketch the system.*
- *List the tasks.*
- *Estimate the size.*

The first concrete step in "getting your arms around" the work is to understand the big picture. When you "scope the work," you give it broad definition, outlining the magnitude of the effort—for example, to develop a new product, undertake a joint marketing program with another company, or reorganize the group you're in. It's a struggle in early stages to establish a "bird's-eye view" of the whole, but it's mandatory.

This is when the back-of-the-envelope sketches and the placemats come into play. A group brainstorms what the project is all about. Then everyone goes to lunch. A few people turn over their paper placemats and sketch how the whole thing fits together. They lay out the handful of components and activities required to give shape to the idea. One Cambridge, Massachusetts, restaurant, the Bennett Street Cafe, recognizes the importance of planning over lunch. Instead of placemats, its tablecloths are pieces of butcher paper, and fat crayons sit on every table next to the salt and pepper.

What, broadly speaking, are the basic tasks? Make a list of what you need to do. Someone goes to the white board, and the group very quickly lists the tasks. Once the list of steps is in front of you, you can begin to see relationships among the tasks.

The last step in this sequence is to estimate the cost of each task. This is not a budgeting exercise at this point. Try to ascertain ballpark figures so that you can understand and communicate the order of magnitude of the effort from a quantitative perspective.

Try this exercise out with your group, with the goal of merging all the models into a one-page sketch.

WHEN?

- *Rough out phases.*
- *Initialize milestones.*
- *Check givens.*
- *Think critical.*

In the rich soup of process, it is *time* that forms the stock, the basic substance in which everything else swims. Above all others, the time element demands repeated iteration. Set and revise. Set and revise. A process is nothing without time.

At the beginning of your process, time seems to stretch forever, into the unknown far future. Use the first run-through of "when" to span the whole distance of the development process. With the complete, high-level picture in hand, then you divide long time spans into *phases*, more manageable chunks. In our first full-day planning meeting for this book, Jim Childs, our editor, went to the white board in the conference room and sketched out the major phases of the book's production, marketing, and sales. When this kind of spontaneous work process design activity gets written down, as it was that day, it becomes a record of the learning and an ongoing management tool.

For teamnets to be successful, this activity is mandatory. The teamnet must chunk its work into explicit phases. Set up a straw set of phases based on the best available current information. This is an excellent way to stimulate further thinking about the whole life cycle of the process.

While chunking out the big phases, also try to set up some initial milestones along the route. Consider periodic reviews, interim products, prototypes, test sites, draft documents, test markets—in short, deliverables, meetings, criteria, and decisions to mark progress toward the goals. Product developers know these milestones as "stable intermediate forms."

Time, in the long sense of "the whole amount of time available for this," often comes with the circumstantial territory: a market window, a budget cycle, quarterly pressures, limited resources, an upcoming trade show. There is rarely enough time. And don't forget the effects of seasons and holidays on the realities of the group doing its work. (Time permeates our whole lives, not just our work lives.)

Time also dictates the order in which to do some work. You need to start some things even before you've fully planned the work or really made your Launch decisions. From the beginning, you already know about some tasks; they sit squarely on the critical path of the project flow. You also know about some long lead items—like real estate, buildings, nailing down known key resources, or critical components. So you need to get started before you're really ready. But beware the fire drill. This reactive mode of project management, which leaps from burning building to smoldering embers, is only crisis management. For prevention and control, you need to take the time to set out the long view.

WHO?

- *Spark of life.*
- *Team types.*
- *Fluid leadership.*
- *Strength of weak ties.*

A process starts with an idea. Perhaps it crystallizes problems and possibilities that have been simmering for some time. Someone, or someones, give voice to the idea, concept, need, change—whatever—with sufficient emotional impact at the right time and the right place. A "spark plug," someone emotionally committed to an idea who shares it with others, first articulates purpose. Spark plugs and other visionaries see what's possible; they are early leaders. Yet if leadership never moves beyond spark plugs, you have hierarchy rather than a network.

Visionaries, risk takers, communicators, negotiators, and exceptionally well-connected people are all at a premium as part of the early mix. Recruit them. The early stages of any business process require significant right-brain capability to supplement the traditional left-brain strength. This is often why consultants and facilitators have a business in new group formation. They bring some extra intuitive and intrapersonal skills into the early stages.

In a prototeam that is not all situated in the same place, "circuit riders" and other communicators can often be found traveling among the core group. They carry the word from person to person and one cluster to another. Percy Barnevik, the CEO of ABB, with dealings in over 100 countries, travels constantly, so much so that his office is his plane. People like Barnevik provide some of the interim face-to-face glue that every teamnet requires.

Besides initiators, communicators, and consultants, other early leaders include key supporters, critical representatives of stake-holder groups, and even an important customer or two. At this stage in the process, everyone is still in the rough camaraderie of peers.

Every teamnet has a periphery as well as a core. All the myriad connections to your core team connect at the edges: reporting connections, professional associations, contacts from previous projects, past jobs, and, of course, family and friends. *Nothing is quite so powerful—and so underutilized—as "the strength of weak ties."*[3] This great insight from social network research reveals the boost and amplification you get from connecting at the *edges* of your network. Look for new information, new leads, new viewpoints, and new insights from the people you don't know well rather than just from the ones you do.

WHERE?

- *Nowhere or somewhere.*
- *Meeting places.*
- *Shared data.*
- *Connection technologies.*

Physical location used to mean everything. Now it means little. The average person can physically travel halfway around the world in 24 hours. A telephone call takes no time at all. A fax takes a minute or two. TV puts us "on the spot, up to the minute." "No sense of place" is the way one writer puts it.[4]

Identifying where the people in your group are and how they can be reached is a key early piece of work. Where does the group meet? Is there any common space? Typically, places where the work occurs belong to members.

An easy, early way to establish the group's sense of place is to gather basic information together and "publish" it as a memo, file folder, presentation, briefing book, or other compilation of diverse material. This is the first edition of your "Teamnet Handbook." Combine *who* and *where* information to create a membership directory.

Phones, faxes, and computer conferencing—which allows people to carry on structured conversations via computer—are good supportive technologies for these efforts. They offer some of the immediacies and contact that help build trust and grease the wheels of interaction. Remember that *where* includes more than traditional mail addresses and physical meeting places, but also electronic addresses of increasing variety and numbers.

Turning Questions Into Answers

Each of the five questions—the five W's—generates an associated set of results—the five T's: targets, tasks, time, team, and territories. Careful tracking of the five T's enables a teamnet to function in an effective, coordinated manner, capturing its learning as it goes.

To initiate a systematic process of designing the work, you must extract "targets" from answers to the "why" question. Targets are tangible results expected by specific dates, such as a prototype up and running by the second quarter. "Tasks" answer "what," like doing a draft of the marketing document. When you attach specific people's names and organizations to targets and tasks, you designate "teams" answering "who"—Richard and Debra take responsibility for the draft. When you answer "when" with "time"—task durations and dates—you make a schedule, the means of coordinating work, i.e., the draft by the end of the month.

Each of the five W's has its corresponding one of the five T's.

Why	>	*Targets*
What	>	*Tasks*
When	>	*Times*
Who	>	*Teams*
Where	>	*Territories*

- *Targets* result from translating *"why,"* the purpose, into specific actionable goals.
- *Tasks* result from answering *"what"* questions that convert purpose into specific chunks of work.
- *Times* result from estimating *"when"* questions for task durations, forming a schedule based on task dependencies.
- *Teams* result from answering *"who"* questions, linking people's names to specific tasks.
- *Territories* result when *"where"* questions are settled, putting names on common places, physical and electronic.

When you tie tasks to targets, you create clear purpose—the essential glue for teamnets—with a focus on work. Your common set of tasks, then, identifies your common process. By focusing on a cooperatively developed set of tasks, your teamnet can see its work through multiple views of relationships among the tasks. This is a very powerful method, made even more so when you apply computer tools.

A common view of the process is the sine qua non of teamnets. Unless everyone has a common view of the work, the distributed committee does indeed design a camel when it means to design a horse. But don't leap to conclusions. A camel is an excellent result from the design process if your goal is to respond to your customers who need reliable transportation across hot deserts.

The Second Run-through

While the first version of the plan is important, it's the second iteration that usually gets you close to a real working plan. Call a Launch session and go through these steps:

---

1. Set the targets.
2. Define the tasks.
3. Estimate the times.
4. Select the teams.
5. Choose the territories.

T1. SET THE TARGETS

All programs begin with purpose. Based on a vision, an idea, an opportunity, a discovery, a challenge, a crisis—something catalyzes a need and crystallizes into a mission.

Getting to clear purpose is not trivial. It is often the first test of a new teamnet's survival, and the last test of an old one struggling with change. Fortunately, there are many methods, techniques, and tools available to assist groups. Here's the point:

Clarify your purpose until goals and overall milestones can be written down as targets. Tasks gain their parameters, personalities, and credibility from goals.

Ideally, you can expand a mission statement into an interrelated set of goals that you can pursue in parallel. Each goal needs to have a concrete outcome attached to it, and a time (however rough) by which it is to be completed. With concrete targets, the qualitative purpose takes on its first quantitative expression.

But setting out targets once is not enough. Purpose remains incomplete unless it communicates easily. A felt sense of shared purpose often precedes any formal purpose statement. Mission statements alone are rarely sufficient vehicles to communicate the "why" of doing the work.

Your group expresses its creativity by coming up with words and visuals that adequately capture your vision. This is an essential part of the process. Pull out the markers, big sheets of paper, tape, scissors, and a copier. One of our favorite slightly higher-tech tools here is a poster maker, which enlarges normal sheets of paper into the size of posters. (It's a tool that lawyers use to produce their visuals for the courtroom.) Graphics and desktop publishing have their places here, too, and multimedia promise even more effective tools.

T2. DEFINE THE TASKS

The next step in Launch is for you to define the tasks. Tasks are "little purposes," micro-missions woven together to achieve an overall macro-mission. Tasks at one level are the breakout of the goals of the level above; they become the purposes of the level below, the nested hierarchical order that gives WPD its small group-to-enterprise scalability.

Although the original transformation of goals into tasks can appear to be magic, it is simply part of the process. Take the first goal and ask, "What do we need to do to make this happen?" Your answer generates a seed set of tasks. Your inevitable incompleteness and overlaps at the start begin to straighten out into a clear picture when you have a sufficient number of tasks on the table.

In this step, you are slicing up the work. *Name the tasks* in mutually understood language. Identify and represent the time sequence *logic of tasks dependencies*. Besides dependencies, task names label a metaphorical folder of characteristics like:

- The purposes served;
- The people involved;
- The duration of the tasks;
- The resources needed;
- The deliverables; and
- The key decision points.

With the capacity to code all this information by task, you have designed the basic conceptual infrastructure for your program management system.

To accomplish simple objectives, you need do little more than write the list of tasks on flip chart or white board, indicate who is going to do them, and when they need to be done. Copy down the list and send it out to all participants and interested parties. For larger, more complex, more distributed projects, you need considerably more than a simple list, but the basic principles are the same. In the MD-12 proposal effort, we used project management tools both for real time capture-process-display and as the longer-term planning medium that tracked tasks, dependencies, schedule, and risks.

T3. ESTIMATE THE TIMES

The next step in Launch is to look at the numbers—both how long it will take and, eventually, how much it will cost. Things become very real with the question of "How much?" How much time, how many people, how much equipment, and how much capital is needed?

Experienced people know approximately how long it takes to do things. Ask them directly for their best guesses. In the thick of a planning session, it is not difficult to get these estimates.

When you add the estimates to the task logic, and assign a start date, you can generate a schedule.

Compare dates with the desired outcome set in your goals and milestones during the purpose stage of planning. Most groups do not hit the milestones in their first iteration—not by a long shot. The discrepancies between the desired and estimated end dates serve as a powerful motivator for the group to revise the plan. One high-end project tool asks people for normal-best-worst case time estimates and generates a *risk profile*, demonstrating how probable it will be to meet desired milestones based on the estimates.

During the first few iterations, use time as a proxy for all costs. As tasks stabilize, however, you can take a detailed look at real costs in time, people, and other resources. As the project becomes more specific, join time-to-market concerns with the realities of scarce resources to understand total cost considerations. This forces further refinements and iterations to bring all these factors into dynamic, doable alignment.

T4. SELECT THE TEAMS

From a distance, the cross-functional picture of a project looks broad and integrated, well matrixed and beautifully networked across the life cycle. Too often, however, the up-close reality is a hair-raising cacophony of competing interests. Everyone, it seems, needs to be involved in everything.

Not so. Most tasks require only a small, albeit cross-functional subset of the whole network at any one time. The trick is to get the right people together on the right task at the right time.

Design two essential activities that enable this to happen:

1. *Name the organizational functions* required to do the work using mutually understood terms; and
2. *Identify the functional dependencies,* the necessary relationships among the people and groups involved to complete each task.

History, politics, and personalities are facts of life in organizations, large and small. Defining work—*independent of who specifically is going to do it*—is important in early iterations. Attaching names and faces to the required work is easier in later stages as the process formalizes.

For each task, name at least one functional owner—and perhaps more—and involve a cross-functional set of participants. Associate deliverables, decisions, and meetings with tasks. Make each task the responsibility of a specific person or function. Participants range from those involved in the input (suppliers) to the tasks, to those who perform them, to those who receive the output (task customers). This cross-functional planning technique is common practice in Japan, and is only now beginning to be used in the West, most often in total quality efforts.

T5. CHOOSE THE TERRITORIES

In traditional organizations, territory is paramount. Guess what? In teamnets, it's the same. One critical element of independence is territory, and teamnet members tend to be quite territorial. Most of the territory important to a teamnet is thus defined by membership. People tend to bring their places with them. Whether country, city, or office, where people are situated is a key, always idiosyncratic, feature of teamnets.

Networks and teams require support. They are not free. The minimal amount of coordination and infrastructure work necessary to maintain a vital process either must be hosted by one of the members, rotated or otherwise shared, or conducted from a place the team calls home.

In the beginning teamnets are almost always hosted by one of the members, often a leader, who provides offices, staff support, a phone number, and access to a copier. At first, work tends to float. As the teamnet and process begin to jell, more permanent solutions appear as part of the overall work plan. When this happens, you know your Teamnet Launch is complete—at least for this round.

The Target Method offers a systematic planning process for small groups and large. For large or otherwise complex situations, some simple tools can augment the method, the subject of the next chapter.

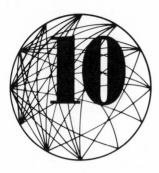

Those That Do, Plan: Bringing Discipline to Teamnets

In an 18th-century farmhouse in the central Massachusetts woods, a handful of engineers huddles around white boards and flip charts. They have gone to their company's retreat center to plan their future. There, they deliberate such things as PLIMS (Product Life Cycle Information Management Systems) and whether they can meet FRS (first revenue shipment) if the TPV (third party vendor) misses Milestone Six by a quarter. To them, it makes sense. Too much so, in fact, because if the plan slips, it's dead.

The PLIMS group faces many challenges. It needs to ship its product in 18 months to be profitable in a very hot new market. To complete the PLIMS product, the group depends on a California vendor for key technology, whose development schedule depends on yet another vendor in Sweden.

Meanwhile, the PLIMS group is in organizational limbo for the moment. It doesn't report to anybody higher in the organization— i.e., they have no boss. The manager of the larger engineering group (in which PLIMS is responsible for software development) has just left for another company. Worse, the PLIMS group needs more software engineers at a time when their company is in the midst of major downsizing in the next year.

In spite of it all, the seven engineers are sufficiently able to concentrate. Within two and a half days, they put together a plan that carries them through to shipping the product. "That planning session saved me a year and a million dollars," the group's manager says six months later.

This particular manager is lucky. He had the sense to understand a simple rule:

Those that do, plan.

There's a very easy way to kill a plan. Ask one group to put it together, then ask another group to carry it out. For plans to work, the people who will have to execute them must put them together. Plans make it possible for teamnets to take on all sizes of tasks. The power of the Teamnet Principles lies in their scalability from small to large. Of course, there are also real differences between small teamnets and large, between simple and complex purposes. Simply put:

- General organizational costs of coordination and communication increase with size.
- The need for explicitness and participatory planning also increases with size, scope, and complexity.

Planning is not about having a neatly bound document sitting on a shelf. Planning is about doing the project right the first time. Plans work because you take the time to mock up, simulate, or otherwise try out the process you will use to accomplish a shared purpose. Planning develops teamnets, where people learn to think together, to make and keep commitments to one another, and to develop personally while building the group.

With size and complexity come data and the need to represent and track changes in them. Complexity increases rapidly with the addition of new members. The more people, the more difficult it is to render common information. Historically, the inability to access common information has been a severe limiting factor for networks. With computers and telecommunications, the complex becomes more manageable. It is an important part of the technological push behind the accelerating use of this organizational form.

The larger the teamnet, the greater the need for conscious planning. The more complex the task, the greater the need for computer support tools.

Purpose Is Where It All Begins

Purpose is a vast natural resource for a group. Like information, a group's purpose is a renewable resource. As people absorb more information, they understand their purpose better. The better they understand their purpose, the more information they can absorb. With use, its value tends to increase rather than diminish. However, as with extracting or harvesting any natural resource, you must combine the purpose resource with human ingenuity to form something useful.

By definition, business networks form for specific purposes. To be successful, they must have a purpose; they must be intentional. Just like any type of business organization, people judge business networks by the normal criteria: effectiveness and efficiency of meeting goals. Business networks succeed by design. A *design* brings clarity and explicitness to business purposes. It is the foundation for carrying out purposes.

A good design gives order to a complex intangible future. When people arrange their detailed purposes systematically, they create handles and hooks to grasp on to. These handles serve to guide people's individual activities within the whole group, as they grope their way through uncertainty.

If a group fails to become intentional about its work, it limits its ultimate potential. The great challenge of teamnets is to be explicit about work. We use the principles of work process design and the Target Method (see "Launching Teamnets," chapter 9) to create explicit plans and put them into action.

Purpose Is Key to Teamnet Management

Purpose is central to all good management practice. For organizations pushing beyond hierarchy and bureaucracy, it is critical. It plays a key role in the power dynamics of human organizations.

In the chaotic modern business environment that extends across boundaries, traditional sources of power—charisma, coercion, and law[1]—collapse. At a distance, personal charisma has its physical limits; the hire-fire power club doesn't work; and legalities are too slow to keep up.

> *The key to coordinating work across boundaries lies in the fourth source of power in organizations: purpose—explicit, common, clear, and detailed.*

Purpose is basic to groups. It is sometimes all they really have. Grass-roots groups demonstrate this: people volunteer because of the group's mission, what it is trying to accomplish.

For most of human history, small groups have done just fine keeping their purposes mostly implicit. Since most of these groups have formed around a particular location—home, community, and workplace—tacit expression of their purposes has sufficed. When people do need to clarify something, they are close enough to talk with one another.

We know what we're doing. We've always done it this way. There is no need to talk about why. When a change comes, word gets around. Somebody takes care of these things.

Boundary crossing introduces a new wrinkle into purpose. The more boundaries to cross, the greater the need to make the purpose explicit. Most specifically, purpose needs to roll out over time. This means that everyone involved needs a shared picture of the work, the schedule, the milestones, and the players.

MAKING THE IMPLICIT EXPLICIT

Strength of purpose is a group's only defense against the inevitable storms of personality and politics that pervade every human organization. How does purpose become a practical tool for group management? By making *some* of the implicit explicit. Note the word "some." It is neither possible nor desirable to make everything explicit. Such a horrible blizzard of information is virtually useless.

There are great rewards in making purpose explicit. From it, people derive tangible drivers for their work:

- *Purposes* translate into targets and goals.
- *Goals* break into task activities.
- *Tasks*, when organized into related sets, become plans.
- *Plans* turn into the ongoing management system.

In teamnets, discipline does not come about through authority or threats. Discipline arises from systematic development of the purpose at the appropriate level of detail and explicitness.

Success requires creating a systematic plan and living it as an ongoing process of change.

Use a light touch to introduce a disciplined systematic process. You don't need to nail down everything to bring sufficient order to real complex work. A disciplined process also helps in the group's dynamics; it introduces structure for planning and gaining agreements, activities that usually stir up conflict.

QUANTIFYING QUALITY

Six sigma. Defect rate of three per million. People familiar with quality management practices know its statistical foundation well. Indeed, many people's views of quality are stuck in numbers. Much how-to literature of the quality movement devotes itself to measurable quantities: methods of planning, gathering, analyzing, and applying data to solve problems.

There is good cause for quality's obsession with data. They provide a systematic way to:

- Uncover customer needs;
- Measure the process of transforming inputs into outputs; and
- Evaluate the customer response to the output.

Qualitative need is intangible; quantitative data are tangible. The combination is powerful. By creative choice of data sources, people can make many "qualities" visible through measures and charts.

Teamnets depend upon data and information. Open, shared, accurate, unbiased information of all sorts forms the basis for peer interaction and decision making. Groups of people who are physically distributed constantly need to receive, evaluate, and digest ever more information. This fundamental information-processing function is one of the prime reasons for the rise of networked organizations.

You can see a hallmark difference between networks and bureaucracies in their approach to data sharing. Compare the relative size and diversity of their common information bases. A person who can control information flow holds a prime lever of power in traditional organizations. It's a major reason why subordinates need direction from superiors. In a successful network, many people have their hands on the information lever; they distribute this power source widely.

In most corporate cultures, access to information is, as they say, a nontrivial issue. The thought of too great an information flow terrifies some people. One fear is that the corporate jewels will soon end up in the hands of the competition. This certainly does not have to be the case, as the experience of more than one open company shows. The more good, useful information that is available to people, the better their decisions. They will be more productive, and the overall business will benefit.

SCIENCE AND THE BOTTOM LINE

The quality movement has brought a great indirect contribution to modern management: scientific method. Today's quality toolbox includes techniques like control charts, Pareto charts, cause-and-effect diagrams, time plots, dot plots, flow charts, deployment charts, scatter diagrams, simple check sheets, and many more.

These very pragmatic, simple "scientific" methods have a modest price tag. Some are done by hand, or require at most desktop computers, yet have features powerful enough to help you uncover the basic laws of your business.

A great teamnet combines science with heart. The heart points the way with a tantalizing target. The science offers a method for getting there based on explicit information.

The Toolbox for Teamnet Support

Finance wants to see numbers. Operations wants to see a schedule. Human resources wants to see the staffing plan. The president wants to know where it's all heading. There is no single "right" view of a process. What it looks like depends on your perspective and the set of relationships you focus on.

Different views of a process accommodate people's different learning styles. Different cultures, disciplines, and personalities favor one type of process picture over another.

While no method can claim completeness, people can draw on and integrate many different views when they have common agreement on a set of tasks. Based on the consistency gained from a common pool of tasks, these views are connected at their roots. Task-based models yield different, consistent, *and* complementary pictures, which enable a variety of people to plan, modify, and manage a process.

MANAGING THE DATA OF CHANGE

Since change is constant in business today, it's wise to assume that your plans will change. To manage the data of change, we string together a set of relatively low-cost software applications. These tools maximize the effect of the teamnet planning process. They make it easy to display and communicate the five-T (targets, tasks, time, team, and territories) answers generated from the five-W (why, what, when, who, and where) questions and their inevitable changes. By capturing the answers in desktop computer tools, you greatly enhance the chances of success in shared management of dynamic distributed processes.

We use portable computers in real-time work process design sessions. The effect is dramatic benefits in the speed of iterations, quality of output, and excitement of participation. With a little experience, you can use them this way, too. Two applications we use are:

- Project management software that supports task sequencing and enables quick schedule forecasting; and
- Cross-boundary mapping tools, based on ideas originally developed at Toyota Motor Company. This allows everyone to quickly see who is responsible for what.

We use different tools and display media to represent data about each of the five-T's, including:

T1 Targets	• Timeline
	• Milestones
T2 Tasks	• Lists
	• Framework
T3 Times	• Task flow diagram
	• Task duration schedule
T4 Teams	• Cross-boundary chart
	• Directory
T5 Territories	• Handbook

Computers function like optical lenses in the organizational sciences. They reduce and enlarge data to help us resolve micro-cosmic details and create macro-cosmic maps. Desktop computer tools enable teamnets to be successful. They make the work explicit through display of detailed information. A medium of distributed work, they keep track of and manage work, and provide a communications structure.

Use the Target Method to build a solid foundation on which to develop more-detailed project management systems. With the target application tools, a small team can capture and organize its own plan, then combine it with larger teamnet designs.

T1: TARGETING TARGETS

When you need to keep the future simple, think of process simply as *steps*. Just think about getting from here to there as a path to be traveled in steps. "Here" is where you are, "there" is where you want to be, representing the purpose. Getting from here to there is a very common, basic human activity.

> *Teamnets pursue purpose over time. Purpose times time equals process. Processes are pursuits of goals, steps toward achieving the purpose. Processes are sets of activities strung together for a reason.*

Purposeful pursuits are the doing, the for-better-or-worse actions performed along the way to produce an outcome. This is the very essence of how groups translate goals into work. The critical success factor in networks is the ability to share work. Great plans are useless without action. You need to map out and track complicated ideas requiring action by multiple players.

Timelines

Habitually, people keep track of things with a mental timeline. When a group gets together to plan, they need to share and make explicit their timeline.

A line with an arrowhead is the most basic image people use to lay out the path of processes. The arrow points simultaneously at a target and the future.

Break up a timeline into steps. This fundamental technique in process planning may be as far as a group needs to go. You can lay out a plan at this level of detail in a few minutes' conversation.

Step-by-Step Timeline

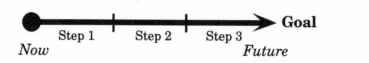

Steps 1, 2, and 3 label the *beginning, middle,* and *end* of a process, the simplest "phases" that a group lives through.

> *Beginning involves what it takes you to get going; the middle is where you do the bulk of the work; and, at the end, you need to wrap things up.*

Define your phases; it's a basic task for launching your team. Phases mark off the big steps for getting the project done. Every planning process segments time into a series of phases. You can array any life cycle model of whatever scale along the line. Every group cuts the process line to suit its needs.

Teamnet Phases of Growth

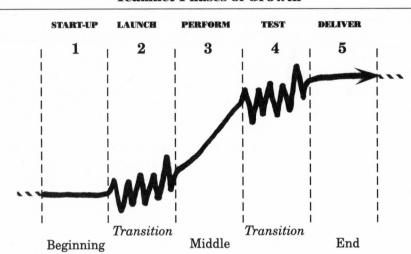

| START-UP | LAUNCH | PERFORM | TEST | DELIVER |
| 1 | 2 | 3 | 4 | 5 |

Beginning   *Transition*   Middle   *Transition*   End

Turbulence

Change rarely moves us harmoniously in a smooth sequence of activities from here to there. Instead, change plays out in fits and starts. To the group experiencing it, this sometimes feels like major turbulence. Turbulence shakes things up at natural stress points in the group's development. It is so common that process professionals can anticipate when it will arrive.

We portray these turbulence points as zigzags. Otto, a member of the Digital MD-12 team, particularly liked this analogy. In a meeting one day, Otto stood behind Ralph, another member of the team, who was loudly complaining about how badly things were going. Although Ralph couldn't see what was happening, Otto, who was standing behind him, started to draw zigzags in the air. Otto's zigzags grew bigger as Ralph got louder. When Ralph finished his harangue, Otto walked over to the group's process chart, which had a prominent place on the wall. "We are here," he said, pointing to the zigzags, as everyone in the room laughed.

Disruptive as it is, turbulence can be a source of energy for the group if you harness it early and properly.

Turbulence first breaks out in the middle of the early stages of a developing process (roughly speaking, in a three-day meeting, it's the end of the first day or morning of the second; in a three-month project, it's week three). People from various factions and with conflicting viewpoints need to work out their differences. To move forward together, they need to sufficiently affirm goals, recognize leaders, and agree on an action plan.

This period is fraught with conflict and potential pitfalls: it always takes longer than anyone estimates or desires; it contains the potential for explosion, *and* it holds the promise of a big reward. If you successfully make it through this stress point, you've launched your teamnet into the performance period—where the real work of the group gets done. This is no small accomplishment.

Turbulence breaks out again toward the end of a change process. Change processes eventually need to level off and stabilize as they approach the inevitable limits to change. Before the change becomes final, you must pilot, test, validate, or otherwise check it. Not every group is successful. Some neglect to figure out how to implement the change. Others skip the critical task of explaining and selling the solution to those who will have to live with it. An engineering group "throws the design over the wall" and calls that its handoff to manufacturing.

Whatever the method, testing introduces turbulence and tries everyone's patience. The more you can anticipate this period of turbulence, the easier it is to live through. Groups who stumble into the second stress period are blindsided by unexpected and sometimes fatal obstacles.

By adding two transitions—times of turbulence—to the basic three stages (begin, middle, end), our general change process has the five Teamnet Phases of Growth: Start-up, Launch, Perform, Test, Deliver. Two transition phases, Launch and Test, punctuate the basic phases, Start-up, Perform, Deliver. Together, these five phases serve as a generic template. Use them to develop a custom phasing strategy for your boundary crossing teamnet.

The Checkout Counter

How do you know when you've gone from one phase to the next? *Milestones* enable a group to set interim collection points for the process as a whole. Milestones are markers, beacons on the path to results. They provide midterm targets that periodically refocus the distributed group on the shared effort. Milestones function like a checkout counter: once you've passed through it, the goods are yours.

Milestones may be deliverables, meetings, or decisions that signify progress toward goals. They are valuable tools for helping a group manage its time.

Consider these milestones as examples:

- **Phase 1. Start-up:** Make an ordered list of customer requirements and write a mission statement.
- **Phase 2. Launch:** Complete a plan and gain commitments.
- **Phase 3. Perform:** Implement a pilot or prototype.
- **Phase 4. Test:** Complete performance check against expectations.
- **Phase 5. Deliver:** Gain enthusiastic customer acceptance.

Exit criteria offer a more rigorous method for passing from one phase to another. Entry and exit criteria, conditions that distinguish where you are in the process, keep track of progress by deliverables, reviews, and decisions as phases inevitably overlap with one another. For example, a group develops preliminary ideas of customer needs in the Start-up Phase. It gathers, documents, and debates perceived customer needs in its Launch Phase. It details a final set of precise requirements as an early task of the Perform Phase. Requirements turn into evaluation checklists during the Test Phase. Thus, the group progressively refines its picture of customer needs, which it can chart phase by phase using exit criteria.

T2: "MINI-PURPOSE" TASKS

Both the visionary and the pragmatist have a stake in defining the tasks correctly. Getting the tasks right is an early vital *task* of any business teamnet. It also is iterative, one that you need to do repeatedly.

Work translates goals into action. Action gets results. The magic comes in dividing the work—*chunking it in the right way.* When this happens, people can commit to concrete tasks. Tasks are the tangible outcome of ephemeral visions and goals.

Each task is a "mini-purpose." It is a little goal, part of the work required to reach a broader objective. Objectives themselves often are part of a larger set of goals that detail aspects of a still-broader mission. Tasks in turn break down into subtasks, as far as necessary—called, quite literally, a *work breakdown structure.*

> *Purposes translate into tasks that people collect into plans. Plans are ways of making purposes real.*

A plan is what it takes for a desired outcome. A process plan may be no more complex than a sequence of tasks in steps. Tasks represent goals, purposes, vision, and values in the work. This is how a conceptual model becomes practical. The plan stands for the vital core spirit of the group.

Never Underestimate the Importance of Lists

The "no frills" way to make a plan is to come up with a list. Even if you do nothing else, do this one step. Lists are invaluable aids to the group's memory. Just making and reviewing a list brings other things to mind. A list is also the critical first step in compiling all the tasks necessary to attaining an objective.

The key to making up a task list is to begin each item with a verb. Verbs indicate activity—create, modify, check, buy, do. Each task represents a chunk of time spent doing something.

The next step is to arrange the chunks in rough time order. For example, "Gather customer requirements" comes before "Introduce new product." At a high level, the task chunks represent a lot of work over a long time. At a detailed level—an agenda, for example—they encapsulate the precise steps the group plans to take over the next hour.

An agenda orders a group's work together. It is an excellent example of the use of task lists and is always worth the effort to put the time into a good agenda. For groups that meet only infrequently, agendas are an extremely important tool of group facilitation and ongoing integration.

Frameworks: Putting a List Into a Bigger Container

Ah, if life were only so simple that lists could do it all. As the group expands both in complexity and time, so does the common work. The group needs a bigger container than a list to hold clearly all that it has to do.

To manage complex processes, arrange your work in a *Task Framework* organized by some consistent format based on the team's purposes and context—a taxonomy. One way to create your framework is to lay out the phases of your project on the horizontal axis and the functions or people performing them on the vertical axis.

- Along the top, you have a rough timeline of major phases.
- Down the side, you have the segments of the team, e.g., people, projects, departments, divisions.

- Populate the cells with tasks, listing each once in the phase and organization where it originates.
- Indicate major steps and milestone dates above the horizontal phase axis.
- Use lists or subframeworks to detail tasks at lower levels.

Task Framework

Phases / Organization	START-UP	LAUNCH	PERFORM	TEST	DELIVER
PROJ MGMT					
MARKETING					
DESIGN			•Task A •Task B •Task C		
PRODUCTION					
SERVICE					
SALES					

The goal in early rounds of planning is to stabilize the information in the Task Framework. Add a variety of details and draw on this common database of elements to construct various models. Do not confuse the collection of tasks—the framework—with the process. A framework is only a well-organized warehouse of tasks. From it, you can construct a variety of interrelated process views.

Change is inevitable. Assume that your plans are going to be messed up. Change has impact to the degree it affects the purpose and activities and your tasks will be modified to reflect external change. By adding, modifying, and deleting tasks, you continue to use the framework to represent the common process. Use it as the basis for redrawing various work perspectives, such as schedules and deployment charts. For the technologically adept, you can use everything from a graphics tool to a simple spreadsheet to a powerful database to draw your framework.

T3: MOVING WITH THE TIMES

Task Flow

A flow diagram is a popular way to represent a project's process. Flow represents the commonsense notion that you need to finish some tasks before others start, while you can do still others in parallel. When you draw lines between boxes, you represent logical relationships of dependency between tasks over time—creating a "task dependency network."

Task Flow Diagram

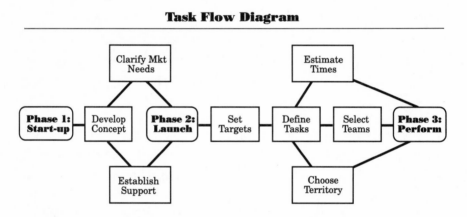

When you have only a few steps, the flow is simple and mainly linear. The more steps you add, the more complex your flow diagram becomes. You begin to see more activities going on in parallel. The connections among the tasks increase and become more varied. It doesn't take too much complexity before a computer comes in handy. Virtually any comprehensive project management software tool—desktop to mainframe—has the facility to link tasks in dependency order.

Task Schedules

Although schedules are an essential part of the planning process, too often people regard them as the only part.

Don't let the schedule drive the plan.

Many a group makes its plan by setting up tasks according to beginning and ending dates. Then it simply collects these dates together into a schedule, letting this hodgepodge serve as the de facto design of the process. Luck is a big wild card in this approach to processes. The key to success is this:

Get the plan to drive the schedule.

Schedules are the means, not the end; they are not the targets. Whether imposed by circumstance or authority, target deadlines are often not negotiable. This is not unusual. All planning takes place within constraints of opportunity, resources, and time. Given the realities, create your plan to maximize advantages, compensate for disadvantages, and take a shot at anticipating the unexpected. The best schedules result from trying combinations of these trade-offs.

To generate schedules from the work process design, add estimates of task durations to the task flow. Every task has a duration that you can express in time units. Ask your group to make its estimates in units of days, weeks, or months according to the scale of the process.

Estimate task durations quickly in the heat of planning, then refine them over time. Group success in estimating task durations depends largely on whether the people participating have sufficient knowledge and experience.

Once you have task dependencies and time estimates, you need only provide a start date, and, presto, you have a *schedule*, often depicted as a bar or Gantt chart. This combination of flow and time is powerful. It provides reality checks for the critical early iterations of planning; moreover, it sets up an infrastructure for managing the long-term process.

Gantt Chart Schedule

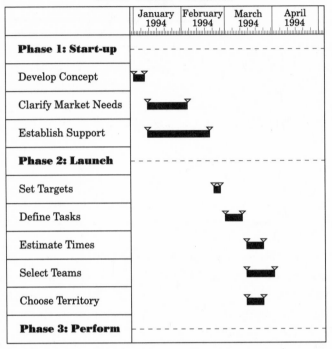

	January 1994	February 1994	March 1994	April 1994
Phase 1: Start-up				
Develop Concept				
Clarify Market Needs				
Establish Support				
Phase 2: Launch				
Set Targets				
Define Tasks				
Estimate Times				
Select Teams				
Choose Territory				
Phase 3: Perform				

When you finally run the first picture of all your tasks, complete with logical dependencies, and time estimates, expect to miss your target milestones. Rare is the group that accurately hits its dates on the first pass. Still, the off-by-a-long-shot exercise plays an important role: it prompts a review of all assumptions—from targets to times to a redesigned process flow. This generates new ideas and eventually a new schedule, which should be closer to your desired outcome, but most likely still will not hit the target.

Experience, patience, and need dictate how many iterations you require for the group to feel that its work is well in hand. Remember: The objective is to make a plan understandable and tangible. It is not a perfect and legally binding document that you're looking for. Rather, it is something that all the key members and process players buy into. The more you involve the team in making these trade-offs, the easier it is to achieve jointly agreed-upon results.

Shared team planning provides vital preparation for the negotiations over real money and resources that unfold during the team's performance.

T4: TRACKING TEAMS

When business archaeologists go digging in our era's midst, they will find cross-boundary charts sorely lacking in Western business practices. They are a critical missing ingredient in the project management repertoire, the absence of which throws everything else askew. Without an alternative way to view interdependencies, people revert to the old, familiar hierarchical organization chart, rarely adequate to display relationships among the parts of a teamnet.

The complexity of tasks is well known. Charts of task logic and task durations are typical features of project planning methods and supporting computer software. However, people do not understand the complexity of teams so well. The gaping hole comes in the management of people.

Cross-Boundary Chart

A teamnet, no matter how small, does its real work in even smaller subgroups—in ones, twos, and threes. Boundary crossing tasks by definition often involve more than one member of the team. Only occasionally, however, does everyone need to be involved all at once.

Participation is both the strength and the Achilles' heel of teamnets. Once the idea catches on, everybody soon thinks they do need to be involved in everything. An everybody-in-everything teamnet of any size soon bogs down, eventually collapsing in confusion. In reality, different people need to work together in different subgroups on different tasks. Horizontal communication is essential. The answer:

Display the subgroup links by tasks so that everyone can understand them.

Toyota Motor Company faced this problem in the early 1960s. Groups had to know what each other was doing because of their interdependencies. To manage, over the past three decades Toyota perfected cross-functional management and invented the cross-functional deployment chart. This is a cross-boundary teamnet chart.

Creating a cross-boundary chart is quite straightforward. Array the names of the people on your team (or the functions they represent) along the horizontal axis. List the tasks down the vertical axis in time order. Indicate which team members or functions the group needs to involve in a given task. Teams form where tasks meet people, the lowest common denominator of teamnet work.

Task teams ideally involve the most effective people in the most efficient way. They are a terrific source of leadership. Each task provides an opportunity for someone to take and/or share responsibility. A cross-boundary chart shows who's involved in what.

The best way to create a chart is with the parties involved. Write your tasks in order on a big white sheet and tape it up in front of the group. List people or functions across the top. Point to the first task and ask the group, "Who will be involved in this task?" Indicate responses by putting X's in the people columns. Circle the member(s) responsible for results. The development of such a chart is a powerful tool for surfacing collaborative opportunities and resolving problems, such as turf and resource conflicts.

Cross-Boundary Teamnet Flow Chart

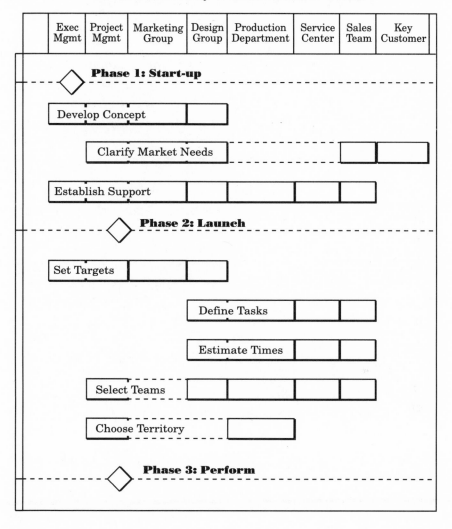

Capture the Learning

Learning is a major problem for modern organizations. Few know how to capture the experience generated by all the ad hoc teams and networks that increasingly populate the business world.

One way to capture group learning is to keep a simple, structured record of a process as it unfolds. This gives the next team that tackles something similar a place to start—a template. Templates are records of experience that you can adapt to new circumstances—not bureaucratic doctrines to follow slavishly. They are an effective way to encode an organization's learning into its business practices without making it a separate bureaucratic function.

It is said that Toyota has 2,000 cross-boundary process templates in use. The company, well known for its world-class business processes, regards these templates as a vital corporate resource and a secret of its success. While you can create serviceable simple charts by hand, TeamFlow, a computer software tool, makes the production of these cross-boundary process pictures easy.[2]

T5: NEW TERRITORIES

Do You Have Your Directory?

Every successful boundary crossing group—every teamnet, every network, every distributed organization—every one starts with a directory. At first, it may be no more than a sign-up sheet from initial meetings. As the group grows, people quite naturally create distribution lists, name and address handouts, and, finally, a directory of members and resources.

A basic teamnet function is keeping track of people and organizations involved. Transform a list of participants into a directory and you have a powerful tool.

Make a formal, researched, printed, and distributed directory the first project of your teamnet. Such a project serves two ends: people get to know one another better, and it gives outsiders a handle on who's involved.

For some teamnets, directories set their boundaries, by distinguishing "insiders" from "outsiders." Some directories also serve as marketing documents. The people listed announce their combined capabilities to the world, giving potential customers a direct line to accessing the best resource to meet their needs.

Directories answer the two most basic questions about members: who and where. People are pointers to places, represented by addresses. Indeed, people point to many places; a person may have home and work mail addresses, a variety of phone, fax, and voice mail numbers, and a host of on-line addresses.

The Team Bible: The Handbook

One team member patted it. "Have you seen our handbook?" Another clutched it. Still another always kept it in her briefcase. People love few objects as much as a new "Teamnet Handbook."

Since boundary crossing teamnets usually have no specific place to call home, you need to compensate. Unlike hierarchical organizations with their corporate headquarters and centralized offices and workplaces, the teamnet is spread out. No matter how distended, every group needs a place to call home. The more distributed the people, the more the group needs another "sense of place."

In the early stages, pull together a handbook to create a simple "place" for your teamnet. Begin by gathering shared information, key memos, and other ideas generated by the group and its members' activities. You don't need desktop publishing to do your team's handbook: scissors, tape, and a copier will usually suffice for early versions.

To expand your handbook, include directories, glossaries, and bibliographies as standard sections. Retain the output from the Launch planning process—from mission statements to schedules. Gather agendas, meeting notes, and action item lists to form the early bulk of a teamnet's joint work. For the rest of the handbook, include selections of key documents, diagrams, and other essential elements that help people keep track of the emerging big picture.

At its best, a handbook is both a map and a resource for the team. It helps capture the learning of the group in process. It is a resource for decision making, providing briefing material for external stakeholders, including customers, suppliers, and the hierarchy. It helps bring newcomers up-to-speed quickly, and provides a record for improving future teams or new cycles of the same process.

To capture your learning, build your information capture system into your process from the beginning. Make the record a natural part of the work. This is useful for the ongoing monitoring, managing, and testing of the immediate process, but additionally of value for the future. After-the-fact documentation is expensive, laborious, and rarely a top priority.

Planning and Managing by Tasks

COMMON PROCESS, MULTIPLE VIEWS

To create different models of your process, you need to have a common way to identify the tasks. Give each task, each minipurpose, its own code. In this way, you can follow each task, with its attributes such as dependencies, time, costs, people responsible, and deliverables, in a variety of models.

Track change—which is inevitable, expected, and continuous in development processes—through tasks. Reflect change by adding, deleting, and modifying tasks and their attributes. Review the effect of change with the team, using each process view— dependencies, time, and teams. Each view offers a different picture of a common process. People find one or another view to be more germane to their part of the whole process, depending on their roles, responsibilities, and learning styles.

The "Concurrent Cube" metaphorically integrates these three

Concurrent Cube— Team, Task, and Time

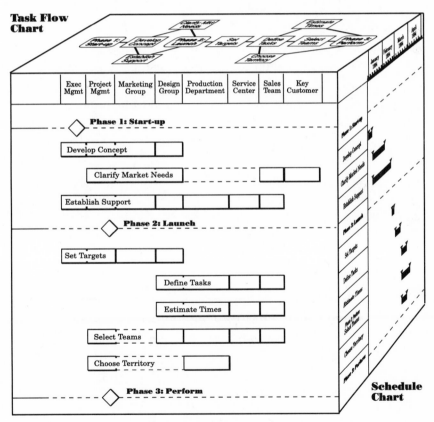

Team Flow Chart

design elements as a common process. Task dependency, time, and teams are the "three faces of concurrency." Change in one dimension affects the picture in others.

THREADING TASKS THROUGH TOOLS

Tasks thread through the tools:

- *Purpose* is the source of work. It expands into
- *Tasks* that are common to a variety of process views. A shared set of tasks is a
- *List*, or a *framework* organized by principles. Arrange the tasks according to their logical relationships to generate a
- *Task flow*. Add time estimates to derive a
- *Schedule* that gives estimated start and finish dates to every task. Then arrange tasks in a
- *Cross-boundary team chart*, according to organizational responsibilities, roles, and dependencies.

The Launch plan sets up an information system for managing later phases. In this way, monitoring is a natural continuation of planning. The data you get from operations greatly facilitate continuous planning, adapting, and reforecasting.

Work process design links planning with program management through its focus on tasks. Program management requires the same essential planning elements: tasks, people, times, and places.

Our Target Method works with existing application software tools. But don't be intimidated by the tools. The concepts are more basic.

Those That Do, Plan: Bringing Discipline to Teamnets

Task-Tool Thread

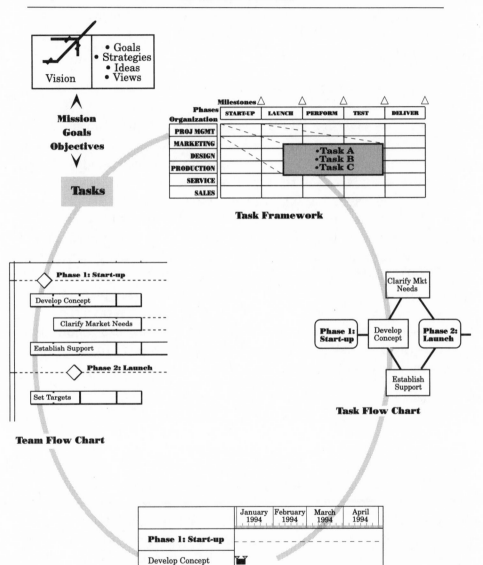

Task Framework

Team Flow Chart

Task Flow Chart

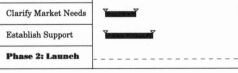

Schedule Chart

For the most part, you can use the ideas on a manual basis in most everyday situations. However, when "big" and "complex" describe your project, computer tools can help a lot.

WORK PROCESS FLOW-DOWN

Work process design (WPD) scales from very small to very large organizations. When most successful, it flows down from the top leadership. The initial high-level planning effort cascades to the next level and so on until it involves all levels of the organization. This is one way hierarchies can learn to network.

As the process unfolds, each level's initial WPD results become the goals, targets, and guidelines for the work process of the next level down. Tasks, along with their associated timing and costs, established at one level become processes and parameters at the next level.

Involve two or more levels of organization in each planning session. In this way, members both buy into and understand the work process requirements at the broader level. They also acquire the experience and skill in WPD that they can then carry to their group as they do the planning at the next level down.

In reality, all levels plan simultaneously, with as much information and influence coming bottom-up as top-down.

Each level plans its own work. Overall purpose, strategy, and targets must come from the top as early as possible. Such clear direction provides a context for all levels of planning. By early and systematic initial scoping plans, you use the first few iterations to sort out the major elements of the plan across the levels.

Some Planning Guidelines

THOSE THAT DO, PLAN

The process of integrating work requires both participation and successive iteration. Those who are going to do the work must plan the work. This process is human interaction-intensive, not technology-intensive.

"Those that do, plan." It's almost a commandment when it comes to successful development of boundary crossing projects. It is not the plan but the *planning* that is the most valuable outcome for a teamnet. Distributed groups depend on their shared views of the work. The best way to understand the common view is to be part of its creation and development.

RULES FOR NOT GETTING STUCK

Some basic rules of work process design and quality help avert the danger of getting stuck in detail that can cause a planning process to go amok or grind to a halt.

1. Plan, Plan, Plan . . . But Only as Necessary

Create minimal but sufficient rules. This original sociotech admonishment heads the list of rules for organizational design. Planning is essential, but good enough is usually good enough. Especially for now.

2. Iterate, Iterate

Get the big picture early and quickly; fill it in later. Start by roughing things out. Make adjustments when the elements are the most fluid. Don't get hung up on completeness and perfection. Processes become increasingly rigid as they mature. Iterate to improve. Learn what's highly leveraged and what's not, then focus on the critical few elements.

3. The 80/20 Rule

Concentrate on a few important things. Attributed to Joseph Juran, one of the quality movement's founders, it means that 80 percent of the trouble comes from 20 percent of the problems, that you can do 80 percent of the job with 20 percent of the effort. It is also known as the Pareto Principle after a simple technique for displaying variants in rank order, so it is easy to pick out critical problems.

4. The 85/15 Rule

If you blame the system, you're probably right. This is the rule that puts blame where it belongs: on the system, more often the source of "the problem" than people. This second Juran rule summarizes decades of evidence: on average, more than 85 percent of mistakes and errors come from the work system, with only 15 percent or fewer being under the individual worker's control.

———

The best principles, guidelines, and tools are never enough. The real world always puts a twist on the tried-and-true. Failure, which shepherds our way toward greater understanding of how people can effectively organize, is the subject of "Rascals in Paradise," the next chapter.

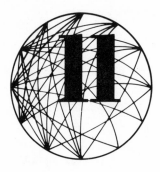

Rascals in Paradise:
Why Teamnets Fail

Known as the "Island of the Holy Spirit" to the Spaniards who landed here in the 16th century, Andros is the largest of the islands in the Bahamas, and a happy destination as we approach it by sailboat in March 1974. We have been sailing for a week now aboard *Atria*, a tiny "31-and-a-half-foot" *Golden Hind* sloop, as its captain, Jim Stamps (father and father-in-law), always describes it. Jim has been aboard for three years, in pursuit of what he calls "the world's *longest* circumnavigation," a record that he well may hold when he eventually moves ashore again after 12 years. *Atria* is the lowest star in the Southern Hemisphere sky and Jim has gone in search of it.

We are eager to reach Andros, where we will go ashore for a meal, and meet up with friends to dive on Andros's legendary Barrier Reef, the third largest in the world. A group of Seminole Indians, runaway slaves from the Florida Everglades, settled Andros in the mid-19th century and until recently it has remained something of a secret. Far enough from Nassau, with little on it for tourists, it is an island paradise, according to the guidebooks.

The Andros Town Hotel, "luxurious gleaming white," the guide-book says, has water and fuel, the only place they are available on the island. So we head for the hotel with near-empty tanks and the vision of tropical luxury in our minds. In passing, we note the warnings of a rare mosquito present only on Andros, and the presence of chickcharnies, the Bahamian version of leprechauns, who can also be mean-spirited to visitors.

In the distance, the hotel appears, a brilliant stark white loveliness against the blue-green sea, not just a single building but a cluster of small, interconnected stucco structures. However, as we approach the dock, all is not as it first appears. There are no boats at the dock, which is falling apart, and no people to be seen. With its broken windows and its front door hanging by a hinge, the hotel is a sorry sight. An abandoned rusted-out Cadillac sits on its rims in the driveway.

Then, out of nowhere, the insects attack. A huge swarm of invisible, vicious bugs assaults us. A more evolutionarily sophisticated version of New England's spring blackflies, each unexpected bite packs the wallop of a small electrical shock. Within a few seconds, we are human feeding grounds for some of the most savage insects imaginable. Neither swatting, cursing, nor insect repellent drives them away.

"Rascals in paradise," Jim says, by way of explaining the sudden onslaught of these evil little creatures. "Just when you think things are perfect, there's always some little horrible thing to mess it up." Not the world's most loquacious man, Jim finds the precise phrase for this horrendous experience.

Rascals in paradise. Ever since our Andros odyssey, we've found Jim's principle at work in many domains, especially teamnets. Far from idyllic organizational utopias, where things always go right, people enthusiastically concur forever, and resources are never constrained, teamnets play host to many rascals in paradise. It is in the nature of life. While we could not escape the "chickcharnies" of Andros, we can warn you about some of the rascals of teamnets.

Public Triumph, Personal Failure

Failure is easier to write about than to live through. Eighteen years later, we are sitting in the Gum Tree Tea Garden at The Rocks, Sydney's tasteful harbor renewal project, drinking cappuccino, more popular than coffee Down Under, talking about things not going right.

It's a fitting spot to think about failure along with its opposite, success. The Tea Garden is just across Circular Quay—the main hub of the city's extensive ferry transportation network—from Australia's astonishing contribution to late-20th-century architecture, the Sydney Opera House.

For two decades, mystery has surrounded this spectacular building, ever since its architect, Jørn Utzon, a Dane, abruptly left the project before finishing it. Incredibly, although millions of people from all over the world have visited the Opera House, Utzon himself has never seen it completed in person. Until now, he has remained silent since his hasty departure.

In October 1992, as the Opera House's 20th-year celebration begins, the architect breaks his silence. In his interview with the *Sydney Morning Herald*, he explains what inspired his unusual design *and* why he left the project. For years, people have believed that Utzon's inspiration for the building's design was the ubiquitous billowing sails in Sydney Harbor. They are wrong, he says. An orange, peeled into sections, was the wellspring of his innovative architecture. From orange peels (which embody enclosure), the sails evolved.

The reason he left the project suddenly, he remembers, was bureaucratic hassles. A publicly funded effort, the Opera House was significantly over budget and behind schedule when a new bureaucrat took charge just as the exterior was being completed. He withheld payment to Utzon, and soon the "Great Dane," as he was known in Sydney society, was unable to pay his employees. With no resolution in sight, Utzon finally packed up his family and returned to Denmark.

Although he went on to many more years as a successful architect in traditional terms, Utzon says no project in his career has rivaled the Sydney Opera House. The Opera House put Sydney—and even the all too unknown continent-country of Australia—on the global map. An extraordinary triumph for the world, in many ways it was a terrible personal defeat for its designer. The bureaucrat and other critics were Utzon's rascals in paradise at his moment of greatest success.

Failures of Process

Is failure the opposite of success? Are outcomes *either* successes *or* failures? Rarely. Have you ever worked on a project that was an unqualified success? Frankly, we have not. Although we can hardly claim title to anything as prominent as Utzon's transformation of Sydney's waterscape, we have worked on projects with considerable reach. In one way or another, most have failed in some respect. From a distance, others would describe few as such, but when *we* scrutinize them closely, we see the failure parts more easily than the success parts. Such is the price for learning on the job.

Since most projects and most teamnet efforts—including the most successful ones—fail in one way or another, we devote the following pages to failure. Teamnets often fail for clear reasons that are preventable. Use failure detection in your own personal experience as a powerful analytic tool. Of course, with every improvement, you will see how you can do better.

Perhaps the most predictable failures occur at the natural stress points in the process of teamnet development, transition phases we call "Launch" and "Test" in earlier chapters. While most change artists know about and anticipate the chaotic, sometimes angry launch period before takeoff, Utzon fell victim to the less well-known stress point in the second transition between the hardest work period and the end point of completion and stability.

While we can give guidebook indications of some of the known rascals in teamnet paradise, they are just words on the page until you live them. What follows is a blow-by-blow description of the ups and downs experienced by one teamnet going through its launch transition.

Living the Zigzags

The transportation industry is in rough shape, a harsh reality that passengers and dispatchers live with daily. Moving people and goods depends on being able to offer sensible times at the right locations with good connections. The basic product of a shipper, railroad, bus company, or airline, then, is its schedule.

After years of preparing its schedule in the same way—as a function of the marketing group at headquarters, a $6 billion international transportation company, TransOceania,[1] decides to take a new approach. The second oldest transportation company in the world, TransOceania, based in Hong Kong, has 14,000 employees in 65 countries. It hires Pointer Associates, one of the premier international "business process redesign" consulting firms, to "reengineer" how it does its schedules. Business process redesign is more than the buzzwords its title suggests: it is the path by which a company looks at how it performs its core processes, then redesigns them so that they work better—much better.

We are unfamiliar with TransOceania's schedule problem until the telephone rings one day. Henrik, a senior officer at Pointer Associates, is calling to ask about our availability for a project. Pointer has been working with TransOceania for the past several months on a schedule project, he explains. Jointly, the TransOceania team and the Pointer consultants have come to this conclusion: to plan their schedules more efficiently, they will need to develop a cross-functional network.

The proposed network will use its companywide expertise to evaluate schedule suggestions from the field. The regional offices, situated on every continent and in several dozen countries, are both close to the customer and to the operations people—those who must work with ports, unions, governments, and the myriad suppliers involved in every departure and arrival. He calls the project TSP—Transportation Schedule Project.

Henrik tells us that the new process will reduce duplication of effort, increase asset utilization, shorten schedule preparation cycle time, and enhance revenue potential. Not only that, both Trans-Oceania's chairman and the CEO support the program, along with its four senior vice president sponsors. Even so, there are significant barriers to success: TransOceania, like all its competitors, is downsizing. Caskers and Longquist, one of the leading head-cutting firms, is working at TransOceania at the same time, reducing head count by the standard 20 percent.

BEWARE THE CHICKCHARNIES

The Transportation Schedule Project team is in the process of wrapping up the first stage of the project when we get involved. They will present their findings and recommendations to the sponsors in a few weeks to seek approval for the project's next stage. Our role at the end of Phase 1 is to educate TransOceania's executives and the TSP team about networked organizations. Then, in Phase 2, we will help the group design and launch its teamnet.

Anthony, the on-the-ground manager from Pointer, and his consulting colleagues have done an excellent job of helping Trans-Oceania develop its own solution to its problem. The TSP team is enthusiastic; the sponsors are receptive; and the project is rolling along.

They complete Phase 1 without a hitch. Except for the general pall surrounding all companies under downsizing, it appears to be a relatively problem-free assignment. A few weeks later, we receive word that the project has its go-ahead from TransOceania's Board of Directors to move from concept phase into launch.

Then, without warning, TSP's rascals in paradise start biting. Within less than a month's time, TSP zigzags through a series of barriers and crises that can befall any new teamnet effort.

Things begin to go awry when, after four continuous months of work, team members take a week's vacation. Cameron, on temporary assignment as TSP's project manager, returns to discover that his boss has given Cameron's full-time job to someone else. Without notice, he's lost his title, his office, and his secretary. Cameron is so depressed that sometimes it's even hard to hear what he's saying.

A few days later, Robert, the vice president who will have the budget for the project's next phase, calls Cameron, Anthony, the consultant from Pointer, and Stephanie, the team's strategic planner, to a meeting. "I'm uncomfortable with 95 percent of the plan," he tells them. Robert particularly objects to the information technology investment, key to reducing the project's cycle time, and asks the team to present an entirely new plan within a week. In the same meeting, he volunteers that he has no budget for the project, the same ambitious plan that the Board of Directors approved a month earlier. Now Cameron, Anthony, and Stephanie all are concerned.

It is these three dejected people who meet us for dinner when we arrive for the second time, expecting to begin work on Phase 2 of TSP. Instead of beginning the next morning to help them design their teamnet, we find ourselves in the midst of a battle for the project's survival.

Day 1—Monday: Down

Unlike our previous visit when the team arrives early for our session, eager to begin, today people straggle in. They are angry that the sponsor is changing the rules and discouraged. Stephanie, in particular, is furious. "We've got to fight this. If we're going under, I want to go down with guns blazing," she says, expressing her determination to fight.

Everyone on the team knows the project is vital to the company, but people are unclear how to proceed. After lengthy discussion, David, a marketing expert who has just joined the team, suggests that they make lists representing the costs and benefits of the project as they appear to each sponsor: What does Robert want from the project? How do he and each of the other three sponsors stand to benefit? What does each fear? Within a short time, they cover the walls with big white sheets of paper—and a rather astute analysis of the power politics at the top of TransOceania.

Then Cameron goes on the offensive. "Don't we have some questions for the sponsors?" he asks. The team decides to ask for clarification of several issues. They brainstorm a list of very specific questions and fax it to the sponsors, requesting a response the following day.

Day 2—Tuesday: Down, Then Up

Unfortunately, the day begins with no response from the sponsors. Richard, the team's information technology expert, suggests that they turn their attention to developing an alternative plan that will please Robert, the budget-holding VP. The team's members have 24 hours to work through the alternatives, before their next sponsors' meeting scheduled for the following day.

The team breaks out into subgroups. Cameron leads consideration of the alternative Robert requested: Option 1 includes no information technology investment. Meanwhile, the other subgroups work through other options, with Richard and Stephanie leading the other two groups. When the whole team reconvenes at the end of the day, they settle on one option as their recommendation, one that will deliver benefits sooner and be less expensive in the long run. It is an alternative to the plan they proposed a month earlier. The team decides to brief each of the sponsoring VPs on its progress before the meeting. Cameron will see Robert, Richard will see Johann, the most sympathetic of the sponsors, Stephanie will see Ned, the newest of the sponsors, and David will brief Neville, the sponsor whose organization will experience the most impact from a change in schedule planning.

Day 3—Wednesday: Some Up, Mostly Down

It is the day of the sponsors' meeting. Set to be an hour long, it goes on for more than three. When it is over, the team invites us to their debriefing in the company's Situation Room. This is the place the executives go in case of an emergency—each seat has a telephone in front of it. The debriefing is not an uplifting experience. Now everyone on the team is very depressed. Yet another sponsor, this time Neville, has expressed reluctance about the project. Although the sponsors agree that two of the options are not viable, they are only lukewarm about the third. Instead of commending the team for all their hard work, they ask them to do more: flesh out their recommended strategy before meeting with them again the following Monday.

Later that evening, the Pointer consultants meet with Johann. He lets them know that the project is in peril of being canceled the following week. The company just has "too much on its plate" at the moment, what with downsizing, the unexpected departure of some senior officers, and falling revenues.

Day 4—Thursday: Up

Even though everyone is down, the day begins with a brilliant idea! For years, TransOceania has been trying to "fix Africa," perceived as a boom market for the only transportation company that serves it directly from Asia. To date, no one has been able to figure out how to develop a robust schedule for the continent. James, the team's member from the sales group, suggests that TSP use Africa as its pilot. If TSP can "fix Africa" with its new schedule planning process, it will instantly demonstrate its value to the company in very palpable terms. Thus, "Project Africa" is born.

Finally, we can get to work in earnest. We lead the team through the process of laying out its basic tasks, estimating how long each will take, and deciding who needs to participate. The team agrees to test-market Project Africa with each of the VP sponsors overnight.

Day 5—Friday: Very Up

Today is the day to determine whether Project Africa is feasible. The first iteration indicates the magnitude of the effort. Looking at the project plan generated the day before, Stephanie says, "Instead of being a smaller project, Project Africa in fact raises the stakes. Even though it will take somewhat longer to 'fix Africa' and cost more at the beginning, it will also deliver benefits sooner and cost less overall than the original plan." Everyone agrees with her that the pilot itself offers a high payback for the company.

By the end of the day, the team has all the documentation it needs to back up its case: a complete Project Africa plan, including a critical path diagram of tasks, a sequenced list of deliverables, a cross-functional team chart, names of representatives from each of the organizations involved, and a schedule. It is Anthony's birthday and the team takes time to celebrate. By the end of the day, reports come back from testing the Project Africa idea with the sponsors: all appear supportive.

Day 6—Monday: Very Down

The day begins with a one-hour meeting with two of the sponsors—Johann, who is generally supportive, and Robert, who still is not. Cameron, still smarting from having lost his job while on vacation, leads the meeting but fails to communicate the new plan effectively. All the sponsors can see is that this is a bigger project. Why does Project Africa take so long and involve so many people? They want more details by Wednesday, before a "final" meeting with all the sponsors on Thursday.

The team is more depressed than ever, but this time they refuse to talk about it directly. They break into subgroups, each going its separate ways to address the sponsors' concerns. Even the consultants meet separately. Together, we run through a set of critical success factors required for big changes in organizations. Our reluctant conclusion is that not enough are in place for TSP to be successful at this time.

Day 7—Tuesday: Down, but Getting Up

To be ready for the next sponsors' meeting, the team needs to fill out the project plan. However, only a few people are on time for the meeting. Before getting down to work, they talk honestly about what they couldn't address the day before. Stephanie opens the discussion with a brutally honest assessment of the team's problems and prospects. It's a very tough conversation, but everyone agrees with her that this is the decisive moment. If they are to succeed, they will have to reshape their strategy relative to the sponsors. Collectively, they decide that the sponsors' meeting the next day is an artificial deadline that will impede the work required for the final meeting. So they do something they've never done before. They cancel the sponsors' meeting; instead, the team invites the sponsors to come help finish their plan for the Thursday meeting. That afternoon, the team works out the next level of detail on Project Africa. By the end of the day, everyone is reenergized and engaged.

Day 8—Wednesday: Up, Way Down, Up Again

Today, planning goes on at a breathtaking pace. The group fills out Project Africa on a week-by-week basis over the next three months. Then, Anthony suggests that they develop a list of minimal criteria required to go forward with the project. Everyone thinks this is a great idea. Just as the sponsors set conditions, so now does the team.

No sooner have they set the criteria than Neville, one of the sponsors, shows up unexpectedly. "I've had a chance to think about Project Africa. I am completely against it and won't allow any of my regional people to participate," he tells a shocked team, then leaves. At the same time, Johann and Robert walk through the door. No one knows quite how to proceed. Cameron decides to press on and attempts to present the team's conditions for going forward, but falters. The team is infuriated. Anthony suggests a break to cool off. After much hallway discussion in twos and threes, the team reconvenes with Johann and Robert. Johann gives a short speech commending the team for its exceptional work. And then a miracle happens! Robert, who has been nothing but a roadblock for the past two weeks, suddenly becomes a believer. He agrees to present the team's criteria for going ahead at the sponsors' meeting the next day. With Johann and the team, he stays to finish the slides for the presentation.

Day 9—Thursday: Up Presentation, Down Decision

It's the day of the senior executive sponsors' meeting. The team performs magnificently. They present their case for the network and its pilot, Project Africa. Everyone agrees that the plan is good. Now, the issue becomes a strategic one: Is this the right time for the project to go forward? The four sponsors disagree among themselves and decide that they have to take the matter to the CEO. They finally meet with him late in the day and he makes his decision: right project, wrong time—he officially defers the TSP project for six months. The team, assembled awaiting the outcome, disbands within moments of hearing the news.

Day 10—Friday: Strangely Up, but Facing a Big Down

Uncharacteristically, the team gathers promptly in the morning. Amidst much debriefing, they decide to package their learning into what they call their "time capsule." In it, TSP members place their detailed project plan, the notebook compilations of their six months' worth of work, and their final presentation. Then they decide to honor Johann, the vice president who most consistently stood behind them. Within a few hours, they organize a party and buy a pen for him, engraved with the words, "Sponsor of the Year." At the party, he voices his "total commitment" to the project, congratulates the team on its excellent work, and acknowledges that the company has made its decision for the right reasons—strategic ones—rather than the wrong—political—ones.

For the team, corporate strategy and external factors over which they have no control are the rascals in paradise. While the content of the project is superior, its timing is premature. By most of its measures, TSP is a success. To the members of the team, however, the overwhelming feeling is one of failure. But not for long. A month later, we receive a long letter from Stephanie, detailing the team's progress during the official period of deferment. In spite of the obstacles, the team remains determined to bring a new transportation schedule planning process to their company.

Five Good Ways to Fail

TransOceania's Transportation Schedule Project is not alone. Most teamnets fail to get off the ground, as most new businesses fail—and for many of the same reasons, including lack of resources, commitments, and luck.

The essence of networking is to keep a dynamic balance between complementary and opposing tendencies. Thus, we can trace many failures to a significant lack or excess regarding one or another of the Five Teamnet Principles.

1. PURPOSE: FROM NO GLUE TO GROUPTHINK

While the TSP team is able to maintain a clear view of its purpose ("to increase profits by redesigning the way the company plans its schedules"), TransOceania the company loses sight of it because the context changes. In just the few months since the beginning of the project, the company becomes involved in a merger and a major downsizing. Perceived short-term needs push long-term benefits aside.

- Without a constantly revisited clear purpose, teamnets collapse. Most teams don't spend nearly enough time talking about it. "I don't have time for that touchy-feely stuff. We have too much work to do," one marketing manager says to us, refusing to participate in the purpose-setting sessions of a new project. So he leaves, convinced that he is doing "real work" while the team is not. Within a few weeks, he is so out of touch with the group that the project manager replaces him.

- On the other hand, too much uncritical agreement and obsession with purpose leads to *groupthink*. This phenomenon, first chronicled with regard to John F. Kennedy's mishandling of the Cuban Bay of Pigs crisis,[2] occurs when people's desire to agree with the group is so great that they do not question truly inappropriate decisions. If everyone must agree on everything to work together, beware—this is a clear sign of purpose gone amok.

2. MEMBERS: FROM NO INDEPENDENCE TO STUBBORNNESS

In many internal teams like TransOceania's in which people come from different parts of the same company, members don't have the autonomy that they need to survive independently. Lacking sufficient autonomy, the team itself never acquires an independent status. External alliances sometimes diminish the independence of the members, perhaps unintentionally through favored relationships that distort market realities.

The most difficult thing for many people is to give up control in favor of influence. The higher you go in the organization, the more difficult this struggle becomes. Executive teams can have the most trouble relinquishing direct control.

- A teamnet cannot function without substantial autonomy. Both the teamnet and its members must be able to stand on their own. If it is just another group that fits neatly into the hierarchy, the teamnet cannot take advantage of the power of voluntary commitments and market mechanisms.
- Alternatively, if the virtues of independence and go-it-alone bravado so consume teamnet members that they overwhelm

opportunities for mutual benefit, teamnets fail. Either they never form or they stagnate in a perpetual state of disintegration, functioning poorly. The dependence-independence-interdependence balance is very tricky.

3. LINKS: FROM NO CONNECTIONS TO OVERLOAD

When the hierarchy appoints all members of the team, relationships tend not to be voluntary. Without open access to information, trust is difficult to establish and maintain.

- Communication is key to teamnet success, and information access is critical to meaningful communication. Voluntary relationships cannot form if members don't have enough information. Nor will the group jell if the information they have is not reliable. Likewise, if they have no easy way to reach one another—meetings are too sparse or communication systems are inadequate—the teamnet will not crystallize.
- The reverse situation also causes teamnets to fail: too much communication, too much information, too much interaction—overload. If all the teamnet does is talk to itself, it will implode from self-induced stress. In the past decade, numerous software companies have introduced products that supposedly "enhance" group communication. Many fail because the overhead of keeping up with the torrent of information swamps the participants.

4. LEADERS: FROM NO LEADERS TO NO FOLLOWERS

Hierarchies and bureaucracies are crumbling because one person can no longer handle it all. Teamnets succeed when they elevate more than one leader. In our experience, many teamnets fail in this transition from the initial spark plug to broader leadership. Some corporate cultures facilitate leadership development while others discourage it. In a culture of high control, middle management does not step forward for fear of making mistakes. The earlier multiple leaders assume position, the more successful the teamnet.

Leadership can expand everywhere, even in the most visible hierarchies in business and government. In a departure from traditional U.S. chief executive style, Bill Clinton and Al Gore positioned themselves in the 1992 campaign as teammates. Here, they take a page from modern business practice, where three times the number of executives share top corporate positions as they did 30 years ago.

- Groups are often short on leaders through no fault of their own. Appointed leaders tend to crowd out and discourage emergence of natural leaders. If you subdivide the work so that only one person rather than a subgroup can do it, then there are fewer opportunities for leadership.
- Is there such a thing as too much leadership? Indeed, old canards like "Too many cooks spoil the broth" point to the obvious problem of everybody's getting an oar in and rowing in different directions. Teamnet leadership also includes followership; good leaders know when to step down or aside as well as up.

5. LEVELS: FROM NO UPLINKS TO NO DOWNLINKS

Many internal teams fail to manage up. At TransOceania, the whole team goes down a notch in status when the hierarchy takes away the project leader's official job. Direct participation by the formal hierarchy in change projects all too often erodes as executives receive more urgent assignments. The entire teamnet needs to manage up across the entire organization. One easy way to ensure that this happens is to use the buddy system—pair up each person on the team with a senior executive.

- When a teamnet neglects to manage up, it fails, an all too prevalent problem. The group gets so caught up in what it is doing that it ignores keeping its superiors closely informed. Or it fears it. "We can't send that to the Board of Directors," a project manager says in horror to us one day. He is referring to the plan for the very large project we are working on together. At every point that he can supply information, he chooses not to keep the Board in the loop. When he finally goes to the Board for after-the-fact approval, they turn him down, saying they don't know enough to commit the company to the project.

• It's as important to stay in touch with the "lower-archy" as it is the hierarchy. When a teamnet fails to manage down, it runs the risk of losing touch with the organization as a whole. External teams often find it difficult to manage the expectations and commitments of their respective internal groups or constituencies.

Avoid failure by keeping the Five Teamnet Principles in plain view at all times. Constantly revisit purpose; use it as a conversation starter to test its currency. Maintain the independence of the members; it is what makes them viable. Invest in communications, both in terms of personal relationships and physical communication systems. Reward multiple leadership; it enables the teamnet to accomplish more work more quickly. Finally, keep the teamnet plugged in at all levels of the hierarchy.

Once these principles become ingrained in your mind, you need to make them part of your daily business practice. It's critical that everyone:

Walk the teamnet talk.

"Transforming Bureaucracies and Systems," the Reference Section, contains more detail on how particular types of teamnets fail. In "Fighting Fire with Organization," the next chapter, we provide clues on how to overcome the obstacles that organizational boundaries present.

Fighting Fire with Organization: Summing It All Up

Command, Control, and Prevention

Right down the street from you, a single organization uses hierarchy, bureaucracy, and networks to accomplish different but interrelated purposes: the local fire department.[1]

- When it fights fires, the fire department is a strict, military *hierarchy*. In crisis, a well-trained unit follows a chain of command. The chief calls the shots. For this purpose, hierarchy is the optimal organization. There is no time to build consensus or work through issues when a blaze is burning out of control.
- When it inspects buildings, the fire department is a typical *bureaucracy*. Administratively, its concern is with building inspections, codes, violations, water mains, and all other laws and policies surrounding the control of fires.

- When it works to prevent fires, the fire department acts as a *network*. Fire department personnel work with other community organizations—media, volunteer groups, schools, hospitals, and even Brownie troops—to spread fire safety information tailored to the specific problems of that locality.

Fire departments also *network* at the community-to-community level. Although fire-fighting units are hierarchical, departments come together as equals in regional "mutual aid" associations. So, if one community has a very bad fire, other surrounding departments send direct aid. Meanwhile, departments on the periphery close ranks to fill in gaps left by departments responding closer.

As with other organizations, fire departments and professionals also form peer-to-peer associations at the state and national levels, *networking* to exchange information and influence policy changes—analogous to the voluntary grass-roots associations dedicated to the environment, consumer rights, and the like. Just as a fire chief cannot order you to be "fire safe," a public education fire prevention team cannot put out a five-alarm blaze with Dick Van Dyke's famous "Stop, Drop, and Roll" commercials from the 1970s.

Fire departments, found in most communities throughout the world, show the three basic forms of organization: hierarchical fire fighting; bureaucratic code enforcement; and peer-based networks of prevention, professions, and mutual aid. Complex organizations today—whether voluntary, business, or government—use all these forms of organization.

Many businesses fail because of their inability to use the right form for the right purpose.

Today's new forms grow from yesterday's. We know, of course, that a "pure" network is hard to find at any level. No one form of organization is right for every part of an organization—not even a family.

Networks, new organizational life-forms emerging at every level, are not fads. They thrive now because traditional hierarchies and bureaucracies cannot adequately cope. The complexity of doing business today in a global economy—which affects everyone from the corner grocer to the globe-spanning multinational—goes beyond traditional organizational capabilities.

Teamnets, Teamnets, Teamnets Everywhere

Boundary crossing teamnets are ubiquitous in business, sharing common characteristics.

Up and Down the Scale

People working in small groups routinely cross boundaries that separate functional expertise domains and command chains. Enterprises struggle to realign work across internal organizational walls. Companies form alliances across the most fortified boundaries of all in business—the enterprise borders.

Size

All sizes of companies cross boundaries. Big firms and small depend upon their small groups for getting work done. Big firms and small organize the basic components of their business into a more flexible form. Both big firms and small form alliances.

Industry

While new technology companies have a high propensity to develop teamnets, the future is not just about high tech. The big news is that teamnets have great success in traditional businesses as well, like textiles, wood, and metalworking.

Global

Finally, boundary crossing teamnets are forming all around the world at an accelerating rate. While American examples of business networking predominate in our survey, there is strong representation from Europe and Japan. Co-opetition—cooperation *and* competition—provides a natural way to balance differences between cultures.

UNITY IN DIVERSITY

The *teamnet factor* is about organizational advantage. The right organization gives you the right edge. However, teamnets are not always the answer. In the wrong context, teamnets offer no advantage; they even can be a disadvantage. Each type of organization maximizes its value under different circumstances and needs.

In the right context, teamnets are indispensable. What qualifies as a teamnet? An organization is a teamnet if it:

- Reflects the Five Teamnet Principles—unifying purpose, independent members, voluntary links, multiple leaders, and interacting levels; and
- Struggles with the Co-opetition Dynamic, the ever-shifting tension between cooperation and competition.

When circumstances require decentralized power and flexibility, there is a teamnet type that will work for you. The Teamnet Organization Scale encompasses the diversity of types.

Teamnet Organization Scale and Examples

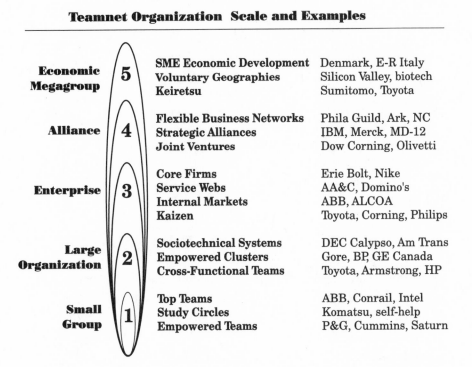

Economic Megagroup	5	SME Economic Development Voluntary Geographies Keiretsu	Denmark, E-R Italy Silicon Valley, biotech Sumitomo, Toyota
Alliance	4	Flexible Business Networks Strategic Alliances Joint Ventures	Phila Guild, Ark, NC IBM, Merck, MD-12 Dow Corning, Olivetti
Enterprise	3	Core Firms Service Webs Internal Markets Kaizen	Erie Bolt, Nike AA&C, Domino's ABB, ALCOA Toyota, Corning, Philips
Large Organization	2	Sociotechnical Systems Empowered Clusters Cross-Functional Teams	DEC Calypso, Am Trans Gore, BP, GE Canada Toyota, Armstrong, HP
Small Group	1	Top Teams Study Circles Empowered Teams	ABB, Conrail, Intel Komatsu, self-help P&G, Cummins, Saturn

The scale of types and examples shows where teamnets appear at different levels. Is your organization like the self-directed teams at Procter & Gamble? Are you a cross-functional team like Armstrong's? Does your organization spread out like a spider web delivering service like Domino's? Are you a flexible business network like Arkansas's 67-firm Metalworking Connection? Are you a player in a new voluntary geography like Silicon Valley and the Red River Trade Corridor?

Each type observes the Five Teamnet Principles and each combines elements of cooperation and competition. Each has both external boundaries (the teamnet whole) and internal boundaries (between the member parts).

*One difference is that each type of
organization has different kinds of
boundaries to cross. Crossing boundaries
from skill to skill is not the same as
department to department, which is very
different from crossing corporate lines,
which differs from crossing national
borders.*

THE MOST COMMON TEAMNET: THE SMALL GROUP

Often found in factories with only a few *levels* of authority, *empowered teams* are the simplest form of teamnet. People come together with a very clear common business *purpose. Members* are peers who interact laterally. *Leaders* emerge from within the group based on expertise and fit with group needs, rather than by superior appointment. Team members work near one another and usually don't face the work-at-a-distance *linkage* problems endemic to more spread-out teams.

- People in these teams usually come from the same broad function. Rather than struggling with internal organizational boundaries, members have to cross *skill* boundaries, cross-training in the multiple capabilities the group requires.
- A finished product or service defines the outer borders of empowered teams. The biggest boundary to a self-directed work team is its interface with the existing hierarchy. Since it is *self-*directed, the group risks alienating the system.

Purposes—both specific work group goals and enterprisewide program visions—guide study circles, which are rooted in the physical workplace. Members are peers whose leaders arise naturally from within the group. While they appear at all levels of an organization, members come from one or two neighboring hierarchical ranks. In circles, everyone works in the same place. People interact through direct face-to-face links.

- A handy way to learn something new or deal with common problems through peer support, you can use circles for anything. A specific location or department typically defines the outer bounds.
- Everybody participates. Everyone is encouraged to contribute. But be careful: Talk about turf wars! Even though circles scale only low walls, hurdles can be considerable. Internal warfare between occupational neighbors can be ferocious.

By their nature, *top teams*, the executives at the top of companies, comprise cross-boundary, independent members with considerable decision-making authority. As major players with fiefdoms, they can be a most difficult team to network. This team "owns" the corporate mission or purpose. By necessity, it copes with multiple levels of organization. In this intense place of corporate power and leadership politics, the CEO holds ultimate hierarchical control over the executive network. Members often have two offices, one symbolizing their peer relationships along the executive corridor, and one symbolizing their vertical position at the top of their department. While some linkages among top teams are optimized for their use within the enterprise, many executive groups still lack the basics: regular meetings and easy-to-use communication systems. Top teams also tend to isolate themselves. A huge moat can separate the vice presidents from everyone else, which teamnets can help bridge.

- Take cover as people lob hand grenades over the wall! In general, internal walls are extremely high and difficult to break down. Top teams cross every major boundary in the enterprise, like functions or divisions.
- For these small groups, the boundary of the whole is the enterprise and its system of external relations.

WHEN A MOB CLICKS: LARGE
ORGANIZATION TEAMNETS

Although there may be no more people in a large organization teamnet than in a study circle, they deal with a much larger universe and confront different boundaries.

Cross-functional teams, perhaps the most commonly known teamnet, appear at all levels of a company—from an isolated temporary team to an institutionalized top management coordinating group. They start with a clear corporate purpose and broad membership from diverse parts of an organization. These teams link horizontally through formal and informal processes and communications systems. Unlike quality circles and self-directed work teams, the coexisting hierarchy usually convenes the cross-functional team and appoints its leadership.

- Watch out for the colliding functions. They can be like bumper cars, involving two or more parts of the company that probably don't work together all that often. The core team must build trust very quickly and transmit it to the constituencies involved.
- While the members may see the shared cross-functional purpose that defines the team's outer bounds, their managers' functional walls may remain high. It's no mistake to call in the voice of the hierarchy here with a memo mandating cooperation among functions.

Empowered clusters are internally networked groups that offer enterprise-level economies of scale. Cluster members are multidisciplinary and leadership is internal. Purpose aligns the corporate vision with the participatory formulation of cluster goals. Well-designed technology and interactive workplaces enable communication links.

- As in empowered small groups, cluster members cross conventional skill boundaries internally, although they typically include a wider professional range.
- Sparks can fly here as the cluster is an administratively autonomous, mostly co-located work unit. Externally, it must interface with traditional administrative functions as a profit center or as a segment of a value chain. Conflicting organizational styles may require significant boundary crossing capabilities.

Sociotechnical systems become increasingly important as the technology of telecommunications and computer networking expands. In 1968, Doug Engelbart,[2] then at Xerox PARC, unveiled AUGMENT, his system for linking technology to organization. Designed on a Perkin-Elmer mainframe, Engelbart's program was more something that you drove rather than ran, with its multiple hand and foot controls, headset, *mouse and pull-down menus*! It was probably the first piece of groupware[3] (computer software designed for use by a group) that maintains common open files, databases, and journals.

Long a proponent of co-designing organization and technology, Engelbart is not alone: high-performance work systems, learning organizations, and knowledge networking all are about empowered multilevel teamnets. Indeed, the teamnet model is ideal for the easier-said-than-done work of creating a good fit between "socio" and "tech." It's much easier to fit technology networks to social networks than to social hierarchies, as untold numbers of companies discover to their great regret.

Teams rather than individuals are basic members of a sociotech system. They derive purposes from customer product requirements or such specific needs as collecting information, sharing databases, and providing electronic services. They link loosely in larger systems of shared information, communications, connections, relationships, and trust. As systems, these organizations are naturally multi-level. While high-performance teams do not explicitly require multiple leaders, they tend to be nonhierarchical and participatory.

- The internal borders of the professions rise like national flags here. The techies and the management types have to work together, as sociotech systems not only cross organizational boundaries, but technology boundaries as well.
- Its vulnerable outer border is highly sensitive to top management, especially since many companies implement technical systems enterprisewide. Unless there's supportive, engaged participation by the top of the house, people will reject sociotech systems.

WHEN THE WHOLE COMPANY IS A TEAMNET

Teamnets permeate some companies. In Japan, companies use the process-oriented management concept of "ongoing improvement involving everyone," called *kaizen*. In kaizen companies, process follows purpose. Small work groups at every level build strong linkages with communication systems as well as culture, participatory planning, problem solving, and the formalized tools and techniques of the quality movement. They involve many members from suppliers to customers. Following the nature of Japanese hierarchy, they depend on multiple leaders.

- What's right for the company is a natural point of reference. Kaizen teamnets also cross time barriers. Kaizen takes a very long view of time.
- There are internal boundaries galore here. Across functions and disciplines, ongoing improvement involving everyone means that identity groups constantly change in dynamic relation to one another.

Kaizen excels in generating *incremental improvements*, such as the 150 successive versions of the Sony Walkman. The American cultural focus on results and individual initiative generates more *breakthrough innovations*, many of which the Japanese successfully commercialize through kaizen processes.

The complementary integration of East-West, process-result approaches, crossing the broadest boundaries of group and individualistic cultures, makes teamnet management principles applicable worldwide.

Really successful boundary crossing teamnets have both a *process* perspective *and* a focus on *results*.

When companies create a large number of internal profit centers, they may develop *internal markets*. Here, members forge internal and external supplier and customer links while seeking advantage through alignment with strategic corporate purpose. A lean hierarchy anchors leadership at top levels, responsibility is pushed down to teams, and staff size is very small. It is amazingly simple to use internal markets as bureaucracy busters: just allow internal units to buy and sell externally.

- The global hierarchy sets the boundaries for the whole and the rules for crossing them. People in the trenches may disagree, which opens up the potential for border disputes.
- In both internal and external markets, members cross incorporation or balance sheet boundaries.

Domino's delivers through *service webs* based on a clear business purpose served by replicable member units. Service webs have few levels and centralized links. Leadership combines a lean hierarchy with entrepreneurial unit owners and/or managers.

- With the enterprise whole bounded from the center by headquarters and its control system, service webs constantly struggle to balance global standardization with local customization.

- While members cross internal unit boundaries by cooperating with enterprise standards, they compete locally with separately owned but similar service firms (often another service web).

Erie Bolt Company sits in the middle of a set of relationships with suppliers and customers. It is the biggest company, and it develops the network. Other members of the *core firm* teamnet take their cue from the business purpose of the major partner. Smaller companies, or small parts of other big companies, link with a larger company, one usually in the middle of a value chain, like a manufacturer. Small owners work with core firm leaders at a variety of levels, depending on the context.

- With the core firm defining the boundaries by its choice of partners, there is little ambiguity about who's in and who's out.
- While members are independent firms operating across enterprise boundaries with one or more major partners, they usually do not do business with other members. These missed opportunities may inhibit the growth of new business.

THE ALLIANCE STRATEGY

When companies deliberately decide to undertake a project together, they create teamnet alliances to link them. Some of these alliance types have been around for many years; others are brandnew. Each poses its own boundary problems to solve.

Joint ventures, like Corning's numerous ones, work best when members and their joint progeny are autonomous at the enterprise level. Voluntary links and joint leadership come from a clear business *purpose* requiring complementary core competencies from the partners.

- The joint venture is quite literally a common corporate whole created by the partners, whose boundaries include internal and

external enterprise relationships. Since many of the people in
the joint venture may come from the partner firms, old firm
loyalty can create barriers.

- Members cross enterprise boundaries to cooperatively create
the venture, but may compete elsewhere in the marketplace.
These confusing sets of relationships can cause impenetrable
walls to go up in the wrong places.

Strategic alliances include a wide array of members linking for
diverse purposes with two or more levels of business relationships.
Top executive leadership is typical, since these often involve major
strategic directions for the company.

- Strategic alliances can draw their boundaries narrowly in tight
exclusive contracts or broadly in philosophical agreements in
principle to work together. The key is to understand the scope
of the agreement, so that property rights, intellectual and otherwise, do not become an issue.
- Alliance members cross both enterprise boundaries *and* some
complementary business boundary that is the basis for the beneficial alliance. Mutual statement of the shared benefit is critical
to avoid transgressing the wrong boundaries.

When many small firms come together to do something they
cannot do alone, *flexible business networks* appear. Individual
firms are the members who communicate and develop relationships
through very voluntary links, hard-won shared purposes, and
very few levels. Diverse leadership comes from individual company owners, industry brokers, or facilitators who know the companies and their businesses, and economic development and other
public agencies, who provide technical assistance and, sometimes,
funding.

- In flexible business networks, the most frightening hurdle for
companies to jump is *cooperating to compete*. Working with a

competitor stops many people cold in their tracks. Once people understand the business justification and learn to trust each other, competition is no longer a barrier.

- Since firms can belong to many flexible networks, not just one, the lines on the map keep changing. When doing business in more than one network, it is mandatory that you keep your separate purposes clear.

REDRAWING THE TERRITORY: ECONOMIC MEGAGROUP TEAMNETS

Something new is happening. Companies are grouping in combinations of previously unthinkable size, across industries and geographies. Together, they create new economic megagroups.

Japan's *keiretsu* are a striking example. Members include large companies and small with countless major and minor strategic links between them serving specific market purposes. In Japan, the core enterprise, one of six banks or the lead manufacturer, exercises leadership. Their cascading levels of relationships extend to the smallest entrepreneurial production units and retail distribution outlets.

- While keiretsu are vast in extent, their membership is clear: you are part of the family or you are not. This makes for extremely closed markets, inhibiting external competition.
- Member companies have cross-ownership as well as supplier-customer relations. People sit on each other's boards. A totally closed keiretsu system could be stifling, but it's not a problem for most, since a typical member does much less than half of its business within the keiretsu.

Voluntary geographies are forming all over Europe, and in many other places as well. The Association of the Eastern Alps, the Association of the Western Alps, the Celtic Arc from Ireland to

Western Portugal, the European Port Cities Network, the Working Communities of the Pyrenees and the Peripheral Maritimes, all are new voluntary geographies that create economic megaregions.[4]

Voluntary geographies are fluid collections of business members of all sizes. They have myriad links among them that nevertheless share some core market purpose. Leaders come from private industry and from public agencies that support the businesses. As loose associations rather than targeted economic engines, they interact with many levels of the private and public sectors.

- Regions are unbounded at the edges, even in physically identified regions, but everyone who participates has a common economic interest. The fuzzy edges of the regions keep the membership issue alive.
- Participants may know one another well because of physical proximity that can produce a side effect of provincialism. The trick is to be just local enough without becoming xenophobic. After all, it's foreigners who are the customers for your exports.

When the public sector becomes directly involved in *small and medium-sized enterprise economic development*, new boundary crossing relationships flourish. With both public and private leadership that links small and medium-sized member companies, they pursue common or complementary purposes in large numbers. Operating across many domains, it's easy to get lost in these levels. Even so, their results are dramatic—whole regions, like Emilia-Romagna in Italy, and the entire country of Denmark—can benefit from concerted joint effort.

- A combination of government policy and private initiatives defines the new economic borders. Since these initiatives draw new boundaries that supersede older ones, it's important to be mindful of falling into old-think traps.
- Members are small and medium-sized enterprises with leaders able to cross the cultural boundaries of rugged individualism.

Unless companies trust one another, they won't work together. The old axiom, "You do business with people you know," is an important one to expand upon. Pay attention to getting to know new people.

Flexible business networks are the heart of economic development for small and medium-sized companies so important to the future of the world's local economies. Rampant downsizing by the world's largest firms, particularly in the United States, is one inevitable consequence of two fundamental trends: greater decentralization and more external alliances. The biggest become smaller as the smallest become more numerous.

> *It's in everyone's interest that the small become smarter and more capable microeconomic engines.*

Taken as a whole, teamnets apply across all the levels, giving companies of all sizes in all industries organizational advantage.

Critical Success Factor 1

Get the purpose right! Structure your organization to meet the purpose. Restructure when the purpose significantly changes. Match organizational type to need. Know your glue:

> *What's going to be the vital something that holds the whole together?*

GLUE BY WARP AND WOOF

Three powerful basic drivers of organizational advantage structure teamnet organizations. They apply up and down the scale for all their infinitely specific purposes:

1. *Complementary needs* create organizations with functional departments, with vertical integration in an industry or market, or with units performing in many contiguous segments of the value chain.
2. *Common needs* give rise to divisional organizations, with horizontal linkages in an industry, or with centralized systems of many similar units.
3. *Mixed needs* try to systematically serve both common and complementary purposes, or markets with both stable and changing features, generating matrix organizations with functions (e.g., marketing, design, production) and divisions (e.g., region, product, project).

This simple set of drivers neatly parallels the most common categories of bureaucracy—functional, divisional, and matrix organizations respectively.

The core giant companies of the past half century and many of the industries they have dominated are breaking up into smaller units—*disaggregating*. To adapt to the 21st century, bureaucracies must break up into smaller parts, forming both internal and external networks.[5] Internal decentralization and external alliances pull bureaucracy in two directions simultaneously.

The columns in the chart represent Critical Success Factor 1, the driver of the organization: complementary, common, or mixed needs. The rows represent the directions bureaucracy is being pulled: the traditional bureaucratic form is in the middle; variations of internal teamnets array along the bottom; and external teamnets are at the top.

From Bureaucracy to Teamnets

	COMPLEMENTARY	COMMON	MIXED
EXTERNAL	**Flex Bus Net/ vertical** (Team Nashua, MD-12) **Joint Venture** (Corning) **Core Firm** (Erie Bolt) ⤊	**Flex Bus Net/ horizontal** (garments, metal, woodworking, e.g., Philadelphia Guild) ⤊	**SME Eco Devel** (Denmark) **Voluntary Geographies** (Silicon Valley) **Keiretsu** (Mitsubishi) ⤊
BUREAUCRACY	**Functional** (most traditional firms)	**Divisional** Automotive (GM); retail (Sears); food (General Mills)	**Matrix** Aerospace (McDonnell-Douglas); electronics (Digital)
INTERNAL	⤋ **Top Team** **Sociotech System** (Digital's Calypso) **Cross-Functional Team**	⤋ **Service Web** (AA&C) **Empowered Cluster** (BP) **Study Circle** (Komatsu) **Empowered Team** (P&G)	⤋ **Kaizen** (Toyota) **Internal Market** (Asea Brown Boveri)

Your teamnet sits somewhere among these levels. Locate its type, then learn from the lessons of other companies that have gone before you. Consider purpose, members, links, leaders, and levels. Ascertain whether you are working internally or externally or both. Sort out whether your needs are complementary, common, or mixed, and whether your teamnet has functional, divisional, or matrix characteristics. Your teamnet is most certainly like someone else's in some fundamental ways—and it is different, always idiosyncratic.

You can creatively address your differences and unique features by "Harnessing the Power of Teamnets," the subject of section II of this book, chapters 8 through 11. By using the tools in different combinations, you can scale and adapt them to virtually any business conditions. Choose your tools wisely and greatly improve your teamnet's chances of success.

With Tools in Hand

It is one thing to understand ideas, and quite another to put them into practice. To help you get your teamnet off the ground tomorrow morning, we offer the Teamnet Interface.

Good software programs have good interfaces. Interfaces are the parts of programs that greet the user, what you see on the screen when you turn on your machine and call up a program. Good interfaces are both intuitive—meaning that they feel natural to the average user—and structured—meaning that they make logical sense from a design perspective. They make it easy to get going and get around. Good interfaces also appeal to people knowledgeable in the application's area of expertise.

The Teamnet Interface consists of three sets of tools, each with five elements:

1. Teamnet Principles

Purpose, Members, Links, Leaders, and Levels

2. Phases of Growth

Start-up, Launch, Perform, Test, and Deliver

3. Target Method

Targets, Tasks, Times, Teams, and Territories

We pair combinations of the three interfaces to organize various parts of the teamnet "how-to" section:

- The Teamnet Principles and Phases organize the Teamnet Activities.
- The combination of the Phases and Target Method identifies Teamnet Information.

- Teamnet Tools integrate the Target Method and Teamnet Principles.

By understanding the underlying planning frameworks that arise from these combinations, you can easily extend many of our teamnet ideas.

TEAMNET ACTIVITIES CHART: FOLLOWING THE PRINCIPLES ACROSS THE PHASES

In "Quick Start," chapter 8, the Teamnet Principles appear immediately as the "Teamnet Checklist," a simple set of diagnostic questions. These questions appear as the first column in the Teamnet Activities Chart.

With these questions, you can rough out the first sketch of your plan as your first phase of activity. For your second pass, the Launch Phase, you sharpen the questions into a set of five focused activities for producing a plan. This shows up as the "Teamnet How-to" in chapter 8, appearing here as the second column of the Teamnet Activities Chart.

Teamnet Activities

	START-UP	LAUNCH	PERFORM	TEST	DELIVER
PURPOSE	Common view?	Clarify purpose	Detail design	Apply criteria	Act
MEMBERS	Colleagues?	Identify members	Utilize skills	Examine quality	Operate
LINKS	Connections?	Create links	Capture learning	Feedback responses	Network
LEADERS	Voices?	Recognize leaders	Lead tasks	Answer challenges	Manage
LEVELS	Inclusion?	Integrate levels	Review progress	Review tests	Implement

When you get to the later phases—Perform, Test, and Deliver—use this chart as a simple device. Think of it as a checklist with a strategy. Consider how the five principles apply at each stage, one by one:

> *Are we still on the beam with purpose?*
> *How have the members changed? Are the*
> *links being used? Where are the new*
> *leaders? How can we connect with the*
> *hierarchy?*

TEAMNET INFORMATION CHART: TRACKING THE METHOD ACROSS THE PHASES

Track the Phases of Growth by combining them with the commonly asked questions of our Target Method (the Five W's: *why, what, when, who,* and *where*; and the Five T's: *targets, tasks, time, team, and territory*). "Launching Teamnets," chapter 9, steps you through the first two phase columns of the Teamnet Information Chart: the first run-through of five-W questions and the second run-through of

Teamnet Information

	START-UP	LAUNCH	PERFORM	TEST	DELIVER
TARGETS	Why?	Set targets	Monitor process	Check results	Measure targets
TASKS	What?	Define tasks	Articulate attributes	Evaluate cost/benefits	Standard tasks
TIME	When?	Estimate time	Report actuals	Evaluate cycles	Document process
TEAM	Who?	Select team	Deploy resources	Review participation	Capture learning
TERRITORY	Where?	Choose territory	Localize work	Check variants	Locally operate

five-T answers. When you complete the first two columns, you are on your way to a workable plan.

Information plays different roles at different points in the process. In the Start-up and Launch Phases, you use information to simulate the future and to populate the planning process. In the Perform Phase, you use information to monitor the group's particular work, based on the categories you establish in the Launch Phase. In the Test Phase, you compare actual output with the goals and criteria set in the early stages. In the final Deliver Phase, you implement change, reject it, or return to begin another cycle of the process.

TEAMNET TOOLS: FOLLOWING THE METHOD ACCORDING TO THE PRINCIPLES

"Those That Do, Plan," chapter 10, makes use of the combination of the Target Method and the Teamnet Principles. Tools manage the information a teamnet generates.

A sturdy foundation for teamnet plans combines tasks, time, and team into four pillars of design:

- Task framework;
- Task flow diagram;
- Schedule; and
- Cross-boundary chart.

Use a framework to capture the *tasks* that elaborate the *purpose*. Break down the framework into more detailed *levels* of tasks. Use cross-boundary charts to show *links*, identifying each task *team* according to *members* involved and who has *leadership* responsibility. You can identify other links by creating a task flow and estimating *times* that together produce a schedule.

To convey *targets*, use words and images in multiple media. To establish *territory*, create a "Teamnet Handbook" of shared information to stand for "where," the group's location. Include directories, mail systems, and maps. Get on-line if possible.

PURPOSE IS THE VITAL CENTER

It is no accident that we place purpose at the beginning of each tool set. Purpose is the vital center. The motivating reason and its objectives overlap in the beginning: Start-up/Purpose/Targets.

Start-up/Purpose/Targets get things going. They are the inspiration that passes from one person to another, the arcs struck by spark plugs, the expression of a group's center when it "clicks."

When you hit it right, you know it. You have the certainty that the process will make it. Keep the purpose out in front for everybody. Ask people to sign the flip chart on which you capture the purpose. Chisel in the date you first get it right.

INVEST IN THE BEGINNINGS

Nothing is more important than getting the beginning right. This is why we focus on the early phases of the process, specifically on the Start-up and Launch stages. The Target Method expands on the critical second stage, Launch, which produces the plan necessary for distributed work. The Target Method's five T's create the momentum the group needs to take off, i.e., to launch.

How Phases Relate to Method

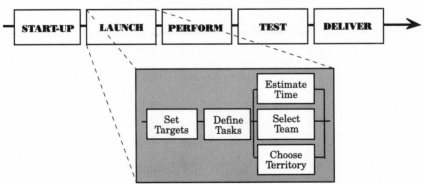

> *Clarify the purpose and divide the work*
> *in the right way.*

We stress this repeatedly because it is the source for all the tasks that make up the plan and drive the process logic. Once you define a task, you can attach attributes to it later in any order. Use your early iterations to complete the task structure, matching it with the needs propelling the work.

In the beginning, planning is fluid: you need to adjust elements interdependently. There is abundant feedback within and between the components of the method and the change process. Initially, keep information in a rough state. At first, order-of-magnitude estimates that scope a whole process will suffice. Clarify and refine the information over time.

NAVIGATING WITH YOUR PLAN

Ray Stata, CEO of Analog Devices, has put "planning as learning" into practice. "I believe our approach to planning as a learning process has greatly facilitated our ability to forge a consensus for change among those who must make it happen. It has also helped reduce the obstacles and resistance to change, that is, outdated beliefs and assumptions created by past success."[6]

To make the complex simple, we naturally create models of our world. Then we filter our daily experience through these models. Groups do the same thing. When a group says it has "a common view of the world," it means that people in the group share certain assumptions about their reality. A plan is a model of the future.

Good, realistic models help groups handle the flood of incoming information. Models provide common categories—such as sales, marketing, invoices, pay periods. They allow people quickly to sort new information into the work flow, i.e., a request for a customer presentation goes to a marketing group, not the accounts payable department. With a clear model, people can then attend to exceptions and pattern changes, the sources of problems and improvements.

When a group of people shares special knowledge about the world, people know what to do in local situations. If the local circumstances fall outside the shared experience, the group receives a signal from people on the scene of the need for new information, resources, or decisions.

The planning process is really all about creating a shared mental model of the teamnet and its work.

At its fullest extent, a richly elaborated shared memory is the essence of the group. It is a specialized organizational culture unique to this set of people.

New plans are seeds for new cultures. Create a shared reality through the common experience of planning. Capture your learning through continuous access to information throughout the life cycle. Extend your learning into the delivery, operations, and service phases of your business process.

USE YOUR PLAN AS AN INTERFACE

Information Age dynamics drive the formation of more organizational networks. Electronic communications and distributed computer capabilities are both a cause and an effect of more teamnets. Electronic distributed work—when people work together apart using computers—adds its own hazards. Chief among them is information overload. When all planning information is widely accessible to everyone, it increases the potential of too much information that is too little processed and too hard to find.

Designing a good work process helps address this problem. Your work process is a mental bridge to the complex shared information space of the teamnet.

Use shared models of the process as menu categories and graphical user interfaces to on-line information.

Employ the work process elements and design visuals to navigate the shared information. Reflect changes in the work as changes in the pointers to the underlying information network, and reap these rewards:

- Flexibility in changing process elements;
- Controllability in maintaining process integration; and
- Ease of use in interacting with the information infrastructure.

Use interfaces and pointers rather than static database designs. In this way, you make the on-line information space navigable rather than a mazelike trap. As the plan and cross-functional associations change, the pointers change as well.

Shared Plan, Shared Interface

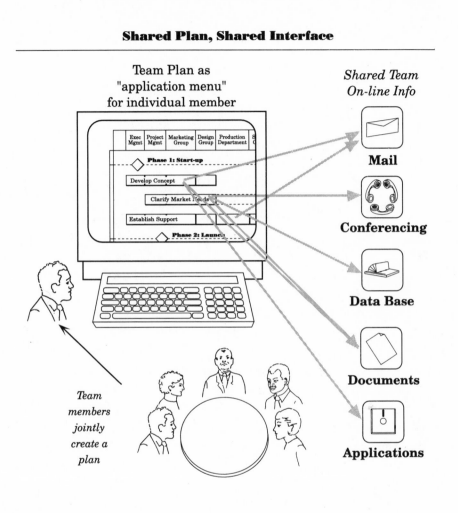

Team Plan as "application menu" for individual member

Shared Team On-line Info

Mail

Conferencing

Data Base

Documents

Applications

Team members jointly create a plan

Imagine conducting this exercise with your on-line system:

Create a cross-boundary chart with icons and names for tasks, deliverables, meetings, decisions, milestones, standards, and functions. Click on a particular deliverable or icon to go directly to associated files wherever they are on the network. Click on meetings, decisions, or milestones to go to information about past or forthcoming events. Click on functions to go to directories of organizations and people, as well as to make electronic connections to them.[7]

Work process design is one critical element in being smart, in improving the complex world of human work. Systems integration programs not only link computers; they also link people and organizations. Few companies or their systems integrators have yet to tackle the organizational aspects of these programs. In the long run, however, technology enhancement efforts fail unless they also address the all-important people integration issues.

It is easier to support networked organizations and work processes with networked information technologies than it is to support hierarchies with them. It wasn't always so. In the old days, centralized mainframe hosts with "slave" terminals ruled the computing roost. They were completely congruent with the traditional organization structure. Times change. Now the advantage is with network architecture, in both organizations and technology.

In the end, better models of the world enable a group to work smarter and more successfully. It is the smart who will inherit the 21st century global market—smart groups, smart companies, smart nations.

What to Do

In the broad shift from hierarchy to bureaucracy to networks, there are some general clues about what to do.

Maintain boundaries and cross them.

Boundaries represent independence. Crossing boundaries is how cooperation happens. Both are important. While some approaches to cooperation demand their removal, the network form requires respect for boundaries. Networks are about learning to live with boundaries by establishing common purpose and interdependent links.

Strengthen the co-opetition dynamic for balance.

Tension is natural and, when not out of control, healthy in a democratic, open economy. Instead of diminishing cooperation or competition to redress imbalances, strengthen both. Measures that encourage cooperation need also to include ways to protect and develop independent leadership and self-reliance. Measures that encourage competition need also to promote cooperative goals and interdependent linkages.

Travel the levels and "walk the talk."

We can all take advantage of the cross-level network principles to apply our learning from one context, level, or scale to another. In particular, in our own "zone of influence," it is of great value to practice what we preach.

Lower the cultural barrier to cooperation.

Most networks and alliances never get past initial hesitations, suspicions, and fears even to begin co-opetition formation. Presidents and other leaders of companies and countries can do something to work on this critical first hurdle by establishing co-opetition as a corporate norm. This is one area where the "bully pulpit" that comes with the top spot can be extremely effective.

Make work fun again.

"I like networks because every one contains a surprise," says Niels Christian Nielsen, one of Denmark's flexible business network strategy architects.[8] "And the owners say they are having more fun in business." When networks work, they are fun and exciting, forming environments of diversity and creativity. People respect one another for who they are and what they do. Working together is fascinating and satisfying. Serendipity happens. The best in people comes out. Of course, when things don't work, all the opposite behaviors appear, and it's not fun at all.

All the more reason to learn how to function in this new style of work, to:

Increase the fun while meeting needs.

Teamnets cross boundaries rarely traversed before, increasing business and creating new opportunities as people cooperate to compete. Are you?

"The Risk of Democracy": Teamnets as the Hope for the 21st Century

The flip chart marked "Concerns" had some interesting words in the middle: "risk of democracy." We had just returned to the room after TransOceania's Transportation Scheduling Project team met with its senior management. The team had proposed setting up an enterprisewide network to run a critical business process. To be more customer-driven meant involving the worldwide field offices. At the senior management meeting, Neville, the vice president in charge of the field offices, objected. He demanded that all field communication filter through his corporate staff. "We're running the risk of democracy here," he said. He didn't want to risk people thinking for themselves.

Unfortunately for him, this vice president is out of step with the times.

> *Successful companies are the ones that*
> *run the risk of democracy.*

They create networks, small experiments in democracy. Teamnets—amalgams of teams working together in networks across boundaries—carry an underlying message. They emphasize both

335

the empowerment of the group and its members—as peers (which is why networks are so often simply contrasted with hierarchies).

Business leads the way in using networks as the cornerstone of a broad new organizational strategy. Grass-roots networks show the incredible power of how ideas galvanize energy at minimal cost. Personal networks enable us to be both local and global in our associations, to play many roles in many stories, sometimes leveraging awesome power. Just ask Bill Clinton.

Revolution by Design:
The Clinton Teamnet

In the 1992 election victory of Bill Clinton over George Bush, the American people sent a clear signal for change. Among politicians, *known* to be astute networkers, Bill Clinton is an extraordinary one. His own vast network of contacts provided the organizational base for his presidential campaign. By tapping into both people and technology networks, he had unparalleled reach.

Fundamentally, Bill Clinton is now and has always been a networker. His story is one of dogged pursuit of a purpose and the disciplined use of networking to get there. We can personally attest to how long he has been honing his networking skills.

Like several hundred other Americans, we (Jeff and Jessica) met as students at Oxford University in 1968. Jeff was a Fulbright Scholar studying political philosophy; Jessica was an undergraduate studying on a one-year exchange. Shortly after Bill Clinton arrived as a Rhodes Scholar in the fall of 1968, Jeff met him at a Rhodes House function on Oxford's Parks Road. After talking a few minutes, Bill pulled out a black address book.

"What are you doing here at Oxford, Jeff?" Bill said.

"I'm at Pembroke on a Fulbright," Jeff said. The Fulbright program had assigned Jeff to Pembroke College, where J. William Fulbright, the Arkansas senator, had studied, even housing him in

Fulbright's room. Ironically, Bill had interned for Fulbright the previous summer.

Bill wrote down the name of Jeff's Oxford college, then asked about his undergraduate school, and his major.

"Bill, why are you writing this down?" Jeff asked a bit skeptically.

"I'm going into politics and plan to run for governor of Arkansas and I'm keeping track of everyone I meet," Bill explained.[1]

Bill Clinton's little black book must be very large now. Today, he can turn to aides, handing them people's business cards, letters, proposals, and even résumés as people give them to him. It is impossible to read an article about Clinton that doesn't reference his prodigious networking skills.

- "The human switchboard" is how one aide describes Clinton a few days after his 1992 election.[2]
- "Clinton comes to the job as the most thoroughly 'networked' politician of his era," David Broder, one of America's most respected political columnists, writes in the *Washington Post*: "He has been part of every major movement in his party from the McGovern campaign on the left to the Democratic Leadership Council on the right."[3]

Clinton's personal networks, now a highly visible group known collectively as FOBs (Friends of Bill), demonstrate the power of overlapping and interweaving different aspects of one person's life:[4]

- His upbringing in his home state of *Arkansas*, population 2.6 million;
- His alma mater, *Georgetown University*, where he was class president in 1968;
- His two years as a *Rhodes Scholar* at *Oxford*, perhaps his most famous network;[5]
- His days at *Yale Law School*, where he met Hillary Rodham

(who was the first student to give a commencement address at her alma mater, *Wellesley College*), whom he would marry;
- His early days in *Democratic Party* politics, first working on Joe Duffy's Senate race in 1970, and then on George McGovern's presidential bid in 1972;
- His years as *governor* of Arkansas, beginning in 1979 (a post he holds for 13 years, with the exception of one loss after his first term), from which he builds a national base;
- His participation in the *Democratic Leadership Council* (DLC), positioned as a "third way" between traditional liberal and conservative politics; and
- His 1992 *presidential campaign*, which put him on the world stage.

Clearly, Clinton had been plaiting his political braid for a long time before he announced his candidacy, weaving together many differing constituencies. Like most campaigns, his depended heavily on networking, informally observing the Five Teamnet Principles.

- A very clear *purpose* focused the campaign. Clinton mentioned it in every stump speech. Someone wrote it on a white board in Little Rock headquarters as a reminder to campaign workers. "We all understood the message, the overarching theme: 'It's the economy, stupid.' Little Rock never wanted us to go off on a tangent," says Bob Randolph, a genuine local FOB who knew Clinton since they were both Rhodes Scholars at Oxford. After going to hear Clinton speak in Seattle, Washington, in early 1992, Randolph, a Seattle attorney, signed up to help, organizing Northwest Business Leaders for Clinton, and serving as deputy campaign director in Washington State.
- Some 3,000 independent volunteers (*members*) poured into Little Rock to help, with many thousands more shoring up the operation in each of the 50 states, then disbanded just as quickly when the campaign was over. "If you looked at the individual parts of the campaign, there were some weak links. Not every-

one in the world could drop everything for five months and move to Little Rock, so there were some people there who were just bodies. What it made me realize is that you don't need rocket scientists, but you do need teamwork and team players," Randolph says.

- Fax machines, cellular phones, and telephone conference calls kept the regional and state operations in constant touch with Little Rock headquarters, providing a very disciplined use of intense two-way communication *links* between Little Rock and the state coordinators every day.
- *Many leaders* populated the campaign, dealing with everything from political strategy to scheduling to fund raising to coordination. "At one point, the Little Rock hierarchy became atomized and factionalized. Running the campaign by committee was too slow. It required too many checks from too many people with too many titles. Finally, they put the political management in the hands of James Carville, the most astute political manager, and it worked," Randolph recalls.
- Multiple *levels* of the existing hierarchy were recruited to endorse and support the campaign—from five-star generals and corporate CEOs to the usual parade of national, state, and local politicians.

Clinton's campaign also combined hierarchical control with the creativity of networks. "It was a damn close-run campaign," Randolph says. "There was no true autonomy. In fact, it was almost like a military organization. We were operating within certain parameters. Loose cannons were not tolerated. But this was also different from a military organization because everyone was a volunteer, not a draftee. We recognized that if you are running a national campaign across 50 states with limited resources, it had to be centralized because there was a tremendous risk of failure."

It did not fail, with networking and hierarchy each playing its appropriate part.

Some Free Advice for the Consummate Networker

Will history remember Bill Clinton, the great facilitator, as the "network president"?

If he ultimately depends only on the power of his personal networks, the answer is no. If he extends his personal networking strength to encompass an organizational networking strategy, the answer is yes. The Clinton administration will fail to achieve its potential if it cannot activate the *teamnet factor* within a federal bureaucracy that interacts with business, labor, education, myriad other special interests, and ultimately all the people. Despite the bad press usually reserved for the federal bureaucracy, countless effective networks function among career civil service workers. A highly effective network at the executive level will empower similar behavior within and among departments that can benefit only from working together. If boundary crossing, horizontal management works for business, it will work for government.

> *Clinton's biggest challenge is not the economy, foreign hot spots, or other domestic issues; rather, it is the ability to organize to do something about these things.*

CLARIFY PURPOSE: "IT'S THE ECONOMY, STUPID"

"Economy" is the single word that stands for focus and *purpose* in the Clinton administration. By clarifying their purpose into a clear set of goals, Clinton and his core set of advisers set out a strategy. Then, they must revisit that purpose often. At the end of 1992,

Clinton sponsored and chaired a two-day preinauguration, 300-person teach-in on the economy, precisely the type of get-all-the-information-on-the-table session that is the first step in launching teamnets. The more cross-government, cross-industry, cross-public task forces working on problems, reorganizing the government, and proposing action, the more successful the Clinton administration will be.

In an enterprise as large as the federal government, with the vast array of, quite literally, suppliers and customers, the top government teams must set clear goals that others can articulate and make specific at every level—by those who need to put them to work. Planning needs to involve the whole enterprise—the refinement and use of the natural network resource of commitment to shared purpose. Planning is most effective when it hears and integrates the "voice of the customer"—a 255-million-person market—from the very beginning.

Participation is a big part of purpose.

---

*Invite everyone, some will show up, and
a few will stay to do the hard work.
Everyone feels involved.*

Getting people involved in figuring out how best to do something is half the battle of getting something done. A well-articulated vision harnesses the power of teamnets, making participatory planning manageable. Research shows that what is most important to people is the feeling that they *can* participate, not that they actually *do* participate.

Don't be afraid to raise expectations. People can do great things by themselves when they have a clear view of the whole. A long-term plan with four-, eight-, and twelve-year targets will help. This future-look provides the context for making short-term trade-offs and decisions.

Plans that sit on the shelf are dead on arrival. Plans need to be living frameworks that people use directly as management tools, then continually revise to reflect the pace of change.

IDENTIFY MEMBERS: 5.5 HANDSHAKES TO EVERYBODY

Clinton's first task before he took office as president was to identify the 3,000 official members of the administration. Technically speaking, the people who occupy the political positions that the White House controls comprise its core network. The administration needs to involve every person who works in or for it, developing the plan around their part of the overall administration purposes.

But Bill Clinton must move beyond Washington, way beyond Washington. Never has a little black book meant so much. Now, he can take another lesson from academia to enhance its power further.

The edges of a network amplify the strongest message, not the center.

"The strength of weak ties" is how Mark Granovetter, the social network analyst who discovered it, describes this strategy.[6] To get the word out, you must get beyond your immediate circle of friends to the edges; the trick is to get to their friends, and then their friends. In a few hops like this, research shows you can reach anyone in the world in 5.5 handshakes.[7] Thus, Clinton, the consummate networker, can amplify his message beyond his current political constituency to reach everyone.

CREATE LINKS: NETWORK SUPERHIGHWAY
FOR TEAMNETS

This is where Vice President Al Gore and the John Sculleys of the world come in. Never has such powerful technology been available to link any administration and the value chain it dominates. And never has U.S. industry been more ready to provide it—except in time of war. Among the earliest members of Congress to understand electronic networking, Al Gore, one of the first candidates to carry around a laptop computer,[8] has proposed a high-bandwidth fiber optic "national telecommunications superhighway." The high-tech companies are ready with the world's most sophisticated networking technology, providing the infrastructure that enables people to work together at a distance.

Technical links by themselves are useless. This is an infrastructure that supports human relationships of every description, economic and social. People don't just need access to the key players in the Clinton administration; they need access all up and down the line and with one another. Imagine that in creating the electronic web we make possible the "Network Nation" that greatly facilitates teamnets at all levels, public and private.[9]

Democracies are about self-rule, about involving people in the decisions that affect them, and free markets of fully informed producers and consumers. Participation is vastly more possible today than it was 200 years ago, both technologically and organizationally. Participation is not just a good idea morally; it is a good idea that contributes to the bottom line and to the quality of life.

MULTIPLY LEADERS: WE DON'T HAVE A
LEADER TO WASTE

While the presidency may seem the ultimate expression of political hierarchy, Clinton promotes multiple leadership through his team relationship with his wife, Hillary Rodham Clinton, and his newer partnership with Vice President Al Gore.

Multiplying leaders simply means recognizing that everyone has a contribution to make, and that no one can solve the world's problems alone.

Successful organizations of the 21st century have more than one leader.

By recognizing all the leaders that are "out there," the country becomes stronger. Each cabinet department, agency, and interest group benefits from regarding itself as a teamnet with many leaders.

Make the 1990s "The Decade of Leaders." It was his trip to the White House—as a teenage leader—that inspired Bill Clinton to become president. Every age group, young to old, every interest group, every skin color, religion, income bracket, trade and profession, has many, many leaders. Recognize, honor, and involve them. "We don't have a leader to waste." We didn't write this line into Clinton's inauguration speech, but we certainly would have recommended it.

INTEGRATE LEVELS: CHIEF HIERARCH
TO CHIEF NETWORKER

The new administration becomes the new hierarchy. It can encourage—or resist—bridges and pathways to business and the rest of the society it serves. Perhaps the most difficult task for any networking effort is to stay connected at all the levels. The purpose of integrating levels is to keep everyone in the loop, minimizing surprises, and involving as many people as possible in an ever-renewing effort.

Unless Bill Clinton can inspire a new type of government management—one that works quickly, transcends partisan differences, and yields bottom line results for the country as a whole, there will be no domestic peace in the United States. The government needs to team with many partners. The more people the government teams with, the closer it will be to its "customer," the people.

This gets back to shared purpose and participatory planning. The Clinton administration can come up with a statement of work that scales from the Office of the President to the loan officer at the Small Business Administration and back up again. Work process design translates the Clinton "purpose" into goals that become the targets for the next level down. These subpurposes translate into tasks that specific people can accomplish by designated dates.

Networking, as a macro-economic development strategy and a way to transform bureaucracy to improve productivity greatly, is remarkably responsive to the power of the "bully pulpit." While President Clinton can't do much about interest rates, he can do a great deal by speech and deed to show the power of teamnets. The president can significantly lower the "it can't work here" cultural barrier and the high costs incurred overcoming it by all newly forming networks.

The most successful organizational transitions are those where the chief hierarch becomes the chief networker.

Teamnets at the Grass Roots

Like many other countries in the world, not only business but also the *people* of the United States are already working in the new style. Big government is the laggard.

In the last three decades, grass-roots networking has mushroomed in the United States. Countless networks involve millions of people across the country who belong to voluntary associations, from self-help groups to special interest groups. Our first book on boundary crossing teamnets, *Networking: The First Report and Directory*,[10] is not about business at all. Rather it chronicles the rise of grass-roots networks in the United States in the 1960s and 1970s, including a directory of 1,500 key networks, many of which still thrive in the 1990s. Fundamentally, America's grass-roots networks are small groups at a local level. They form all manner of larger coalitions that in turn aggregate into multileadered movements.

Teamnets form on all sides of issues. Regardless of ideology, voluntary networks have common organizational features, and they use similar tools to connect their members. Richly networked groups can be highly effective, both inside and outside hierarchies. America's history as an individualistic democracy is nevertheless also full of numberless groupings and associations, a characteristic of such remarkable note that the famous commentator on early America, Alexis de Tocqueville, wrote in 1840:

> The political associations that exist in the United States are only a single feature in the midst of the immense assemblage of associations in that country. Americans of all ages, all conditions, and all dispositions, constantly form associations. They have not only commercial and manufacturing companies, in which all take part, but associations of a thousand other kinds—religious, moral, serious, futile, extensive or restrictive, enormous or diminutive.

Since we began our research in 1979, we have corresponded with networkers in more than 70 countries and have observed networking grow from a local grass-roots activity to a global mainstream activity. Networks have impact everywhere in the world, and many networks are global in their reach.

THE GODDESS OF DEMOCRACY

The closing days of the 1980s left the world reeling from unprecedented events. Eastern Europe shed a half century of Soviet Communist rule, literally tearing down the wall that separated East from West. Inexorable forces unleashed in that remarkable year moved on at blinding speed to nonviolently sweep Communism from power at its very roots, the now former Soviet Union. The Cold War collapsed.

It is hard to remember how sudden this all seemed at the time. "If I had sat here on January 1, 1989, and told you that a million people would occupy Tiananmen Square for a month, you would have said I was crazy," NBC News broadcaster Tom Brokaw said at the end of 1989 on the air. "If I had told you that I would come back to the United States with pieces of the Berlin Wall in my suitcase, you would have had me committed." That is exactly what happened, seemingly overnight.

Nowhere is this clearer than in the spring of that year in Beijing. There, Hu Yaobang, a Chinese reform leader much admired by China's long-standing democracy movement, dies. At exactly the same moment, Mikhail Gorbachev, the symbol of Communist reform, lands in Beijing, making the first Soviet state visit since Nikita Khrushchev's trip in 1959.

Instead of covering official events, reporters, who have traveled to China from all over the world to cover the Gorbachev visit, find a completely different story unfolding before their eyes.

In response to the death of Hu Yaobang, the Chinese university students and supporters of the country's prodemocracy movement, at least a million strong, occupy Tiananmen Square. No one orders them to come there and the government doesn't want them to stay. Spontaneously, the students arrive from everywhere, and before they know it, they are international heroes, standing in front of television cameras linked to satellite dishes, being interviewed by the world's press.

"Did you have any inkling this was coming?" Dan Rather asks his colleague, the two standing in front of the Goddess of Democracy. The Goddess is the students' rendition of the Statue of Liberty, one output from this phenomenal experiment in self-organization. The students form three major groups: one negotiates with the government; another carries out the highly media-visible hunger strike; and a third manages logistics in the square itself (green plastic garbage bags are much in demand).

Communication explodes: wall posters, newsletters, radios, bullhorns, cassettes, photocopiers, video, fax, cellular telephone, computers. Universities, businesses, and even government offices in China allow their fax machines to send and receive. Foreign corporations, with operations in China, permit the use of their computers to send electronic mail messages. International telephone calls in and out of China increase dramatically.

It is perhaps the largest political demonstration in human history and certainly the most high-tech one. And the world is watching— live. Media feedback loops soar to a new level.[11]

- A Beijing University biology student, who heads the student delegation negotiating with the government, delivers a speech by bullhorn in Tiananmen Square.
- A Canadian television crew broadcasts the speech live, then interviews him.
- In Montreal, a television producer digitizes the video signal, and prints out a still photograph of the student.
- Chinese students studying there at McGill University then fax the photo back to their former classmates at Beijing University.
- The students in Beijing write a short story beneath the picture and photocopy it, enlarging it as they do. Then they hang it up as a wall poster.
- The wall poster, in turn, is broadcast on television again in an

eyewitness report about how students are communicating in Tiananmen Square.

Amplified bullhorn, broadcast TV, digitized photograph, phone and fax, photocopier to wall poster, and back on TV again. Just one of many full-circle feedback loops of interacting electronic technologies.

Suddenly, June 3–4. The Army opens fire on unarmed demonstrators and kills many. As the shooting continues, survivors run back and forth to telephones. Eyewitnesses phone out accounts all around the world. Reporters switch on their cellular telephones in Beijing and broadcast live and the world is watching.

When Business Is Like Politics

The China story underscores the potential power unleashed at the intersection of people and technology networks, culminating in an epic clash between raw hierarchy and a democracy movement. It also shows how the voluntary response by individuals directly plugs into participation in the great events of our time. The captains of industry all around the world share the same problems as the old leaders of China. The world is changing fantastically right before their eyes and they really don't know what to do about it. So some resort to primitive ways—brute force and rigid control hierarchies. It is only a temporary measure. The guard is changing and no one can stop it.

TECHNOLOGY AND ORGANIZATIONAL NETWORKS INTERACT

More global networks lead to an increasingly interdependent global economy, largely based on business-to-business and person-to-person relationships, rather than on state-to-state linkages. The number of international companies and organizations has sky-rocketed in the past two decades.

To play in the world economy requires open communications. So, China's leadership, desiring to be part of the global economy, opens up communications. China did this technologically, by installing a new national telephone system, and socially, by sending large numbers of students abroad. More than 100,000 were believed to have been in other countries in 1989.

Open communication in turn stimulates a desire for democracy, for a more-open political system. In China, communications and politics created an accumulating positive feedback loop. Events escalated to the dizzying hope expressed by the Goddess of Democracy, and then crashed in the horror of the massacre.

Tiananmen Square sends a message to hierarchies everywhere: the risk of democracy.

Organizations and societies must change to effectively use new information technologies and to be part of the global economy. To be more competitive, closed societies will need to open up more. More open societies eventually lead to more democratic organization.

Does this apply to American business? Will accelerating use of electronic and digital technologies within a company lead to more decentralized and networked organizations? Will more peer-to-peer communications and distributed work drive corporate organization to less hierarchical and more democratic forms?

Imagine Deng Xiaoping, the leader of China, as the CEO of a multinational. Up from the ranks, this diminutive CEO has been a reform-minded leader, credited with saving the company years ago. Then, he installs an enterprisewide, globally distributed computer network that puts everyone in direct touch with everyone else. He pushes down decision making, encourages creativity, stimulates joint ventures, and cuts red tape.

When push comes to shove, this CEO also insists on traditional hierarchical control. He centralizes power in the hands of a small group of loyal executives. The contradictions fed by the new technologies lead the company into turmoil. Mass firings result. The "old boys" win, but the company's finances and morale are in shambles. It has severely compromised its ability to compete internationally.

It doesn't have to be this way. Rather than fighting the driving forces, put them at your back. Make them work for you. Let them provide new energy for getting where you want to go.

Corning chairman James Houghton consciously restructured his company from a traditional corporate hierarchy to a "global network" over a six-year period. He did this because it is necessary to provide the "flexibility and strength" to meet growing international competition, he says.[12]

PARTICIPATORY DEMOCRACY

In the broad cultural context, global networks are both the stimulus for and the sociological response to electronic and digital technology. Networks are the singular organizational response to the driving forces of information, just as hierarchy developed in the Agricultural Era and bureaucracy matured in the Industrial Era.

There is a new politics that has not come from the barrel of a gun but from communication and shared visions. Networking is the basis for a new participatory democracy that extends the bureaucratic representation system to everybody. Information and the sources of control are no longer scarce resources. It is structurally and technologically possible to participate directly in the processes of self-governance on a local, national, and global level.

Networks link peers for a purpose. There is immense power in myriad people voluntarily interacting to effect a common cause. Teamnets emerge as people engage with others based on their values.

There is more opportunity for more people to be leaders. Networks need more leaders than hierarchies and bureaucracies. Leadership cannot depend upon force or policies for control. Networks link work to personal values, the most compelling source of motivation without coercion. When teamnets work, people feel good about their contributions, feel valued by peers, and have an increased sense of self-worth.

The teamnet approach dynamically balances and creatively strengthens both individuality and cooperation. Rosemarie Greco, a nun-turned-CEO of a $5.7 billion bank, sums this up as one of her essential learnings:

There is unlimited power in the fusion of organizational vision and individual fulfillment.[13]

Networking is a natural way for people to work and function in the polity. Still, we need new skills and ways of thinking about groups to take advantage of the transforming forces of our time.

THE BIG BOOM

The way to play follow the leader today is to turn around and see who's behind you. In 1993, a new generation takes power, represented by a youthful president. The evidence is in that a new generation of change agents is indeed emerging.

The symbolic beginning of the baby boom generation is 1945. That year is fraught with meaning—the atom bomb drops on Hiroshima and Nagasaki, the United Nations signs its initial charter in San Francisco, and ENIAC, the first electronic computer, is switched on in Philadelphia. The baby boom grows up in the after-effects of these events: haunted by the specter of thermonuclear war; aware of an interdependent global society balanced on a fragile planet; and the first to grapple with computers and electronic communication.

To understand the unusual impact of this generation, you need only look at the numbers. Demographers often use the image of a python swallowing a pig to describe the post–World War II population bulge moving through the age brackets all around the world. Besides history, issues, and technology, the sheer numbers of this generation promote the formation of networks. So many people reach for so few traditional positions that they create an additional force to multiply positions in politics, business, and every other institution. The reason is simple:

Hierarchies limit the number of power seats.

Demographers call the baby boomers an "unfavored" generation. In "favored" generations, such as the group just leaving power and the one that follows the baby boom, the number of contenders to the thrones is fewer. A relatively high proportion of a relatively small number of people fills the choice leadership positions. Conversely, in "unfavored" generations, like the baby boom, relatively few can reach the tiny top ranks of organizational pyramids. In a hierarchical world, the "boomers" are the most unfavored in history.

As the moment for taking power arrives for this generation, the "Plum Book" looks frightfully thin.[14] Not only are the seats at the top limited, but the American workplace also is eliminating middle management. Between the twin forces of corporate downsizing and the simplistic flattening of organizational structures, the power spots are shrinking.

Without teamnets, this generation faces intragenerational warfare and the waste of extraordinary human resources. With teamnets, we can greatly expand leadership and encourage true empowerment.

GLOBALLY DISTRIBUTED GLOBAL WORK

Work-at-a-distance is not only about doing business better. It is also about how we collectively can address the really big issues of our time. People are, after all, naturally distributed around the planet. We cannot solve the world's problems by bringing everyone together face-to-face in one place.

The great promise of today's networks lies in their ability to accomplish work with physically distributed groups, work traditionally done by people in the same place.

By linking physically dispersed peers—whether people, groups, organizations, or countries—local interests can engage in global purposes. Local and global are complements in networks, both intrinsically important.

Distributed work offers flexible use of resources, access to limited resources, and load balancing. Human resources in particular benefit in a globally networked organization. Access to a global workforce will progress from a value-added convenience today to an absolute necessity tomorrow. By being able to draw on a broadly based resource pool, networks also have access to a richer and more diverse skill set than is available to a collocated group.

Speed in getting new work started and speed in dissolving teams upon completion of a purpose are differentiators in the marketplace. Organizations that tap people's skills while leaving them physically in place have great competitive advantage. This flexibility translates into more responsiveness and better solutions.

Both the organization and the individual benefit from distributed work. A networked workforce is a happier and less stressed one. By greatly reducing the pressures for relocation, the costs in dollars, family stability, and community support are enormously relieved. People are happier because distributed work requires personal commitment to a project, and thus some alignment of team goals with individual goals.

Only by learning how to do networked work can everyone

affected by a complex problem come together to solve it. Humanity can avoid the inevitable alternative of authoritarian control and perpetual crisis. By creating effective teamnets, we can solve our collective problems.

What we are looking for here are planetary benefits. The synergy of the whole. A networked planet would be truly extraordinary.

NETWORKS OF NATIONS

As generational transition transpires in Washington, we see the empires and superpowers of the Industrial Age completely losing their hegemony. In the early 1990s, the Soviet empire disaggregates internally and externally. Though feeling the effects of the global recession, Japan and other Asian countries are on the rise. The European Economic Community is coming of age. Leaders of the world are addressing concerns that they can resolve only on a global basis: the interlocked economy, global warming, ozone depletion, AIDS, nuclear proliferation.

If there is not to be one world government, or one or two dominant superpowers, what is the vision of how to live together on this one planet? What is a mode of world governance that will in fact work? Does a World Hierarchy served by a Global Bureaucracy seem right?

With the little-noticed death of the internationalist dream of a One World Government in the past few decades, there is a pregnant vacuum waiting to birth a new vision of global governance.

The emergence of *networks of nations* is upon us. This vision of the future sees multiple international networks where the members are sovereign nations. Each nation integrates into the global whole and yet remains an independent entity with its own integrity and substantial self-reliance.

Networks are a natural for nations, even very hierarchical ones. They protect sovereignty while increasing cooperation and benefits. Teamnets of nations are peer-based and relationship-rich ways to deal with our world's megaproblems. Myriad international relations at all levels—grass-roots, academic, trade, professional, religious, cultural, and personal—thicken the links among the people of the world.

LEARNING ACROSS BOUNDARIES

Here are some of the ways governments can take a page from business and grass-roots networks:

- Learn from business how to apply discipline to networks, leverage smaller bureaucracies, and operate in leaner, flatter hierarchies.
- Learn from the grass roots how to deliver what people want for the lowest cost with the broadest access and highest participation.
- Learn from the pioneers on the electronic frontier how to leverage new network technologies to involve people at every level of decision making. Electronic town meetings only scratch the surface of what's interactively possible.
- Learn how to quickly develop and use a global telecommunications highway to enable faster, better networking in every sector.

Here are some of the ways teamnets will affect business in the 1990s and beyond:

- Jobs, jobs, jobs. By revitalizing small and medium-sized companies through flexible business networks, employment will increase. Rebuilding local communities and regions through large-scale economic network development—including focus on the smallest and poorest levels through micro-enterprise development—will bring unemployment down further.
- The trend to restructure organizations from hierarchy to networks will accelerate. Driven by the clear business benefits of speed, flexibility, and power, networks enable companies to compete successfully on the global stage.

- As the baby boom generation gains power, corporate governance will become more democratic. The pressure from sheer size to increase leadership will combine with learning gained from grass-roots networks.
- The major social issues of the 1960s—such as minority and female participation at all levels and greatly increased awareness of environmental factors—will permeate business in the 1990s. Business will pay more attention to the "double bottom line," focusing on companies' social as well as financial performance.
- The never-ending, ever-faster technology change driver will continually add to networking capability in the years ahead as far as can be seen. As always, networks driven by technology will leap out ahead and pull on organizations to reorganize into more flexible and smarter forms.

Global People Network

The world today needs a vision. We need to believe that with honest work our lives can improve, our children can prosper, and our environment can flourish.

- *"Small is beautiful,"* the economist E. F. Schumacher pointed out.
- *"Do more with less,"* the design scientist Buckminster Fuller advised.
- *"Think globally, act locally,"* the Pulitzer Prize winner René Dubos inspired.

To this short list, we add a phrase that is the essence of our networking vision:

- *"Global people network."*

We live in global times—personally, environmentally, and economically. Teamnets enable people to reach across differences. Networking solves problems in a way that contributes to the metasolution of the global *problématique*: it enables people to work together better.

We are one planet and many networks—the organizations of the future in a world that works.

REFERENCE SECTION

Transforming Bureaucracies and Systems

For the truly deep divers in organizational design, this section is for you. If your job involves navigating complex bureaucracies or trying to change prevailing systems, you will find this material helpful.

- Bureaucracies spawn three major types of teamnets: functional, divisional, and matrix. Compare your teamnet with these types and become familiar with the risks associated with each.
- Each of the Five Teamnet Principles has a systems principle corollary. This offers hooks into the vast literature of systems approaches to business and management, as well as immediate handles on distributed systems of all types—economic, social, and technological.

If you already consider yourself a systems thinker, you can regard this section as a new way to approach systems principles. If your interest is more general, think of this section as providing deep background on the essential ideas of the book. Even if systems thinking has never appealed to you, you might find helpful extrapolations that connect with other ideas you hold dear.

Bureaucracies and Teamnets

For many centuries, technology and organization have been engaged in a complex dance. Advances in technology spawn new forms of organization that encourage the development of new technology. One great wave of change comes on the heels of the European Renaissance and the invention of mechanistic science. Steam engines follow Isaac Newton's laws of motion, as do bureaucracies. Specialized, formal, machinelike organizations and assembly lines clack along behind the steam engines and their energetic offspring. In the movie *Modern Times*, Charlie Chaplin satirizes the human cog in the Industrial Age machine.

This organizational machine mentality fights to retain supremacy as another great wave of change breaks over the 20th century. The fertile minds of Albert Einstein and his colleagues first glimpsed a new age in the early part of the century. It fully bursts forth in the waning days of World War II as nuclear knowledge explodes over Hiroshima and Nagasaki in 1945. By mid-century, the use of television and computers fully reveals the outlines of the technological drivers of fundamental change.

As we speed toward the 21st century, we are living the Launch Phase of the Information Age. Today, global networks are emerging in the wake of new knowledge, technologies, and the world economy. Networks do not replace hierarchy and bureaucracy; rather, they include them. To understand better where teamnets came from, we look more closely at hierarchy and bureaucracy.

CENTRALIZED HIERARCHY AND
SPECIALIZED BUREAUCRACY

Traditional 20th-century organizations derive the coordination of centralized control from hierarchy and the power of replicable specialization from bureaucracy.

The separate uses of these two organizational dynamics—*centralization* and *specialization*—are clearly visible in the military: everyone has (a) hierarchical rank and (b) a specialized function. Similarly, the organizational title "vice president for finance" identifies both dynamics: a rank (vice president) and a function (finance).

"Specialization" is an abstract term that translates into jobs. Your job is your specialty. At the level of the firm, specialization defines the business you are in and what differentiates you from other companies. Specialization is where purpose gets specific.

In "Fighting Fire with Organization," chapter 12, we highlight the importance of getting the purpose right. Purposes come together in three basic ways: through complementary needs, common needs, or through a mix of both. These three ways of combining specialization correspond to three basic types of bureaucracy: functional, divisional, and matrix.

• Hierarchy	• Centralization
• Bureaucracy	• Specialization
– Functional	– Complementary
– Divisional	– Common
– Matrix	– Mixed

Complementary departments are the basis for the *functional* form of bureaucracy. These one-of-each-kind organizations combine capabilities such as marketing, design, production, service, and sales. Historically, the pure classical railroad-and-steel-type bureaucracy works best for producing standard products in a slowly changing market. Where these conditions don't prevail, the legacy of functional bureaucracy—awesomely exaggerated in government—plagues every aspect of society today. People are not joking when they call them dinosaurs.

> *A functional bureaucracy is a set of
> different specialties that come together as
> a special-purpose machine under central
> control.*

In the early 1900s, bureaucracy begins to spawn a significant varia-
tion on the classic form. Faced with the need to achieve even greater
economies of scale—particularly for capital utilization—the largest
of firms forge *divisions*. At General Motors in the 1920s, Alfred P.
Sloan invents large, semiautonomous operating units, each with its
own complete complement of functions. To the public, these divisions become well known by their product names—Chevrolet, Pon-
tiac, Buick, Oldsmobile, Cadillac, GMC Trucks. After World War II,
divisions proliferated in many large companies, usually organized
either by related products or services, or by marketing regions.

> *A divisional bureaucracy is a centralized
> cluster of similar special-purpose
> machines.*

As the Information Age reaches early adolescence in the 1960s
and 1970s, conventional functions and divisions proved increasingly
inadequate in fast-moving industries. So the third child of bureaucracy formed: the *matrix*. Instead of inserting a divisional layer and
duplicating functions, companies maintain relatively stable functions, intersected by a number of relatively quickly changing divisional markets or products. With its dual reporting structure—one
to the function and one to the project under way (or product, or
region)—the matrix enables organizations to adapt more quickly to
markets.

A matrix offers the stability of functions and the flexibility of divisions.

WHY BUREAUCRACIES FAIL

Each bureaucratic form has a tendency to fail in different ways.[1]

Functional firms fail when they grow beyond their ability to fully use all their special skills and machines. Sometimes failure occurs insidiously slowly, as a company loses its ability to tell how well a function does its job or how much value it contributes to the whole enterprise. While sheer size alone overloads a functional organization, so does widening the scope of products or services beyond the capabilities of centralized management. It is far too easy to take on too much as the pace of change accelerates. Success—and giddy bureaucratic growth—are often the precursors to dramatic and seemingly sudden failure.

Divisions have a different problem. While sharing some of the autonomy found in networks, divisions suffer from the weakness of their centralized superstructure. Typically, corporate executives *force* cooperation across divisions, undercutting the self-reliance and market sensitivity of the business unit. While self-initiated cooperation across divisions works, mandated cooperation—something of an oxymoron—does not. Divisional bureaucracies also overreach themselves when they buy or create new divisions that stray too far from their core expertise.

Matrix organizations have yet different weaknesses. Subject to the vagaries required to balance between stable and changing factors, the matrix manager has considerable difficulty serving two masters. Either the functions are too strong, and the projects are too weak—or vice versa. Centralized control and the complexity of the interrelations do not an easy mix make. What they do create is many middle managers with much responsibility but little authority. The complexity of matrix management too easily overloads central control mechanisms. When companies exert a centralized effort to maximize global enterprise benefits, they also tend to limit the adaptability of local units.

BYE-BYE BUREAUCRACY

People often contrast networks with hierarchy, and even hold them in opposition to one another. The clash between centralization and decentralization is epic and sometimes brutal in specific circumstances. From a distance, however, it appears to be much more a dance of dynamic balance. In the end, there are always aspects of both in any successful human organization.

---

*Networks do not eliminate hierarchies—
they balance and reduce them.*

While hierarchies are likely to be leaner in well-networked organizations, bureaucracy may be decimated altogether. Networks offer a more direct challenge to bureaucracies because they offer an alternative way of organizing specialized units, promoting autonomy rather than dependence.

---

*For many purposes, networks replace
bureaucracy.*

As traditional companies find themselves pushed to become more networked, they can move beyond bureaucracy in both internal and external ways. Whether attention is on internal or external changes, or both, companies need to carefully create and nurture the Co-opetition Dynamic. Healthy networks integrate and sustain the forces of *competition*—independent members and multiple leaders—with the forces of *cooperation*—unifying purpose and voluntary links.

Problems in particular teamnets follow from both excesses and deficiencies in the forces of co-opetition. To develop a "failure detection device," we look at the weaknesses of different teamnet types in terms of competition and cooperation.

The teamnet types discussed here follow the same form as those presented in "In It Together," chapter 4, and "Inside-Out Teamnets," chapter 5, and summarized in "Fighting Fire with Organization," chapter 12, particularly in the chart "From Bureaucracy to Teamnets." Here, they appear for easy comparison with their bureaucratic progenitors.

TEAMNETS OF THE FUNCTIONAL PERSUASION

Teamnets that develop among functions thrive on *complementary* needs. Together, these functional components form an economically viable whole:

- Internally, through cross-functional teams, sociotechnical systems, and top teams; and
- Externally, through core firms, joint ventures, and vertically integrated flexible business networks.

Internal Functions

Cross-functional teams, such as Conrail's Strategy Management Group, in which a companywide cross-section of managers makes strategic decisions, or Digital's Calypso team, are the most common type of teamnet that springs up in bureaucracies. They thread across the company's functions, choosing one from Column A, one from Column B. Usually operating under hierarchical oversight, cross-functional teams coordinate activities among multiple specialties.

Internally, functional networks are at risk for many competitive reasons:

- Turf wars, the all too familiar situation where organizational territory takes precedence over corporate strategy;
- Decision making so protective and cross-functionally feeble that it grinds to a halt in gridlock;
- Disenfranchisement, in which cross-functional teams receive so little legitimacy from the hierarchy that they end up as just another committee.

There are also cooperative reasons for failure, such as:

- Excessive involvement, where people think everyone needs to be consulted in everything, which, of course, brings all progress to a halt; and
- Groupthink, where people lose their critical thinking faculties, resulting in bad decisions.

External Functions

Functional networks also form across company lines, often driven by big companies in trouble. This was exactly how Harry Brown found Erie Bolt when he took over the Erie, Pennsylvania, bolt maker. It was losing money and "looked like a mini-GM," he said. As part of a value chain, Erie Bolt, the producer, forms market-based relationships with a few upstream suppliers and downstream distributors. In Denmark, Alphabetica, a network of small firms, provides complete interiors for buildings—from interior design to delivering the plants for the lobbies. These networks, whether organized by a core firm or a group of complementary firms, provide diverse expertise with reduced risk. Responsibility for assets spreads across all the firms, separately stimulating each partner to make full use of his own capabilities by maintaining other relationships outside the network.

Intercompany functional teamnets fail for competitive reasons when:

- Upstream and downstream businesses unduly rely on one core firm and unhealthy co-dependencies emerge; and
- In a small group of firms, total dependence on one another for business success leaves them subject to the same inefficiencies as a rigid functional bureaucracy.

They fail due to cooperative weaknesses, including:

- Pressure of excessive coordination, compromising the creativity of specialized partners, or retarding a swift response to market changes.

DIVISIONAL TEAMNETS

Common needs are the basis for teamnets with divisional structures, in contrast to the complementary needs that bind functional teamnets.

- Inside companies, divisional teamnets include service webs, empowered clusters, study circles, and empowered work groups; and
- Externally, divisional teamnets appear as horizontally articulated flexible business networks and the numerous industry associations of "like" companies.

Internal Divisions

When a company creates divisions and reaggregates as internal networks, it does so by reducing business units to the smallest independently viable size. At Procter & Gamble, this means forming many self-directed work groups. In British Petroleum's clusters, units of 40 to 50 people effectively perform all administrative functions. W. L. Gore & Associates limits a new factory to 200. These internal units operate within their hierarchy's guidelines; their relative autonomy and small size enable them to cope rapidly with diverse local conditions and global market changes.

Divisional networks are competitively weak inside companies when:

- The autonomous parts have too little understanding of the whole enterprise; and
- The effort to maximize the unit's economic results means suboptimizing the corporate whole.

Divisional networks fail in the cooperation domain when:

- The hierarchy, ever lurking with the executive impulse to control, takes over in a crisis, and crises seem to multiply; and
- Units adhere to a too-detailed strategy that squelches incentives for local initiatives.

External Divisions

The Philadelphia Guild is a group of businesses that has designed a line of home office furniture. They differentiate around unique pieces of the line, while they pool their common needs as woodworkers. These small business "divisional" teamnets typically form in industries with limited economies of scale and circumscribed opportunities for vertical integration, such as garments, metalworking, and woodworking. Such teamnets also are common in industries with a high rate of change and a dependence on very skilled people, like high-tech and bio-tech.

Such divisional networks have competitive weaknesses when:

- Partners become overspecialized, burrowing into a niche so small that other firms with broader expertise take over the role.

Among externally divisionalized networks, cooperative failures arise from:

- Linkages that persist with no economic advantage even after circumstances have changed; and
- Opportunities are missed because of preexisting exclusive relationships.

MATRIX TEAMNETS

Matrix teamnets are the most complex. They use the glues of both functions, which are stable and complementary, and divisions, which are changing and common, in very fast-moving environments:

- Internally, they appear in kaizen management approaches and development of internal markets; and
- Externally through keiretsu, voluntary geographies, and SME economic development.

Internal Matrix

Very large, very lean organizations that require large capital investments are the ultimate in internal matrix networks, the purported direction of the new decentralized IBM of the 1990s. Internal market mechanisms calibrated by the external market test the value of multiple commonly owned business units. Internal market controls replace perpetually out-of-date administrative procedures, as the electrical equipment business of Asea Brown Boveri attests. Matrix teamnets fail competitively when:

- Internal units with specialized assets produce more than the internal market can absorb at competitive advantage over external sources.

Cooperative weakness of the internal matrix is inevitable when:

- The residual hierarchy cannot control the temptation to issue commands instead of using influence and incentives to guide component operations.

External Matrix

The external matrix teamnet is a dynamic environment where many independent firms create multiple relationships drawing from a large number of possible partners. Relationships form, dissolve, and re-form based on both complementary and common needs. Japanese keiretsu are an early form of subnational matrix teamnets: many separate firms in different industries with multiple interdependencies cluster around a common bank. Emilia-Romagna and Denmark are dynamic economies of many flexible business networks, a development strategy for countries or regions with many small firms.

These large-scale dynamic teamnets are prone to competitive paralysis because:

- People all around the world initially respond to the idea of business networks in the same way: "We are too independent to cooperate."

Cooperative failure at this level results when:

- A "we'll do it for you" attitude on the part of core firms, brokers, or other leaders results in an unhealthy number of dependency relationships and subsequent distortion of economic realities; and

• Overzealous public agencies or strategic planners at a lead bank slip from a suggestive into a directive role.

This section summarizes the taxonomy of teamnets and their risk points. This is an example of using systems theory to manage complexity: it pulls a disparate variety of cases into an integrated framework to leverage common principles. We expand upon the systems infrastructure next.

Holism for the Left Brain

"Network" is a general concept like "system." Networks of molecules, neurons, waterways, transportation, television stations, and computers share common features, such as nodes (members) and links.

Consider the next few pages an extremely short course in systems thinking. Use it to help you simplify complexity. Each of the network concepts has an analog in general systems theory. By associating these concepts with one another, we leverage the phenomenal power of such complexity-busting tools as the systems principle of hierarchy:

NETWORK PRINCIPLE	SYSTEMS PRINCIPLE
• Network	• System
• Purpose	• Synergy
• Members	• Holons
• Links	• Relationships
• Leaders	• Representation
• Levels	• Hierarchy
• Co-opetition	• Complementarity
• Phases	• Logistic growth curve

NETWORKS ARE SYSTEMS

Systems theory the world around permeates advanced management techniques such as the quality movement and sociotech approaches. When W. Edwards Deming, the father of quality, turned to science, he did not borrow from the traditional reductionism of Frederick Winslow Taylor. Rather, he viewed science holistically, as do other great systems scientists, such as Herbert Simon and Kenneth Boulding. Deming's business systems model is very straightforward:

Every value-producing organization receives inputs from suppliers and provides outputs to customers.

Networks are systems, pure and simple. Anywhere a systems concept will work, so will a network concept. Indeed, for many systems, particularly social systems, networks are an easier sell.

In the social world, people do not much love the word "system." It's easy—and often justified—to hate "the system." Some people hate it so much that they are blind to their aversion.

Little wonder. Most traditional systems are "black boxes." Think of the tax system or the international monetary system or even the municipal garbage system. Most systems portray themselves as beyond the comprehension and control of ordinary mortals. Traditional systems science is much the same. It also offers an obfuscating self-portrait of systems as black boxes, unfortunately too complicated for just anyone to understand.

With networks, you can take the wraps off systems. Instead of "black box" systems, create "glass box" networks. Make the outer boundary of the whole transparent. See inside to the parts—the members—and to the relationships—the links—between the

Black Box, Glass Box

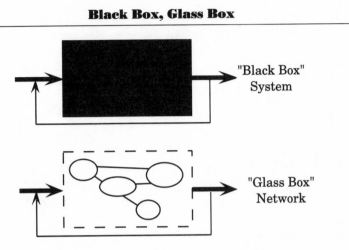

"Black Box"
System

"Glass Box"
Network

parts. The more clearly you lay out the network-system elements, the easier it is to understand.

It is difficult to "see" a physically distributed organization. Turn this liability to advantage by promoting "whole systems awareness." Emphasize how all the parts interrelate. A systems view enables you to grasp a network as naturally as the hand of a friend.

PRINCIPLE 1: SYNERGY BECOMES YOU

"The whole is more than the sum of the parts." This systems principle is so popular that it's almost a cliché. In networks, purpose is the "more than" that defines the whole, what Buckminster Fuller called "synergy." Purpose is what enables a group of independent people to do something together that they cannot do alone. Together, synergy is possible; in isolation, it is not.

> *To function, your system—no matter how minimal—has to have some synergy or purpose.*

Purpose relates very practically to how people become legitimized in networks. In a simple hierarchy, you gain legitimacy from the authority structure, with its system of rewards and punishments. In bureaucracies, control comes from charters and all manner of legalities and policies. In networks, legitimacy is an altogether different animal. You gain real legitimacy through contribution to the shared purpose.

Develop purpose as a resource for your team, just as people develop procedures and policies using law as a resource. Encourage your members to participate in planning and decision making to internalize the purpose for themselves. Externalize the purpose through explicit plans, information access, and by creating symbols—logos, nicknames, acronyms. Instead of controlling one another through one-way orders or endlessly detailed policies, boundary crossing teamnet members exercise control through their shared process.

PRINCIPLE 2: THE BEST MEMBER IS A HOLON

Each of us is a *whole* person who plays a *part* in businesses, families, and communities.

What sorts of things are simultaneously wholes and parts? Everything. Arthur Koestler, the author and systems thinker, coined the word "holon" to stand for this whole/part characteristic of everything.[2] This "systems within systems" feature of nature is fundamental to understanding complexity.

View teamnet members as holons. The autonomy of teamnet members means that they are independent parts; they have their own integrity and own life processes of survival and growth. This is true whether the members are alliances of firms or individual peers on a team.

Parts and wholes have names. Companies, departments, divisions, functions, projects, programs, and teams all have names. From a systems perspective, these names label *categories*. They differentiate the parts of complex systems. Bureaucratic boxes and network nodes both function as categories; they both collect people, things, and activities into coherent clusters. In real life, we are all parts of many categories, many social clusters, many boxes. Sometimes, the same name represents both a bureaucratic box and a network node: an engineering group is both a node in the product development boundary crossing teamnet, and a bureaucratic departmental box at the same time.

There are important differences here. While you play multiple roles in multiple networks, in hierarchies you appear in one and only one box. As a network member, you are relatively independent and demonstrate strong tendencies to autonomy. In a bureaucracy, you are relatively dependent and look for precision fit. When it comes to the independence-dependence continuum, network nodes and bureaucratic boxes lean to opposite poles.

PRINCIPLE 3: THE INTERCONNECTED WEB OF RELATIONSHIPS

Relationships are elusive things. For some people, they are real; for others, they are not. Some people literally cannot see relationships, even indirectly. These people do well in organizations with a rule to govern every aspect of behavior. They don't fare well in teamnets. Relationships are at a network's core.

There are so many relationships involved in life, and so many different kinds of them everywhere you look. To simplify this vast interconnected mess, traditional organizations have many one-way signs. Hierarchies and bureaucracies take an extremely limited approach to how parts interconnect. Generally speaking, orders and information flow in a minimal number of formal channels. Information flows up and commands flow down. This traffic pattern gives rise to the walls, stovepipes, silos, and other hard-to-penetrate boundaries in organizations.

By contrast, in networks, connections are many rather than few. Information and influence flow both up and down the levels through links, as well as horizontally within levels. What is the situation with your boundary crossing teamnet? Do information and influence flow along a two-way highway, or are people stopped for going against the traffic?

Systems thinking has historically emphasized relationships. Peter Senge's book, *The Fifth Discipline*, is an excellent example of a systems approach to complexity for business based on understanding processes and relationships.[3] Gregg Lichtenstein, one of the leading facilitators of flexible business networks, wrote about "the significance of relationships in entrepreneurship" for his doctoral dissertation in social systems science.[4] June Holley and Roger Wilkens have developed a systems dynamics model of flexible networks to guide the development of networks of small manufacturers in southern Ohio.[5]

PRINCIPLE 4: REPRESENTATIVE LEADERSHIP

Nothing in groups is as complicated as leadership. One way to simplify complex wholes is to grasp a part that represents the rest. For example, Wall Street is shorthand for America's financial system; the White House stands for the executive branch of government; the Oval Office represents the White House.[6] In the search for simple ways to "grasp a group," leaders come in handy. Leaders are people who stand for a group.

All organizations have leaders, even self-directed groups, where leadership comes from within rather than from without. Networks are rife with leaders. By definition, leaders are partial representatives whose views others need to supplement.

To Americans, hierarchies in the social sense are single-pointed pyramids. Unfortunate as the burden is impractical, in a hierarchy everything supposedly comes together at the top in one perfect person. In a hierarchy, the rule is the fewer the leaders the better—with as little change as possible for as long as possible.

The same is not true in networks. As we stress repeatedly, the more leaders the better. In the best of networks, everyone is a leader. Everyone provides guidance in specific realms of expertise, their talents and knowledge all contributing to the success of the group. People alternate between leadership and followership roles in fast-moving networks with many parallel interconnected activities.

PRINCIPLE 5: HIERARCHICAL LEVELS

While in some ways boundary crossing teamnets are very different from hierarchies, in others they are the same. Do not despair. This is not some sort of depressing truth that makes us want to say, "See? I knew there was nothing different here, after all." Consider it instead a great source of comfort. Since you already know a great deal about hierarchies, draw on your experience as a source of strength.

Were you schooled in the analytic, "break-it-down," mechanistic, one-size-fits-all strategy approach to anything complicated? We were, and so was nearly everyone else in the West. This half-brained approach to thinking has its strengths but also its limitations in solving life's problems. From a systems perspective, it ignores the parallel value of synthesis, the "build-it-up" holistic strategy, critical for all living systems, including human ones.

What systems am I part of? What environments is the team part of? What contexts is the company part of? What systems . . .

One of the great ironies of systems science lies in the term "hierarchy." Hierarchy is the most common principle threading through the multitude of systems theories.[7] Every comprehensive systems theory uses it, regardless of its native discipline. According to Herbert Simon, the father of information science, hierarchy is nature's "architecture of complexity."[8] Confusion over the word, which literally means "priestly rulership," has kept this idea from being widely understood where it is needed most, in human affairs.[9]

Hierarchy is what we mean by *levels*.

The social use of the term "hierarchy" includes the scientific one, levels of organization. Unfortunately, when people apply the word to organizations, they also add another characteristic: vertical control. In social hierarchies, the higher you are, the better off you are, and the more power you have; the lower you are, the worse off you are, and the less power you have.

As true as this may be in your local hierarchy, let us say most emphatically that *top-down* is only one of many possible relationships between levels. Exclusive one-way control is *not* natural in nature's hierarchies. Rather than dominating one another, levels are interdependent. More inclusive levels have critical dependencies on lower levels. Molecules would have a tough time without atoms. Organisms wouldn't be much without cells, which rely on molecules. The life of cells follows its own rules quite apart from an organism's life, which has its own special rules. These are all examples of hierarchy in the natural scientific sense.

Complex boundary crossing teamnets *are* "systems of systems within systems." Every teamnet is a hierarchy of wholes and parts. Teamnet members are systems of systems. The systems principles of segmentation and inclusion apply every time a group splits up into task teams or an alliance jells.

LOVE AND MARRIAGE, HORSE AND CARRIAGE: THE COMPLEMENTARITY OF CO-OPETITION

"Co-opetition" brings the complements of cooperation and competition into one word. This dynamic between the self and others is one of many ways *complementarity*, the second fundamental principle of systems (after hierarchy), shows up in networks.[10] When you see your teamnet as both structure and process, you see complementary views of the same thing.

Both hierarchy and complementarity appear everywhere in nature and society. They are grand boundary crossing concepts that cross many terrains of knowledge. Physicists use complements like positive and negative charges, matter and antimatter, and right and left spins. They see fundamental reality as both particles and waves at the same time. In biology, we see life and nonlife, birth and death, male and female, as basic complements. In society, people struggle between *self* and *group*, a natural dynamic that is central to families, communities, and nations alike.

Tension erupts when complements begin to grate against one another. In reality, the tension of duality is always there. When the system begins to shake, stress becomes noticeable as relationships form, break, and re-form. You can use the principle of complements as a simple tool in many teamnet situations. For example, you can take a complementary approach to conflict, using such simple homilies as "There are two sides to every story."

PHASES OF GROWTH

The teamnet concept of process derives from a key pattern recognized by general systems theory. "General systems"—initiated half a century ago by the biologist Ludwig von Bertalanffy and the economist Kenneth Boulding among others—is a scientific discipline that focuses on common patterns, mathematical and otherwise, found in physical, biological, and social systems.

The S curve, also known as the "logistic growth curve," which we use to represent the change process, appears in the original paper von Bertalanffy wrote establishing the field of general systems.[11] It was his first example of an "isomorphy," a general principle that holds across scientific disciplines. *An isomorphy is a boundary crossing principle.*

Timeline

Time

To track the cumulative progress of some change over time, add a second dimension to the simple time line. Now, the straight-arrow process path looks like an S curve. It generates a *plane of change,* a very typical result when you plot change data against time.

Change Line

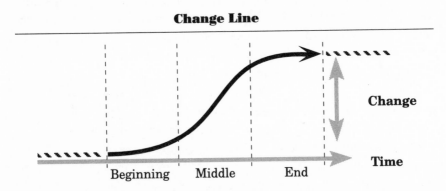

The S curve does equally well at charting the growth of bacteria in a petri dish and the rate at which new technology spreads, for example, the penetration of a cable television franchise into a new area.[12] "Limits to growth" is the common factor in these processes, a major law of all life on this planet.[13]

> *The S curve charts the common dynamic when change starts small, develops slowly, then "suddenly" takes off, rapidly filling out the available opportunity, slowing as it reaches limits, and stabilizing into a new slow- to no-growth pattern.*

Well understood in a wide variety of disciplines, the S curve represents great acquired knowledge, available to those who want to deepen their understanding of process.

The S curve becomes the "stress curve" when you pay attention to the turbulence associated with the two bends in the curve (see "Teamnet Phases of Growth" in chapter 10). The stress curve is a very handy pocket tool for anyone involved with teamnets. Use it as an extremely valuable process aid to plan meetings and conferences of all sizes. Look to the points of turbulence in the process. Use them as alpine skiers do the bumps on the downhill trail: racers anticipate and prejump the bump, leveraging momentum from the bump's back side rather than being thrown for a loop by flying off the front.

Smarter Groups

Human evolution has progressed by substituting brain for brawn.

We see the possibility of much smarter groups as new forms of teamnets integrate with the electronic world of technology networks. Remember:

Only a few generations of humans have had instantaneous electronic communications, and only now are we launching groups linked with the historically unique cognitive (digital) technology of computers.

In the broad cultural context, electronic and digital technology stimulates and shapes the sociological response of global networks. Networks are the unique response to the driving forces of information, just as hierarchy developed in the Agricultural Era and bureaucracy matured in the Industrial Era.

But we don't have to wait for tomorrow for smarter groups. Most people have at some time or another been a member of a group that really "clicks"—a family, work, political, religious, or volunteer effort. Most people intuitively know the tremendous personal satisfaction that is possible with high group performance. Only a small but critical general improvement in people's ability to think and act collectively may have a great impact on solving all the world's problems.

Notes

Introduction

1. For more on the shift from hierarchy to networks, see *Megatrends: Ten New Directions Transforming Our Lives*, by John Naisbitt (New York: Warner Books, 1982).

Chapter 1

1. Denmark spent $50 million on its network programs, 1/2,000th of its annual $100 billion GDP.
2. Quotes on co-opetition from television report from "World News Tonight with Peter Jennings," ABC News, May 18, 1992.
3. Siemens Nixdorf quote on co-opetition from a June 8, 1992, press release distributed by Copithorne & Bellows, Cambridge, Massachusetts, for Siemens Nixdorf Information Systems, Burlington, Massachusetts.
4. Luc de Brandere of Brussels Bourse quote on co-opetition from "Public Sector Gets Private Incentive," by Lucy Kellaway, *Financial Times*, June 18, 1990, p. 28.
5. Ray Noorda quote on co-opetition from "Preaching Love Thy Competitor," by Lawrence M. Fisher, *New York Times*, March 29, 1992, section 3, p. 1, column 2.
6. Ted Engkvist's quote on co-opetition from "NYNEX Information Solutions Group Inc.'s Ted Engkvist Explains Why Systems Integrators Need to Be Specialists," *Systems Integration*, October 1990, p. 19.
7. The emotional nature of cooperation was raised by Darryl Landvater, president of Oliver Wight Publications, in an interview, July 27, 1992, Essex Junction, Vermont.
8. View of Arthur D. Little, Inc., from an interview with ADL Board member Robert Kirk Mueller, published in *The Networking Book*, by Jessica Lipnack and Jeffrey Stamps (New York: Viking Penguin, 1986), pp. 35–44.
9. Subtitle "Small Is Bountiful" is taken from *Old World, New Ideas*, a report by Joseph Cortright on the Northwest Policy Center tour of flexible manufacturing networks in Europe issued April 1990.

(Northwest Policy Center, University of Washington, 327 Parrington Hall, DC-14, Seattle, WA 98195, 206-543-7900.)

10. Joseph Roberts's company, Advanced Circuit Technologies, is one of 10 firms comprising Team Nashua. The firms' individual annual sales range from $500,000 to $20 million and range in size from 8 to 10 employees to 200 people. (Team Nashua, 118 Northeastern Boulevard, PO Box 547X, Nashua, NH 03061, 603-880-6000; fax: 603-880-1785.)

11. MD-12 market projections from "MD-12 Revealed as Taiwan Signals Approval for Tie-up," *Flight International*, May 6, 1992.

12. Quote about the future of the MD-12 from a commentary entitled "New Meaning for 'Worldwide Company,'" by Jessica Lipnack and Jeffrey Stamps, *St. Louis Post-Dispatch*, December 22, 1991; also quoted in *Liberation Management: Necessary Disorganization for the Nanosecond Nineties*, by Tom Peters (New York: Knopf, 1992).

13. View of Japanese networking movement from "Vision of the Alternative Society Described by Networking" keynote speech by Jessica Lipnack and Jeffrey Stamps to the Japan Networkers' Conference, November 12, 1989, Tokyo, Japan.

14. Alfred Peterson's comments on "barbecued sushi" reported in "Managing Paradoxes," by A. W. Demmler, Jr., *Automotive Engineering*, Society of Automotive Engineers, December 1990, vol. 98, no. 12, p. 32.

Chapter 2

1. Computer conferencing "builds on the more familiar features of electronic mail—adding the capability of electronic spaces where groups of people can exchange views, develop plans, manage projects, and coordinate group and team efforts," according to Metasystems Design Group, Inc., 2000 North 15th Street, Suite 103, Arlington, VA 22201, 703-243-6622; fax: 703-841-9798.

2. The Calvert Social Investment Fund, with $1 billion in assets, is the largest of the socially responsible mutual funds; it invests only in companies that pass a series of financial *and* social screens. We've been members of the Advisory Council since the fund was started in 1982.

3. Comment about joining a network fostering independence from manuscript margin notes written to us by Charles Savage, author of *Fifth Generation Management* (Digital Equipment Corporation: Digital Press, 1990).

4. "Working Together Apart" is the subtitle of *Enterprise Networking*, by Ray Grenier and George Metes (Digital Equipment Corporation: Digital Press, 1992).
5. Comment about doing business with the people you know from a telephone interview with Jerry Nagel, Red River Trade Corridor, Inc., 208 Selvig Hall, University of Minnesota, Crookston, MN 56716, 218-281-6510, ext. 458; fax: 218-281-5223.
6. For more on chaos theory, see *Chaos: Making a New Science*, by James Gleick (New York: Viking Penguin, 1987).
7. In "Causes of Failure in Network Organizations" (*California Management Review*, Summer 1992, vol. 34, no. 4), Raymond E. Miles and Charles C. Snow stress this voluntary aspect of network relationships. (*California Management Review*, 350 Barrows Hall, University of California, Berkeley, CA 94720, 510-642-7159.)
8. "Node" is the technical name for a member of a network.
9. "You really need to emphasize the quality of messiness in teamnets," Lisa Carlson of Metasystems Design Group said in a phone interview. "Usually, the same people don't stay on the team the whole time. This makes for comings and goings. It's fuzzy and it's messy." When asked why this was a good thing, she said, "I don't know if it's good or not, but it's true."
10. For more discussion of leadership, see references to Japan's "blunt hierarchy" in "Quick Start," chapter 8.
11. Virginia Hine's classic four-page article, "The Basic Paradigm of a Future Socio-Cultural System," appeared in *World Issues*, Spring 1977 (Center for the Study of Democratic Institutions, Santa Barbara, California).
12. Elizabeth Lorentz's comments on leaders as followers from mss. margin notes. (Lorentz Laboratory for Collaborative Enterprise, 180 South Broadway, White Plains, NY 10605.)
13. "Authority is not bad," Pam Johnson of Digital Equipment Corporation said in response to a draft of this chapter. "An authoritarian way of expressing it *is* bad. Allowing everyone into everything breaks the rule of independence."
14. "The Architecture of Complexity," by Herbert Simon, *General Systems Yearbook*, Society for General Systems Research, 1965, explains the elegant principle described in the article's title.
15. "Hierarchy" is the awkward name for the systems principle of

successive inclusion, meaning systems of subsystems composing supersystems. See "Transforming Bureaucracies and Systems," the Reference Section, for more on the systems context.

Chapter 3

1. Quotes on Armstrong's networks from "How Networks Reshape Organizations—For Results," by Ram Charan, *Harvard Business Review*, September–October 1991. (HBR Publications, Operations Department, Harvard Business School, Boston, MA 02163, 617-495-6192; fax: 617-495-6985.)
2. Henry Bradshaw quote from ibid.
3. For more on The Philadelphia Guild, see "The Philadelphia Woodworking Initiatives: Manufacturing Networks as a Model for Improving Industry Performance," by Gregg A. Lichtenstein and Anthony J. Girifalco, January 1992. (The Delaware Valley Industrial Resource Center, 12265 Townsend Road, Suite 500, Philadelphia, PA 19154-1286, 215-464-8550; fax: 215-464-8570.)
4. Quotes by Percy Barnevik from "The Logic of Global Business: An Interview with ABB's Percy Barnevik," by William Taylor, *Harvard Business Review*, March–April, 1991.
5. Quote about ABB from *Liberation Management: Necessary Disorganization for the Nanosecond Nineties*, by Tom Peters (New York: Knopf, 1992). Note that all ABB statistics are from Peters's 1991 interviews.
6. For more on the pressure of internal comparisons, see sidebar article, "Power Transformers—The Dynamics of Global Coordination," by William Taylor, *Harvard Business Review*, March–April, 1991.
7. Quote from Karlsson on interplay among countries from ibid.
8. Arthur Koestler was one of the earliest systems thinkers to recognize the importance of complementary dynamics in living systems. In *The Ghost in the Machine* (London: Hutchinson & Co., 1967), Koestler describes inward-looking "self-assertive" (competitive) tendencies entwined with outward-looking "integrative" (cooperative) tendencies. Several of his books have such paradoxical titles: *Darkness at Noon* and *Janus*, for example.
9. The phrase "winning combinations" is from the book by that name: *Winning Combinations: The Coming Wave of Entrepreneurial Part-*

nerships between Large and Small Companies, by James W. Botkin and Jana B. Matthews (New York: John Wiley & Sons, 1992).

Chapter 4

1. Conrail quotes from "How Networks Reshape Organizations—For Results," by Ram Charan, *Harvard Business Review*, September–October, 1991.
2. *Forbes* cites W. L. Gore & Associates in "Where to Find the 400 Largest U.S. Private Companies," December 9, 1991, p. 272.
3. For a profile of Robert Gore, see "No Bosses. And Even 'Leaders' Can't Give Orders," by Joseph Weber, *Business Week*, December 10, 1990, p. 196.
4. We published Bill Gore's paper, "The Lattice Organization: A Philosophy of Enterprise," by W. L. Gore, in *Networking Journal*, Spring/Summer 1985, vol. 1, no. 1, p. 24. (The Networking Institute, Inc., 505 Waltham Street, West Newton, MA 02165, 617-965-3340; fax: 617-965-2341.)
5. For an excellent view of corporate culture, see *Organizational Culture and Leadership: A Dynamic View*, by Edgar H. Schein (San Francisco: Jossey-Bass Publishers, 1985).
6. For many years when he was at Exxon Chemical Company, Bill Paul, now of Deltech Consulting, sent a monthly packet of leading-edge management articles to about 100 people. We were on the list, and one of his packets contained "Entrepreneurship Reconsidered: The Team as Hero," by Robert B. Reich, *Harvard Business Review*, May–June 1987.
7. For the ultimate skunkworks story, see *The Soul of a New Machine*, by Tracy Kidder (Boston: Little Brown and Co., 1981).
8. Quote on the vision of a team from *Leading the Team Organization: How to Create an Enduring Competitive Advantage*, by Dean Tjosvold and Mary M. Tjosvold (New York: Lexington Books, 1991).
9. For more on self-directed teams, see *Empowered Teams: Creating Self-Directed Work Groups That Improve Quality, Productivity, and Participation*, by Richard S. Wellins, William C. Byham, and Jeanne M. Wilson (San Francisco: Jossey-Bass Publishers, 1991).
10. Impediments to success discussed in *Self-Directed Work Teams: The New American Challenge*, by Jack D. Orsburn, Linda Moran, Ed

Musselwhite, John H. Zenger, with Craig Perrin (Homewood, Illinois: Business One Irwin, 1990), p. v.

11. "A quality control circle is a small group that voluntarily performs quality control activities within the workplace," writes Masaaki Imai, author of *Kaizen: The Key to Japan's Competitive Success* (New York: McGraw-Hill Publishing, 1986), the influential book on Japanese management practices.

12. For more on self-help networks, see *Networking: The First Report and Directory*, by Jessica Lipnack and Jeffrey Stamps (New York: Doubleday, 1982).

13. Statistics on executive team growth from *Passing the Baton: Managing the Process of CEO Succession*, by R. F. Vancil (Boston: Harvard Business School Press, 1987).

14. Definition of executive team from "Teamwork at the Top: Creating Executive Teams That Work," by David A. Nadler and Deborah Ancona, in *Organizational Architecture: Designs for Changing Organizations*, by David A. Nadler, Marc S. Gerstein, Robert B. Shaw, and Associates (San Francisco: Jossey-Bass Publishers, 1992), p. 212.

15. John Manzo of Digital Equipment Corporation uses this initiation exercise for cross-functional groups.

16. For more on the history of functions in organizations, see *The Seamless Enterprise*, by Dan Dimancescu (New York: Harper Business, 1991), p. 27.

17. Statistics on Hewlett-Packard's success with teams from ibid., p. 18.

18. Quote on hierarchy as an obstacle from *Rebirth of the Corporation*, by D. Quinn Mills (New York: John Wiley & Sons, 1991), pp. 3, 8, 30.

19. Use of clusters in GE Canada from ibid, p. 286.

20. For more on the effective use of technology and its relationship to organizational design, see "Designing High-Performance Work Systems: Organizing People, Work, Technology, and Information," by David A. Nadler and Marc S. Gerstein, in *Organizational Architecture: Designs for Changing Organizations*, p. 118, note 14.

21. Statistics on American Transtech from ibid., p. 110.

22. In regard to technology's not solving problems: One major chemical company did a study of its $2 billion information technology investment and concluded that it could not attribute a single performance increase to its use.

23. Judith Campbell quote in regard to technology's helping organizations from *The Impact of Information Networking on Organizational Design and Strategy,* published by SEI Center Reports at the Wharton School, p. 13. (SEI Center for Advanced Studies in Management, The Wharton School of the University of Pennsylvania, Suite 1400, Steinberg Hall-Dietrich Hall, 3620 Locust Walk, Philadelphia, PA 19104-6371, 215-898-2349; fax: 215-898-1703.)
24. Michael Useem quote on errors from ibid., p. 14.

Chapter 5

1. Quote on big company joint ventures from "Corning Ventures Prove Togetherness Pays," by James Flanigan, *Los Angeles Times,* February 4, 1990, page D1.
2. Statistics on layoffs from "The Job Drought: Why the Shortage of High-Wage Jobs Threatens the U.S. Economy," by Brian O'Reilly, *Fortune,* August 24, 1992, pp. 62–74. This article looks at worker training, job displacement, lowering of income, and education, and includes examples of Fortune 500 companies solving these problems "by banding together" to increase exports, experiencing dramatic gains in areas like Huntsville, Alabama, where exports have increased at twice the national average.
3. In the United States, Fortune 500 companies now employ the same number of people as do businesses owned by women—12 million, according to the May 1992 issue of *Inc.* Figure of 3.6 million job losses from "The Economy: Problems," *New York Times,* February 14, 1993.
4. Description of IBM from "Out of One Big Blue, Many Little Blues: Chairman John Akers Thinks Shock Therapy Will Get IBM Moving," by John Verity, *Business Week,* December 9, 1991, no. 3243, p. 33.
5. Quotes on Corning from James R. Houghton's article, "The Age of the Hierarchy Is Over," *New York Times,* September 24, 1989, Forum section.
6. Quote on liquid crystal displays from "Corning's Class Act," by Keith H. Hammonds, cover story, *Business Week,* May 13, 1991, no. 3213.
7. Statistics on Corning from ibid.
8. Quote from Houghton on his quality initiative from ibid.
9. Corning and Dow Corning revenues from "Dow Corning's Billion-Dollar Crisis," by Bill Vlasic, *Detroit News,* March 8, 1992.

390

Notes

10. Quote on Corning's treating partners fairly from *Partnerships for Profit* by Jordan D. Lewis (New York: Free Press, 1990).
11. Quote on networks as egalitarian organizations from Houghton, "The Age of the Hierarchy Is Over," note 5.
12. Umbrella bullets and definition of kaizen from *Kaizen: The Key to Japan's Competitive Success*, by Masaaki Imai, p. 4. See chapter 4, note 11.
13. According to legend, J. M. Juran's lectures on "quality control management," during a visit to Japan sponsored by the Japan Union of Scientists and Engineers in 1954, pushed the quality movement to an overall management approach.
14. Quote from Philips's Dr. Wisse Dekker from *Kaizen*, note 12, p. 225.
15. Ackoff quote from "Creating Market Economies Within Organizations: A Conference on 'Internal Markets,'" by Jason Magidson and Andrew E. Polcha, *Planning Review*, January–February 1992, pp. 37–40.
16. Observation on use of information in service organizations from "Technology in Services: Creating Organizational Revolutions," by James Brian Quinn and Penny C. Paquette, *Sloan Management Review*, Winter 1990, pp. 67–77.
17. Applicability of service webs to simple and complex organizations from ibid.
18. Quote on the hollow corporation from "The Hollow Corporation: The Decline of Manufacturing Threatens the Entire U.S. Economy," by Norman Jonas, *Business Week*, March 3, 1986, no. 2935, p. 57.
19. Description of Nike from "Causes of Failure in Network Organizations," by Miles and Snow. See chapter 2, note 7.
20. Observation on outsourcing as positive influence on organizations from "Technology in Services," pp. 79–87 (see note 16). "Service technologies smash overheads through outsourcing," they write.
21. Statistics on longevity of joint ventures from *Teaming Up for the 90's: A Guide to International Joint Ventures and Strategic Alliances*, by Timothy M. Collins and Thomas L. Doorley III, (Homewood, Illinois: Business One Irwin, 1991), p. 9.
22. Statistics on merger from ibid., p. 242.
23. Observation on importance of partner autonomy in joint ventures from "Building Strategic Partnerships: Creating and Managing Effective Joint Ventures," by Charles S. Raben, in *Organizational Archi-*

tecture: Designs for Changing Organizations, p. 93. See chapter 4, note 14.

24. First five major categories in which companies work together to pursue joint strategies from *Teaming Up for the 90's*, see note 21.

25. Information about McKesson Corporation from "Beyond Vertical Integration—The Rise of the Value-Adding Partnership," by Russell Johnston and Paul R. Lawrence, *Harvard Business Review*, July–August 1988, vol. 66, no. 4, pp. 94–101.

26. Description of corporate venturing from "Building Strategic Partnerships: Creating and Managing Effective Joint Ventures," by Charles S. Raben, in *Organizational Architecture: Designs for Changing Organizations*, p. 183. See chapter 4, note 14.

27. Quote on Euroventures Fund from Collins and Doorley, note 21, p. 186.

28. Definition of vertical supply alliances from Raben, note 23, p. 264.

29. Advantages of large and small company alliances from Botkin and Matthews, p. 10. See chapter 3, note 9.

30. For more on virtual corporations, see "The Virtual Corporation," *Business Week* cover story, February 8, 1993, and *The Virtual Corporation: Structuring and Revitalizing the Corporation for the 21st Century*, by William H. Davidow and Michael S. Malone (New York: HarperCollins, 1992).

31. Quote from TRW's Joseph Gorman from "Learning from Japan," by Kevin Kelly, Otis Port, James Treece, Gail DeGeorge, Zachary Schiller, and bureau reports, *Business Week*, cover story, January 27, 1992, pp. 52–60.

32. Proposal for a Euro-American keiretsu from "Computers and the Coming of the U.S. Keiretsu," by Charles H. Ferguson, *Harvard Business Review*, July–August 1990.

33. Quote on cooperation and competition from "Regional Networks and the Resurgence of Silicon Valley," by Anna Lee Saxenian, *California Management Review*, Fall 1990, pp. 89–111.

34. Description of biotechnology industry from "Technology in Services: Rethinking Strategic Focus," by James Brian Quinn, Thomas L. Doorley, and Penny C. Paquette, *Sloan Management Review*, Winter, 1990, pp. 79–87.

35. Classic studies on relationship of environment of change to organizational structure by Tom Burns and G. M. Stalker, *The Management of Innovation* (London: Tavistock, 1961).

36. Quote on networks as offering competitive edge for 1990s from Charan. See chapter 3, note 1.
37. Observation on relationship of internal structure to uncertainty from Paul R. Lawrence and Jay W. Lorsch, *Organization and Environment* (Boston: Division of Research, Graduate School of Business Administration, Harvard University, 1967).
38. Quote by USS Fairless Works' Eugene E. Harris from "Looking for— and Building—a Few Good Heroes," *Industry Week*, October 15, 1990, p. 16.

Chapter 6

1. In regard to use of terms, we prefer "flexible *business* networks" (to "flexible *manufacturing* networks") since nonmanufacturing firms also participate in and benefit from the idea.
2. Statistics on Denmark from May 13, 1991, testimony of Niels Christian Nielsen before the Oregon House Committee on Trade and Economic Development considering a networking approach to economic development.
3. Erie Bolt's Harry Brown quotes from "Make Love Not War: How Competitors Are Joining Forces to Create Opportunities They Wouldn't Get on Their Own," by Tom Richman, *Inc.*, August 1988, p. 56.
4. Observation on Erie Bolt from *Catalog of U. S. Manufacturing Networks*, by Gregg A. Lichtenstein, Ph.D., 1992, available from State Technology Extension Program, National Institute of Standards and Technology, A343 Physics Building, Gaithersburg, MD 20899, 301-975-4520; fax: 301-975-2183.
5. Quote on why businesses join networks from ibid.
6. Quote on East Brooklyn having enough metal shops to build a car from "Network: East Brooklyn, NY: Cooperation Is Reviving an Old Industry," *Inc.*, August 1988, p. 58.
7. Regarding small industrial pockets all over the United States: In 1973, we moved our office to the remodeled Futurity Thread Company, in Newton's Nonantum neighborhood. Until earlier that year, women were still spinning thread in the factory, soon to be the offices we would occupy. Futurity Thread was located just a few blocks from Roberts Printing.
8. Statistics on number of flexible business networks in the United States

from "Networking Comes to America," *Entrepreneurial Economy Review*, Spring 1991, vol. 9, no. 3. (Corporation for Enterprise Development, 777 North Capitol Street, N.E. Washington, D.C. 20002, 202-408-9788; fax: 202-408-9793.)

9. Reasons why heat-treating companies joined network from "Heat in Ohio: The Difficult Birth of an American Network," by Dennis J. Giancola in ibid., p. 19.

10. "Manufacturing Networks and State Policy in North Carolina," by Stuart A. Rosenfeld, Raymond Daffner, and William P. Meade, April 1992. (Southern Technology Council, 5001 South Miami Boulevard, P.O. Box 12293, Research Triangle Park, NC 27709, 919-941-5145; fax: 919-941-5594.) Rosenfeld is now executive director of Regional Technology Strategies (P.O. Box 9005, Chapel Hill, NC 27515, 919-933-6699) and publisher of *Firm Connections*, a bimonthly newsletter about flexible manufacturing networks, available from his office.

11. Information about STC's pilot programs from *STC Regional Forum*, December/January 1992, vol. 5, no. 5., a newsletter by Southern Technology Council (see address in previous note).

12. For more on ASTA, contact Arkansas Science and Technology Authority, 100 Main, Suite 450, Little Rock, AK 72201, 501-324-9006.

13. Quote on Arkansas networks from "Rural Perspectives: Linking Networks and Economic Development," by Stuart A. Rosenfeld, *Entrepreneurial Economy Review*, Spring 1991, p. 29.

14. For information on the Arkansas Wood Products Trade Group, contact Arkansas Rural Enterprise Center, Winrock International, Route 3, Box 376, Morrilton, AR 72210-9537, 501-727-5435.

15. For more on Woodworkers Manufacturing Network, contact Felton Lamb, Venture Resources, Inc., Little Rock Technology Center, 100 South Main, Suite 416, Little Rock, AK 72201, 501-375-2004.

16. Quote on Catawba Valley Hosiery Association mills from "Manufacturing Networks and State Policy in North Carolina: Introducing Change" (see address, note 10).

17. Description of TEEMS project genesis from ibid., p. 21.

18. Quote on why TEEMS needed a network from ibid., p. 11.

19. Floppy disk (DOS version) of "Flexible Manufacturing Networks: What, Who, Why, and How," by Paul Sommers, May 22, 1992, (Northwest Policy Center, University of Washington, 327 Parrington DC-14, Seattle, WA 98195, 206-543-7900; fax: 206-543-1096.)

20. To order *Catalog of U.S. Manufacturing Networks* by Gregg Lichtenstein, see address in note 4.
21. Definition of flexible manufacturing network from *Flexible Manufacturing Networks: Cooperation for Competitiveness in a Global Economy* by C. Richard Hatch, ISBN: 0-9605804-8-4, published by the Corporation for Enterprise Development (see note 8).
22. Nielsen quote on independence from his testimony to Oregon Joint Interim Committee on Forest Products Policy, April 12, 1990, p. 8.
23. "NIST Network Brokers Handbook," by C. Richard Hatch, is available from State Technology Extension Program, National Institute of Standards and Technology (see address, note 4.)
24. For more information on the center, contact Anne Heald, Center for Learning and Competitiveness, University of Maryland, School of Public Affairs, College Park, MD 20742, 310-405-6350.

Chapter 7

1. For a synthesis of the International Labour Organization study, the Emilia-Romagna experience, and developments among businesses in Silicon Valley, see "Can Small Business Help Countries Compete?" by Robert Howard, *Harvard Business Review*, November–December 1990, p. 4.
2. Description of Emilia-Romagna renaissance from a firsthand observer. See Hatch's *Flexible Manufacturing Networks*, chapter 6, note 21.
3. Cambridge University forecast on Emilia-Romagna from "Bologna Looks Set to Boom in Next Decade," *Estates Time Supplement*, Reuter Textline, March 6, 1992.
4. Statistics on banking industry in Emilia-Romagna from "Rural Savings Banks in Emilia-Romagna Region Perform Well in 1991," *Il Sole*, June 11, 1992, Reuter Textline.
5. Conclusions drawn from the work of C. Richard Hatch, Stuart Rosenfeld, and other observers.
6. Quote on the benefits of networks from "The Ties That Bind: Networks and the Making of Denmark's Competitive Edge," by C. Richard Hatch in *Entrepreneurial Economy Review*, Spring 1991, p. 13 (available from CFED, see address in chapter 6, note 8).

7. Quote from Niels Christian Nielsen on Denmark's success with networks from interviews with him, May 7–8, 1992, by Jessica Lipnack and Jeffrey Stamps in Washington, D.C.

8. Data on Oregon's employment situation from "Twelve Innovative Ideas for Economic Development, 1990," by Joseph Cortright and Tami Miller. (Joint Legislative Committee on Trade and Economic Development, State Capital, Room 132, Salem, OR 97310, 503-378-8811.)

9. For a copy of Oregon Senate Bill 997, State of Oregon, 1991, contact address in note above.

10. Quote on the power of targeting markets from *Old World, New Ideas*, by Joseph Cortright, April 1990. See chapter 1, note 9.

11. Quote on how governments aid business networks from ibid.

12. Quote on using appropriate language with business people from Ray Daffner, who also reports one businessman congratulating him at a meeting because "this isn't one of those *networks*," telephone interview, December 16, 1992.

Section II

1. For the term "computerless software," we are grateful to Rick Berenson, a Boston area entrepreneur, attorney, and former McKinsey & Company consultant, who first described our work this way.

Chapter 8

1. To obtain a copy of the "Four Hour House" video, contact Building Industry Association of San Diego County, 6336 Greenwich Drive, Suite A, San Diego, CA 92122, 619-450-1221; fax: 619-552-1445.

2. Quote on how much planning goes into the four-hour house from "BIA Needs But 172 Minutes to Build Home," by David Whitwer, *San Diego Daily Transcript*, October 11, 1983.

3. Quote on cooperating during planning phases from "BIA Four-Hour House Not Just Two-Ring Show," by Rob Schupp, *San Diego Daily Transcript*, September 22, 1983.

4. Re: Habitat's blitz builds. Blitz builds are high-profile events, usually attended by celebrities to publicize Habitat's efforts. Former U.S. president Jimmy Carter volunteers a week each year. But blitz builds

are not typical. Usually, Habitat builds houses over a series of consecutive weekends. (Habitat for Humanity, Habitat and Church Streets, Americus, GA 31709-3498, 912-924-6935.)

5. Habitat plans to build 300 to 500 houses in South Florida by 1994 in response to the 75,000 homes damaged by 1992's Hurricane Andrew.

6. This is one of Stephen Covey's *Seven Habits of Highly Effective People* (New York: Simon & Schuster, 1989).

7. Gardner quote from his Remarks to Independent Sector, 1984 Annual Membership Meeting and Assembly, October 17, 1984, Boston, Massachusetts.

8. Derivation of the word "polycephalous" from Hine's "The Basic Paradigm of a Future Socio-Cultural System." See chapter 2, note 11.

9. Business process redesign is also known as "business reengineering"; see *Reengineering the Corporation: A Manifesto for Business Revolution*, by Michael Hammer and Jim Champy (New York: Harper Business, 1993).

10. Books on teams hit some kind of zenith of popularity in the 1990s, but their principles have been around for many years, often known by different names.

11. Four styles of team members from *Team Players and Teamwork: The New Competitive Business Strategy*, by Glenn M. Parker (San Francisco: Jossey-Bass Publishers, 1991).

12. Quote on different kinds of leadership from *Fifth Generation Management*, by Charles Savage. See chapter 2, note 3.

13. Much of this material was inspired by Bruce W. Tuckman's "Development Sequence in Small Groups," in *Psychological Bulletin*, 1965.

Chapter 9

1. CALS stands for "Computer-assisted Acquisition and Logistic Support."

2. Bernie DeKoven of the Institute for Better Meetings displays the cost of meetings by minute for all participants to see. In big companies, these numbers are staggering: a two-day meeting of 15 technical people can cost a company in excess of $12,000. (Institute for Better Meetings, 2972 Clara Drive, Palo Alto, CA 94303, 415-857-1757; fax: 415-493-1417.)

3. "The Strength of Weak Ties," by Mark S. Granovetter, Johns Hopkins

University, originally was published in *American Journal of Sociology*, vol. 78, no. 6, pp. 1360–1380.

4. The phrase "no sense of place" comes from Joel Meyrowitz's book by that name: *No Sense of Place: The Impact of Electronic Media on Social Behavior* (New York: Oxford University Press, 1985).

Chapter 10

1. Max Weber first identified charisma, coercion, and law as the three sources of power in organizations.
2. A desktop computer software tool that charts cross-boundary process is TeamFlow, designed by Ron Cordes. (For more information, contact The Networking Institute, Inc., see chapter 4, note 4.)

Chapter 11

1. By request, the identity of TransOceania remains anonymous.
2. For extensive treatment of groupthink and specifically the Cuban Bay of Pigs invasion, see *Groupthink: Psychological Studies of Policy Decisions and Fiascoes*, by Irving L. Janis (Boston: Houghton Mifflin Company, 1982).

Chapter 12

1. In regard to the structure of fire departments: For three years in the 1970s, we helped the U.S. Department of Commerce set up America's first national fire prevention agency.
2. For more information on his work, contact Doug Engelbart, 89 Catalpa Drive, Atherton, CA 94025, 415-322-9087.
3. Peter and Trudy Johnson-Lenz first coined the term "groupware" in 1978. (Institute for Awakening Technologies, 695 Fifth Street, Lake Oswego, OR 97034, 503-635-2615.)
4. Jerry Nagel, executive director of the Red River Trade Corridor (it runs along the Red River, one of only three rivers in the world that run north) of western Minnesota, eastern North Dakota, and the province of Manitoba, identifies voluntary geographies in North America, in varying degrees of development: the Midsouth Common Market, covering the 50- to 60-county, seven-state trade region around Memphis;

the Pacific Northwest Region; the Toronto-Buffalo Commerce Corridor; Man-Valley Tri-State Network of western Pennsylvania, eastern Ohio, and West Virginia; the Rocky Mountain Trade Corridor reaching from Edmonton, Alberta, through Montana to Denver; the Arizona-Sonora, Mexico, Commission; and the Red River. Nagel also supplied the European list. See chapter 2, note 5.

5. Miles and Snow believe different types of networks develop out of the different types of bureaucracy. See their article, "Causes of Failure in Network Organizations," chapter 2, note 7.

6. Ray Stata quote on planning as a learning process from his article, "Organizational Learning—The Key to Management Innovation," in *Sloan Management Review*, Spring 1989, vol. 30, no. 3.

7. The specific product described here is TeamFlow (see chapter 10, note 2).

8. Quote from Niels Christian Nielsen on each network's containing a surprise from interviews with him, May 7–8, 1992, by Jessica Lipnack and Jeffrey Stamps in Washington, D.C.

Afterword

1. Jan Brenning, another friend from the Oxford days, later told us how Bill Clinton would sometimes arrive late for dinner because he was busy transferring the day's names to his card file. (See "Most Likely to Succeed," by Alessandra Stanley, *New York Times Magazine*, November 22, 1992, for another account of this Clinton habit.)

2. Quote on Clinton as "human switchboard" from "In Transition, Information Is Power," *Washington Post*, November 15, 1992.

3. Quote on Clinton as the "most thoroughly 'networked' politician of his era," from "He's Not Another Carter," by David S. Broder, *Washington Post*, November 15, 1992.

4. *Newsweek* was one of many publications that took a stab at trying to identify the many Clinton networks in "Clinton's Team: The Inner Circles," October 26, 1992.

5. Forty-six Leckford Road (in what was then a working class and now is a gentrified Oxford neighborhood) was a landmark for Americans studying at Oxford in the late 1960s. Jeff Stamps originally rented the three-story brick row house in January 1968, and lived there until he left Oxford to return to the United States in December 1969. Frank

Aller, the Rhodes Scholar profiled in "Most Likely to Succeed" (see "Afterword," note 1), moved into the house before Jeff left. Then Clinton and Strobe Talbott, now Ambassador at Large for the former Soviet Republics, moved in.

6. For more on the power of "the strength of weak ties" see Mark S. Granovetter's article by that name. See chapter 9, note 3.

7. In a famous study, Yale's Stanley Milgram found that anyone in the world could reach anyone else through 5.5 handshakes.

8. During his 1988 presidential campaign, Al Gore carried around a laptop, which had been outfitted for him by Metasystems Design Group, according to Lisa Carlson, one of the company's founders.

9. Starr Roxanne Hiltz and Murray Turoff first used the phrase in their book by that title, *The Network Nation: Human Communication via Computer.* (Reading, Massachusetts: Addison-Wesley Publishing Company, Inc., 1978.)

10. For more on grass-roots networks, see *The Networking Book* by Jessica Lipnack and Jeffrey Stamps (New York: Viking Penguin, 1986).

11. For an excellent account of the media feedback phenomenon in Tiananmen Square, see "When Global Pen Meets Chinese Sword," by Marilyn Lewis, *San Jose Mercury News,* June 11, 1989, Perspective section, p. 1.

12. Quote on why James Houghton reorganized Corning, Inc., into a global network from his article, "The Age of the Hierarchy Is Over." See chapter 5, note 5.

13. Quote on the power of fusing "organizational vision and individual fulfillment" from Rosemarie B. Greco's article, "From the Classroom to the Corner Office," *Harvard Business Review,* September–October 1992, vol. 70, no. 2, p. 54.

14. The "Plum Book" is the name for the directory of 3,000 political appointment jobs in federal government.

Reference Section

1. The observation that bureaucracy fails in one of three ways from Miles and Snow. See chapter 2, note 7.

2. Koestler created the word "holon" from the Greek "holos," meaning "whole" and "-on" meaning "part." See *The Ghost in the Machine.* See chapter 3, note 8.

3. For more on a systems view of business, see *The Fifth Discipline: The Art and Practice of the Learning Organization*, by Peter Senge (New York: Doubleday/Currency, 1990). Some systems theories, like Jay Forrester's Systems Dynamics, are almost purely relational.

4. For more on the topic of its title, see "The Significance of Relationships in Entrepreneurship: A Case Study of the Ecology of Enterprise in Two Business Incubators," a doctoral dissertation by Gregg Lichtenstein presented to the faculties of the University of Pennsylvania, 1992. (Gregg Lichtenstein, 7348 Malvern Avenue, Philadelphia, PA 19151, 215-473-5393.)

5. June Holley and Roger Wilkens have written extensively on a systems view of flexible networks. See *Creating Flexible Manufacturing Networks in North America: The Co-Evolution of Technology and Industrial Organization*, published by Appalachian Center for Economic Networks, 94 North Columbus Road, Athens, OH 45701, 614-592-3854.

6. Cognitive science has a term for the part standing for the whole: "metonomy."

7. For a study of the common principles among general systems theories, see *Holonomy: A Human Systems Theory*, by Jeffrey Stamps (Seaside, California: Intersystems Publications, 1980). (Available from The Networking Institute, Inc. See chapter 4, note 4.)

8. For the Simon article, see chapter 2, note 14.

9. Confusion over the word "hierarchy" has been a subject of periodic sore debate ever since British systems theorist Lancelot Law Whyte first raised the issue in 1949.

10. For a comprehensive treatment of the principle of complementarity, see Stamps, *Holonomy*, note 7.

11. For the original work that established the field, see *General System Theory*, by Ludwig von Bertalanffy (New York: Braziller, 1968).

12. For further discussion of the S-curve, see *Diffusion of Innovations*, by Everett M. Rogers (New York: The Free Press, 1983).

13. The limit to growth of the S-curve is represented by the asymptote of the curve.

Index

ABC News, 11
ABN/Amro, 166
ACEnet, 17, 140, 153
Ackoff, Russell, 116
Acquisitions, 105
ADP, 120
Advanced Circuit Technologies, Inc., 18–19
Advanced Fabrication Technology, Inc., 148
Agendas, 268
"Age of the Hierarchy Is Over, The" (Houghton), 108
Agfa, 125
Ahlen, John, 145
Airbus, 20–21, 25–26
Akers, John, 107
Alabama, flexible business networks in, 143
ALCOA, 116–17
Alliances, 36, 69, 72, 76, 77, 86, 88, 90, 105, 106, 107, 121–27, 181–82, 307, 316–18
  boundaries of, 87, 121, 316–17
  strategic, 90, 122–27, 134, 317
  see also Flexible business networks; Joint ventures
Alphabetica, 173, 366–67
American Transtech, 102
Analog Devices, 328
Ancona, Deborah, 96
Anderson Consulting, 227
Antitrust issues, 181
Appalachian Regional Commission, 144
Apple Computer, 15, 21–22, 72, 106, 126, 129
Arkansas, flexible business networks in, 6, 144–47
Arkansas Enterprise Group, 146
Arkansas Industrial Network Project, 144
Arkansas Rural Enterprise Center, 147

Arkansas Science and Technology Authority (ASTA), 145
Arkansas Technology, Inc., 146
Arkansas Technology Manufacturing Network, 146
Arkansas Wood Products Trade Group, 146–47
Armco, 116
Armstrong World Industries, 16, 17, 53, 54–57, 62, 67, 71, 309
Arnston, Catharine, 164
Arthur Andersen and Co. (AA&C), 118
Arthur D. Little, Inc., 17
Asahi Glass, 111–12
Asahi Journal, xxvii–xxviii
Asea Brown Boveri (ABB), 3, 4, 8, 28, 53, 61–67, 68, 89, 96, 97, 100, 116, 124, 242, 370
Associated Press, 31
Association of the Eastern Alps, 318
Association of the Western Alps, 318
AT&T, 22, 102, 122
AUGMENT, 313
Australia, clothing industry in, 152
Auto industry, 27–28, 129
  cross-functional teams in, 15, 98–99
  joint ventures in, 9, 11
  see also specific auto makers

Baby boom generation, 352–53, 357
Barnevik, Percy, 61–67, 93, 96, 242
Bayer, 125
Bay of Pigs invasion, 300
Bay State Center for Applied Technology, 141
Beginnings, investing in, 233–34, 327–28
Berenson, Rick, 181
Bertalanffy, Ludwig von, 379
Biotechnology, 130
Biotechology 91, 22
Boeing, 20–21, 24, 25–26, 93, 107, 140

404

About the Authors

Jessica Lipnack and Jeffrey Stamps are founders and principals of The Networking Institute, Inc. (TNI), a consulting, research, and professional services company based in West Newton, Massachusetts. Founded in 1982, TNI has a global reputation for its work with corporate, government, nonprofit, and grass-roots networks in the United States, Canada, Europe, Japan, and Australia.

TNI's mission is to help people work together better by understanding, planning, and managing teamnets. We offer consulting services, education, publications, and software to aid the development and operation of teamnets. We speak frequently at public and private events.

TNI is creating a database of people and organizations using teamnet principles. Please send us information about teamnets you know about and your teamnet experiences—the problems you encounter and how you go about solving them—and we'll find a way to connect your example to others.

The Networking Institute, Inc.
P.O. Box 66, Drawer TN
505 Waltham Street
West Newton, Massachusetts 02165 USA

617-965-3340 (telephone)
617-965-2341 (fax)

Teamnet @ world.std.com (Internet)
Teamnet / MCI ID: 589-8615 (MCI Mail)
177000,507 (CompuServe)